Writing Animal History

WRITING HISTORY

The *Writing History* series publishes accessible overviews of particular fields in history, focusing on the practical application of theory in historical writing. Books in the series succinctly explain central concepts to demonstrate the ways in which they have informed effective historical writing. They analyse key historical texts and their producers within their institutional arrangement, and as part of a wider social discourse. The series' holistic approach means students benefit from an enhanced understanding of how to negotiate the contours of successful historical writing.

Series editors: Stefan Berger (Ruhr University Bochum, Germany), Heiko Feldner (Cardiff University, UK) and Kevin Passmore (Cardiff University, UK)

Published:

Writing Medieval History, edited by Nancy F. Partner
Writing Early Modern History, edited by Garthine Walker
Writing Contemporary History, edited by Robert Gildea and Anne Simonin
Writing Gender History (second edition), Laura Lee Downs
Writing Postcolonial History, Rochona Majumdar
Writing the Holocaust, edited by Jean-Marc Dreyfus and Daniel Langton
Writing the History of Memory, edited by Stefan Berger and Bill Niven
Writing the History of Crime, Paul Knepper
Writing the History of Nationalism, edited by Stefan Berger and Eric Storm
Writing Transnational History, Fiona Paisley
Writing History (third edition), edited by Stefan Berger, Heiko Feldner and Kevin Passmore
Writing Visual Histories, edited by Florence Grant and Ludmilla Jordanova

Writing Animal History

TIMM SCHÖNFELDER

BLOOMSBURY ACADEMIC
LONDON • NEW YORK • OXFORD • NEW DELHI • SYDNEY

BLOOMSBURY ACADEMIC
Bloomsbury Publishing Plc, 50 Bedford Square, London, WC1B 3DP, UK
Bloomsbury Publishing Inc, 1359 Broadway, New York, NY 10018, USA
Bloomsbury Publishing Ireland, 29 Earlsfort Terrace, Dublin 2, D02 AY28, Ireland

BLOOMSBURY, BLOOMSBURY ACADEMIC and the Diana logo are
trademarks of Bloomsbury Publishing Plc

First published in Great Britain 2026

Series design by Grace Ridge
Cover image: duncan1890 via Getty Images

A catalogue record for this book is available from the British Library.

A catalog record for this book is available from the Library of Congress.

ISBN: HB: 978-1-350-46847-4
PB: 978-1-350-46848-1
ePDF: 978-1-350-46850-4
eBook: 978-1-350-46849-8

Series: Writing History

Typeset by Integra Software Services Pvt. Ltd.
Printed and bound in Great Britain

For product safety related questions contact productsafety@bloomsbury.com.

To find out more about our authors and books visit www.bloomsbury.com
and sign up for our newsletters.

If history were taught in the form of stories, it would never be forgotten.
– Rudyard Kipling

Contents

1

Why look at animals?
On the evolution of a
burgeoning field

In 2010, social anthropologist Garry Marvin cautioned: 'If the task of writing the history of just one species is an impossibility, I cannot imagine historians will ever possess the breadth of knowledge to write about the thousands of species of nonhuman animals now existing on the planet and for this to be *the* history of animals.'[1] During the past three decades, animal history – or rather *human–animal history* – has been growing into an almost insurmountable thicket. It is rich in underbrush, with deep roots, and a cacophony of colourful voices young and old. It is home to a multitude of different animals that human observers try to categorize, not least to discern and better know themselves. Welcome to the jungle.

Yet what is such a jungle if not a well-ordered system that one is simply unable to grasp in all its complexity, as Marvin's quote suggested? Throughout this book, paths are presented that may prove worth following through this thicket of animal history while warning of possible dead ends. What is most important, however, is that its readers ultimately feel encouraged to find their own ways. As will be seen, this young field is not only alive and kicking but it is evolving at a staggering pace. Its boundaries are constantly remade, and traditional dividing lines between nature, culture, the human and the non-human are overcome. In the process, creative forms of thinking and writing about beastly companions are found. This first chapter aims to establish some of the underlying philosophical ideas before introducing the reader to the

---

[1] Garry Marvin, 'Wolves in Sheep's (and Others') Clothing', in Dorothee Brantz (ed.), *Beastly Natures. Animals, Humans, and the Study of History* (Charlottesville and London: University of Virginia Press, 2010), pp. 59–78, here p. 61.

larger themes of the book. It shines a light on animals as protagonists and discusses ways of framing their experiences in relation to human interaction.

'Animals are born, are sentient and are mortal', the art critic John Berger wrote in his essay *Why Look at Animals?* 'In these things they resemble man. In their superficial anatomy – less in their deep anatomy – in their habits, in their time, in their physical capacities, they differ from man. They are both like and unlike.'[2] To further refine our view, we differentiate wild and domesticated species; carnivores, herbivores and omnivores; working animals, pets, livestock and prey; companions and pests. For millennia, humans have been speaking *of* and *for* animals, only seldomly overcoming our anthropocentric bias. Just as in Rudyard Kipling's *Jungle Books*, we often do this allegorically with animals as stand-ins for human issues. But what is the human–animal boundary if not a discursive invention? Only recently has this been reflected more methodically.[3] And what if we could truly understand animals? What if their language and behaviour could be read with ease?[4]

Philosopher Thomas Nagel famously argued that it is ultimately impossible for humans to perceive the world the same way as animals do; we are limited by our inadequate minds and bodies that differ too much from those of other species.[5] This has not stopped us, however, to come up with stories that fill whole libraries. 'You must not deny your relatives, the other animals. Their history is your history', Jack London wrote at the beginning of the twentieth century. 'What you repudiate in them you repudiate in yourself.'[6] More than one hundred years later, authors like Melanie Challenger have provided a popular answer to the age-old question *How to Be Animal*. According to her, it is about finding our place in the world and giving meaning to our existence: 'This is an impossible task without first accepting that humans are animals. This should be straightforward, yet it isn't. In truth, we live inside a paradox: it's blindingly obvious that we're animals and yet some part of us doesn't believe it.'[7] After anecdotally skipping through the history of evolution that ends with DNA-tinkering, cybernetic organisms and artificial intelligence, she advocates grounding ourselves: 'For now, humans are Earth creatures, still born of flesh, conscious, emotional and mortal (...) still, we remain animals. We are the selfsame star-stuff we have always been.'[8]

---

[2]John Berger, *Why Look at Animals?* (London and New York: Penguin, 2009), p. 13.
[3]See, for example, Margo DeMello (ed.), *Speaking for Animals. Animal Autobiographical Writing* (New York and Oxon: Routledge, 2013).
[4]Cf. Alastair Pennycook, *Posthumanist Applied Linguistics* (Oxon and New York: Routledge, 2018).
[5]Thomas Nagel, 'What Is It Like to Be a Bat?' *The Philosophical Review* 83(4) (1974), pp. 435–50.
[6]Jack London, 'The Other Animals', in id., *Revolution and Other Essays* (New York: The Macmillan Company, 1910), pp. 237–66, here pp. 265–6.
[7]Melanie Challenger, *How to Be Animal. What It Means to Be Human* (Edinburgh: Canongate, 2021), p. 9.
[8]Challenger, *How to Be Animal*, p. 230.

Unfortunately, the answer to the question *What is an animal?* is not that simple. As the philosopher Keekok Lee has observed in 1997, responses differ greatly between what she labels the 'lay public' and scientists.[9] For the uninitiated majority, the main question is about distance: which creatures do we see and interact with in everyday life? Here, we quickly arrive at a group of animals that is at times referred to as *charismatic megafauna* – elephants, tigers, pandas, lions, giraffes, great apes, whales, dolphins and other symbols of conservation. They are followed by their smaller animal kin, like cats, dogs, hamsters and budgies that humans keep as companions. People are then quick to point at the skies with their majestic hawks and bald eagles or at ducks and geese on nearby lakes. They would also remember what they eat and wear and think of cows, pigs, chicken, fish, sheep and maybe horses. Reptiles do already feel sketchy to many, and ticks and mosquitoes are seen as a nuisance at best – not to speak of bed bugs, lice, fleas and cockroaches. 'The further down the (historical) evolutionary scale an animal or species is, the less it is perceived to be an animal', Lee writes.[10]

By and large, they stick to a commonsensical understanding of the traditional two-kingdom schema and would have no difficulty classifying squirrels as animals and conifers as plants. They would not have heard of protozoa and if asked whether bacteria or fungi are plants or animals, they would have no opinion because of their total ignorance about such matters.[11]

The fact that people are typically aware of only a few dozen types of animals is all the more astonishing, considering that the estimated number of different species is in the millions, even if we exclude microbes.[12] *Writing Animal History* is prone to committing the same mistake of focusing on the animals that humans are most acquainted with. This is only exacerbated by Marvin's observation that '[w]orking from the perspectives of the humanities, researchers are not generally equipped with the expertise to write about the animals themselves or the animals' side of the relationship except in human terms'. He continues:

My view is that the creatures of interest to those of us in the humanities are always socially and culturally constructed: animals that, in terms of our interests and perspectives, have only a tangential relationship with the

[9]Keekok Lee, 'An Animal: What Is It?' *Environmental Values* 6(4) (1997), pp. 393–410.
[10]Lee, 'An Animal: What Is It?', p. 404.
[11]Lee, 'An Animal: What Is It?', p. 396.
[12]Lee, 'An Animal: What Is It?', p. 398. See also John J. Wiens, 'How many species are there on Earth? Progress and problems' *PLOS Biology* 21(11) (20 November 2023), doi: 10.1371/journal.pbio.3002388.

animals in and of themselves. I do not believe that scholars in the humanities can have much, or anything, of significance to say about animals outside any human context.[13]

While this almost sounds like a capitulation, Marvin's proposed solution is to include voices from other disciplines that may have a better understanding of the social life of other animals. This includes the natural and social sciences along with anthropological works that study our close relationship to the animals around us. This introduction is aware of the anthropocentric bias already mentioned at the beginning of this chapter. But it is also devoted to dealing one or the other 'left-handed blow' to the field of history, in the words of Erica Fudge, in the way it approaches the agency of human and animal protagonists. Against her postulation, however, it shows that we are in no way 'attempting to write histories without some of the fundamental ingredients of history', namely empirical source material.[14] All the works discussed herein are deeply steeped in archival findings, literature and often also in field studies with boots on the ground around the world.

Scandals and scoundrels

A good indicator for a burgeoning field is the scandals it produces. These show not only that its theses are perceived, but also that they spark a reaction and create discursive tension. In the case of animal history, two examples concerning German shepherd dogs and Russian hares serve to illustrate this. The first, and probably more famous one, blew up in 2016 when it became known that an article published by the Hannah Arendt Institute for Totalitarianism Studies in Dresden in their renowned journal *Totalitarismus und Demokratie* was a hoax. It followed in the footsteps of one of the most famous examples in the humanities, namely the so-called 'Sokal affair' of the mid-1990s that broached the logical aberrations of postmodern thought from the perspective of the natural sciences. Here, the physicist Alan Sokal managed to publish a largely nonsensical article in the well-known journal *Social Text* that was to unmask the field's empty phrases and lacking scientific

---

[13]Marvin, 'Wolves in Sheep's (and Others') Clothing', p. 62.
[14]Erica Fudge, 'A Left-Handed Blow: Writing the History of Animals', in Nigel Rothfels (ed.), *Representing Animals. Theories of Contemporary Culture* (Bloomington: Indiana University Press, 2002), pp. 3–18, here p. 6.

rigour (see also Chapter 8).[15] The direction of the 'shepherd dog hoax', labelled a 'plea against academic conformism' in the short manifesto of confession that was published online, proved to be more contentious, however.[16]

Penned using the fake name of 'Christiane Schulte', who claimed to be a recent PhD student in history, it aimed to understand 'the German-German shepherd dog' as 'a contribution to the history of violence in the century of extremes'. What sounds rather inconspicuous at first, proved to be a bombshell. Schulte, in truth a collective of dissatisfied academics, claimed that canines used by the East-German National People's Army (*Nationale Volksarmee* or NVA) along the inner German border between 1961 and 1989 had descended from dogs that had been used in Nazi concentration camps. Claiming to 'illustrate the ambivalent role of animals in the history of violence in the 20th century' with 'huge implications' for its continuity after 1945, it argued to show the merits of presenting a human–animal perspective.[17] Based on a conference paper and greenlit by the editorial board, several cynical remarks and hidden jokes throughout should have alerted reviewers, like the alleged breed of the 'altdeutscher Einhoder' ('Old-German cryptorchid'), an obvious reference to the often-purported rumour about Hitler having only one testicle.[18] Nonetheless, it was the authors themselves who uncovered their deed shortly after publication.

The damage dealt to human-animal studies and especially animal history in German-speaking academia was notable, as the incident became a laughingstock among supposedly more serious and conservative scholars. Yet, it was by no means permanent; the debate in its wake remained modest, even for German standards as a culture of thick monographs rather than strong thesis-driven treatises (which, in turn, is why more creative approaches seem to shine more brightly).[19] While this case reveals 'politically motivated

---

[15]Alan D. Sokal, 'Transgressing the Boundaries: Toward a Transformative Hermeneutics of Quantum Gravity' *Social Text* 14(46/47) (1996), pp. 217–52, and, for an overview on the evolving discussion, Alan Sokal, *Beyond the Hoax. Science, Philosophy and Culture* (Oxford: Oxford University Press, 2008).

[16]The original document is no longer available. A qualified overview and commentary can be found in Florian Peters, 'Von totalitären Schäferhunden und libertären Mauerkaninchen. Alles von Relevanz? Ein Beitrag über zweifelhafte wissenschaftliche Standards und die angezogene Handbremse in der akademischen Debattenkultur' *Zeitgeschichte-online* (1 February 2016), https://zeitgeschichte-online.de/kommentar/von-totalitaeren-schaeferhunden-und-libertaeren-mauerkaninchen [accessed on 14 May 2025].

[17]Christiane Schulte, 'Der deutsch-deutsche Schäferhund – Ein Beitrag zur Gewaltgeschichte des Jahrhunderts der Extreme' *Totalitarismus und Demokratie* 13 (2015), pp. 319–34, quote p. 320.

[18]Schulte, 'Der deutsch-deutsche Schäferhund', p. 328.

[19]Cf. Enrico Heitzer and Sven Schultze (eds), *Chimära mensura? Die Human-Animal Studies zwischen Schäferhund-Science-Hoax, kritischer Geschichtswissenschaft und akademischem Trendsurfing* (Berlin: Vergangenheitsverlag, 2018).

wishful thinking on various sides of the academic spectrum', as the historian Florian Peters observed, it also underlines 'the central importance of open and controversial debates in the humanities':

> it is highly problematic for the culture of academic discussion if no one has the courage to take issue with colleagues – after all, they could be the reviewers of their own next project proposal. Where there is a lack of courage to disagree and a desire to argue, academic habitus ultimately counts for more than actual scientific knowledge.[20]

What it means for scholars when such critical exchange is no longer possible is shown in the second example on *The Minister and the Hare*. In June 2013, the Russian Minister of Culture Vladimir Medinskii (2012–20), himself notorious for promoting a nationalist understanding of history and culture, expressed disdain during a radio interview about a supposedly state-funded five-year study on the 'philosophy of the hare' – a project that, in fact, never existed. This, he thought, was only wasting precious government roubles and did not have any merit. In response to such absurd fabrications and as an act of defiance against state intervention, the Institute of Russian Literature (also known as the Pushkin House) of the Russian Academy of Sciences in St Petersburg organized a three-day conference in June 2014 that was dedicated to this new field of interest. Contributions ranging from 'The Fauna of Morality' in Russian Classics to 'The Image of the Hare in Nazi Propaganda' were later published in the journal *Novoe literaturnoe obozrenie* ('New Literary Observer') as a cluster titled 'The Minister, Hares, and Memes, or How Scholarly Communities Are Formed and How They Persist'. It is an important tongue-in-cheek document of a time when the humanities in Russia experienced increasing pressure to submit to the regime's radicalized patriotic narratives.[21] In response to the conference, Medinskii published a letter stating he was 'sure that issues discussed at the symposium are particularly important and relevant for millions of ordinary taxpayers'.[22]

---

[20]Peters, 'Von totalitären Schäferhunden und libertären Mauerkaninchen'.

[21]All repression withstanding, the special issue is still openly available online: Konstantin A. Bogdanov (ed.), 'Ministr, zaitsy, memy, ili kak sozdaiutsia i chem derzhatsia nauchnye soobshchestva' *Novoe literaturnoe obozrenie* 140(4) (2016), https://www.nlobooks.ru/magazines/novoe_literaturnoe_ obozrenie/140_nlo_4_2016/ [accessed on 14 May 2025]. For an update on the state of the art in Russia and beyond, see 'Forum: Liudi i drugie zhivye sushchestva' *Antropologicheskii forum* 62 (2024), pp. 11–224.

[22]Timm Schönfelder, *Animals in Russian and Soviet History* (Oxford Bibliographies, New York: Oxford University Press, 2026), doi: 10.1093/obo/9780197768709-0058. N. N., 'Hare today and gone tomorrow' *openDemocracy* (7 July 2014), https://www.opendemocracy.net/en/odr/hare-today-and-gone-tomorrow [accessed on 14 May 2025].

A field in bloom

While the hoax of the German shepherd can be read as a self-critique of academic culture, the Russian hare is an example of the struggle for academic freedom and self-determination. Both cases highlight two significant traits of human–animal studies within the humanities: they are deeply grounded in literary and cultural studies, and they are met with scepticism by more conservative individuals. In her foreword to an excellent German-language introduction to the field, Margo DeMello maintains in 2017 that even though 'Christiane Schulte and friends' caused a great deal of embarrassment to the community, she still sees human–animal studies 'as a rigorous and important form of critical inquiry' that transforms animals 'from *objects* of academic inquiry into *subjects*, in and of themselves'. This is even more important, she adds, considering that 'until the rise of the field in the 1990s, the invisibility of animals in scholarly inquiry was perhaps as great as the presence of animals themselves in our daily lives'. Although she notes connections to the animal protection movement, which dates back to the nineteenth century and brought forth organizations like People for the Ethical Treatment of Animals (PETA) or militant groups like the Animal Liberation Front (ALF), she stresses that (unlike the field of *critical animal studies*) it is not interested in animal advocacy per se.[23]

Organizations like the Animals & Society Institute, which was created by Kenneth Shapiro in 1983 and decided to close in 2025 for financial reasons after more than forty years of work, played a major role in shaping the field not least through its journal *Society & Animals* (since 1993), which followed the path-breaking *Anthrozoös*, founded in 1987. Early protagonists have time and again underlined the transdisciplinary character of the field which also took its cues from environmental history and anthropological studies in the way they investigate the interaction of humans and nature along with the commodification of animals as resources which made them 'a backbone of civilizational development'.[24] This has provided fertile ground for lively debates

---

[23]Margo DeMello, 'Vorwort' in Gabriela Kompatscher, Reingard Spannring and Karin Schachinger, *Human-Animal Studies. Eine Einführung für Studierende und Lehrende* (Münster and New York: Waxmann, 2017), pp. 7–9, quotes p. 7. On critical animal studies, see the first textbook in the field: Margo DeMello, *Animals and Society. An Introduction to Human-Animal Studies* (New York: Columbia University Press, 2012), pp. 17–8.

[24]Lloyd Price, 'Environmental and Animal History', in Stefan Berger, Heiko Feldner and Kevin Passmore (eds), *Writing History. Theory and Practice* (London: Bloomsbury Academic, ³2021; first published in 2020), pp. 253–72, quote p. 261.

on animal ethics and sustainability.[25] One of the most inspiring examples that proved to be defining for the field was Peter Singer's 1975 treatise on *Animal Liberation*. Here, the philosopher argued from a utilitarian perspective that human privilege over animals is not justifiable. Such *speciesism* (coined in analogy to racism and sexism) that discriminates against living beings simply because they are not read as human is morally untenable if they are capable of suffering. Singer also highlights a range of contradictions that entered the focus of animal history concerning the use of animals in agriculture or in scientific experiments. He then poses the provocative question whether we would do the same to our own kind.[26] Singer's ideas, though not outright accepted by every representative of the field, have become common ground for discussions.[27] They were, of course, part of a much larger conversation reaching from Jeremy Bentham's (1748–1832) question whether animals can suffer, posed in 1789, to the foundation of the Society for the Study of Ethics and Animals by the American Philosophical Association in 1980, which in the words of the ethicist Paul Waldau was 'among the first academic groups to offer organized discussion at professional meetings of issues going beyond resource-focused use of other-than-human animals'.[28] In 1983, Tom Regan made *The Case for Animal Rights* which, in contrast to Singer, argued that animals as sensing, thinking and feeling 'subjects of a life' had intrinsic value independent of our use of them.[29] 'What is important is that animals, such as humans, have interests', Margo DeMello summarizes his argument. 'Neither humans nor animals should be eaten or experimented on' regardless of 'whether or not the greater good would be met by this'.[30]

As a consequence of this shifting focus, animal studies has gone beyond classical teachings *ex cathedra*, and 'by its very nature, systematically seeks out and takes lessons from both the people inside universities and those whom universities have historically ignored, as well as nonhuman animals

---

[25]For an anthology of defining texts, see Linda Kalof and Amy Fitzgerald (eds), *The Animals Reader. The Essential Classic and Contemporary Writings. Second edition* (London and New York: Routledge, 2022). A critical discussion in German 'on the societal nature of human-animal relations' can be found in Chimaira – Arbeitskreis für Human-Animal Studies (ed.), *Human-Animal Studies. Über die gesellschaftliche Natur von Mensch-Tier-Verhältnissen* (Bielefeld: transcript, 2011).
[26]Peter Singer, *Animal Liberation* (London: Bodley Head, 2015; first published in 1975).
[27]One example of this would be Donna J. Haraway, *When Species Meet* (Minneapolis and London: University of Minnesota Press, 2008) where Peter Singer is not mentioned once, even though she engages with related ethical and moral questions in human–animal interactions.
[28]Paul Waldau, *Animal Studies. An Introduction* (New York: Oxford University Press, 2013), p. 121.
[29]Tom Regan, *The Case for Animal Rights* (Berkeley and Los Angeles: University of California Press, 2004; first published in 1983).
[30]DeMello, *Animals and Society*, p. 388.

themselves'.[31] The *animal turn*, as it has gained traction especially since the 1990s, introduced a new category of protagonists. This attempted change of perspective is maybe best exemplified in a text by the poststructuralist philosopher Jacques Derrida (1930–2004). In his essay *The Animal That Therefore I Am*, originally the introductory part of a long lecture given in 1997 at Cerisy-la-Salle titled 'L'animal autobiographique', Derrida starts with a rather personal encounter: the penetrating gaze of his cat as he stands naked in front of it.[32] The fact that he feels shame although animals 'don't notice their own nudity' as 'there is no nudity in nature' triggers the seemingly simple question: 'Since so long ago, can we say that the animal has been looking at us?'[33] This would imply subjectivity in the animal other and put our anthropocentric worldview into question. From this equalization of humans and animals as it is further elaborated in Derrida's lecture by a selective reading of philosophical and religious texts, an important take-away is the explicit focus on *animal agency*.

Looking at animals

More than a decade after the first publication of parts of Derrida's musings on the animal in French, many historians still struggled to accept non-human agency and include animals into their narratives. The idea that they can directly transform human structures, Dorothee Brantz remarks, 'necessitates a radical rethinking of the project of history, which is in many ways synonymous with the project of modernity'. This continues to be a daring endeavour, as it calls to overcome 'the epistemological separation of nature and culture' that is still deeply engrained in much of historiography: 'For historians, animals seemed to matter only insofar as they supplied the material resources necessary for the advancement of human societies.'[34] Following in the academic footsteps of such pathbreaking and still authoritative works like Harriet Ritvo's *The*

---

[31]Waldau, *Animal Studies*, p. 294.

[32]Derrida's lecture was posthumously collected in Marie-Luise Mallet (ed.), *Jacques Derrida. The Animal That Therefore I Am* (New York: Fordham University Press, 2008; first published in French in 2006), pp. 1–51, 162–7 (footnotes). The introduction 'The Animal That Therefore I Am (More to Follow)' first appeared in an abridged English version in the Winter 2002 issue of the journal *Critical Inquiry*. Other parts soon followed in translation, e.g. Jacques Derrida, 'And Say the Animal Responded?', in Cary Wolf (ed.), *Zoontologies. The Question of the Animal* (Minneapolis and London: University of Minnesota Press, 2003), pp. 121–46.

[33]Mallet (ed.), *Jacques Derrida. The Animal That Therefore I Am*, pp. 3–4.

[34]Dorothee Brantz, 'Introduction', in Dorothee Brantz (ed.), *Beastly Natures. Animals, Humans, and the Study of History* (Charlottesville and London: University of Virginia Press, 2010), p. 3.

Animal Estate (1987) and John M. MacKenzie's *The Empire of Nature* (1988), animal history kept slowly evolving.[35] In 2007, six volumes edited by Linda Kalof, Brigitte Resl, Bruce Boehrer, Matthew Senior, Kathleen Kete and Randy Malamud provided *A Cultural History of Animals* in Antiquity, the Medieval Age, the Renaissance, the Age of Enlightenment, the Age of Empire and the Modern Age. Organized to offer a comparative perspective *à travers les époques*, each book addresses the sacred and the symbolic, hunting, domestication, entertainment and exhibitions, science and specimens, philosophical ideas, and artistic representation with valuable introductory chapters and a strong focus on 'the West'.[36]

The ensuing decade of the 2010s saw a growing number of reference works and introductions that dealt with a broad set of themes and were increasingly geared towards the historian. The pioneering *Routledge Handbook of Human-Animal Studies* edited by Garry Marvin and Susan McHugh surveyed the field in 2014.[37] It was followed three years later by Linda Kalof's *The Oxford Handbook of Animal Studies*.[38] In 2015, Arianna Ferrari and Klaus Petrus published a German-language *Encyclopaedia of Human-Animal Relations* that satisfies both adherents of human–animal studies and critical animal studies with a range of contributions from architecture to zoomusicology.[39] Leaning towards intersectionality and posthumanism, Lynn Turner, Undine Sellbach and Ron Broglio edited *The Edinburgh Companion to Animal Studies* in 2018. It is organized in alphabetical order and includes less-prominent topics like abjection, affection, animation, biopolitics, death, fragility, meaning, microbes, queer theory and voice next to established ones such as arts, ethics, farming, science, technology and law.[40] The following year, Hilda Kean and Philip Howell published *The Routledge Companion to Animal-Human History* that offers in-depth chapters on nationalism, political history, heritage, conservation, ethics, visual culture, as well as animal agency, literary representation, emotions, breeding and consumption.[41] In 2022, Mieke Roscher, André Krebber and

[35]Harriet Ritvo, *The Animal Estate. The English and Other Creatures in the Victorian Age* (Cambridge: Harvard University Press, 1987), and John M. MacKenzie, *The Empire of Nature. Hunting, Conservation and British Imperialism* (Manchester: Manchester University Press, 1988).

[36]Linda Kalof, Brigitte Resl, Bruce Boehrer, Matthew Senior, Kathleen Kete and Randy Malamud (eds), *A Cultural History of Animals*. 6 vols. (Oxford and New York: Berg, 2007).

[37]Garry Marvin and Susan McHugh (eds), *Routledge Handbook of Human-Animal Studies* (London and New York: Routledge, 2014).

[38]Linda Kalof (ed.), *The Oxford Handbook of Animal Studies* (New York: Oxford University Press, 2017).

[39]Arianna Ferrari and Klaus Petrus (eds), *Lexikon der Mensch-Tier-Beziehungen* (Bielefeld: transcript, 2015).

[40]Lynn Turner, Undine Sellbach and Ron Broglio (eds), *The Edinburgh Companion to Animal Studies* (Edinburgh: Edinburgh University Press, 2018).

[41]Hilda Kean and Philip Howell (eds), *The Routledge Companion to Animal-Human History* (London and New York: Routledge, 2019).

Brett Mizelle eventually edited a *Handbook of Historical Animal Studies* that discusses a range of core themes and conceptual frameworks with a more global outlook that explicitly addresses the area studies (although expertise on countries like Russia is lacking).[42] Providing a more globalized perspective that aims to include hitherto marginalized voices has been acknowledged as a serious desideratum, which is evidenced not least by Helen Louise Cowie's *Animals in World History* (2025).[43] Also worth mentioning is the widely read Animal series published by Reaktion Books which goes far beyond the scope of this introduction with its more than one hundred species-specific single treatments that comprise such creatures as nightingales, crabs, jellyfish, bees, worms, turtles, leeches, hyenas, hedgehogs, wild boars and – last but not least – humans proper.

Even though it is still a young sub-discipline, the number of works that explicitly or implicitly deal in 'animal history' has grown into its own jungle in recent years, to reuse the metaphor at the beginning of this chapter. This includes monographs that boldly describe *longue durée* evolutions like the anthropologist Brian Fagan's *The Intimate Bond* that draws a trajectory of human–animal interaction from prehistory to the present through selected case studies.[44] On a more critical note, such overviews naturally tend to oversimplify complex developments. For this reason, and not to overstretch the core expertise of the author, this introduction decided to set its focus on the nineteenth and twentieth centuries, with slight deviations when it comes to the conquest of the Americas and the exchange of people, flora and fauna. In doing so, it stays close to defining works of animal history and its related disciplines by emerging scholars as well as established academics.

Writing Animal History is organized in a thematic fashion. It aims to exemplify how animal history can be told by retracing narrative arcs and by discussing on what sources authors base their theses and arguments.

---

[42] Mieke Roscher, André Krebber and Brett Mizelle (eds), *Handbook of Historical Animal Studies* (Berlin and Boston: De Gruyter, 2022). For the Russian Empire and the Soviet Union, see Jane Costlow and Amy Nelson (eds), *Other Animals. Beyond the Human in Russian Culture and History* (Pittsburgh: University of Pittsburgh Press, 2010) as well as Helena Holzberger and Timm Schönfelder (eds), 'Special Issue: Crossing Boundaries. Human-Animal Relationships in Tsarist Russia and the Soviet Union' *Slavonic and East European Review* 103(1) (2025).

[43] Helen Louise Cowie, *Animals in World History* (New York and London: Routledge, 2025).

[44] Brian Fagan, *The Intimate Bond. How Animals Shaped Human History* (New York and London: Bloomsbury, 2015). For a sweeping essay on the place of the animalistic in Western philosophy, see Oxana Timofeeva, *The History of Animals. A Philosophy* (London: Bloomsbury Academic, 2018; first published in Russian in 2017).

Since a single book cannot represent the exponentially growing field in all its complexity, it rather critically evaluates the individual approaches to human–animal relations regarding eminent historiographical questions about agency, acculturation, gender roles and power hierarchies in modern societies. While all the chapters can be read independently, they are structured to argumentatively build and expand upon each other. Thus, the reader is provided a narratively framed discussion on methodological approaches, the use of sources, as well as on the theoretical preconceptions of the respective works in accordance with their situatedness in academic discourse. For this, they are contrasted with a larger body of literature. Overall, this book hopes to awaken the curiosity of the reader not only to pick up the works presented, but to ask their own questions and to bravely stray from the suggested paths into the unknown.

Following this introductory chapter that has broadly sketched the evolution of animal history, we will focus on its relationship with environmental history. 'Wilderness and civilization: Animals at the nature-culture divide' uses the example of wolves to discuss the varied representations and transfigurations of the 'wild beast' and its 'savage gaze' which serve an important role in establishing and reproducing social boundaries and structures as it is not least mirrored in religious beliefs and cultist practices. Then, 'Coevolution and domestication: Companion species in everyday interaction' takes a wider perspective on the relationship of humans and animals in predominantly urban contexts. It connects some of the more classical texts of animal history to ongoing debates both in the field and in neighbouring disciplines. The practices of everyday interaction with companion species do not only make us ask how urban spaces are created at their interplay, but they also force us to re-evaluate the controversial status of emotions in historiography. 'Global exchanges: Species transfer and the making of new worlds' broadens its perspective on the Columbian Exchange of flora and fauna as a pivotal moment of global history. Conquest, colonization and imperial exploitation were accompanied by intentional and unintentional introductions of species ranging from horses to microbes. Repopulation policies transposed practices in animal husbandry and agriculture that recreated local environments. Not only did this challenge Indigenous traditions and ways of life, but it also brought whole ecosystems closer to extinction. As an example of global interconnectedness, this chapter pays attention to the understudied 'subaltern voices' in contact while also considering the cultural and economic impacts on Europe.

'Killing game: Hunting and the legacy of colonialism' then focuses on the African continent. The chapter treats the complex role of animals in histories of imperialism, colonialism and the sometimes-resulting controversial projects of wildlife conservation. Here, 'Western' ideals of progress, science-based innovation and supposed rationalization have created a vast array of social and environmental problems that inform ongoing conversations on sustainability and reconciliation. Furthermore, it sheds light on prevailing relations of gender and power in such masculinized practices like the ritualized killing of game. 'Commodifying animals: Whaling and the exploitation of the oceans' presents what now appears to be a derelict business done away by advanced technologies and activism for marine mammal protection. It was, however, once at the heart of the Industrial Revolution: whale oil was used to illuminate streets, homes, workshops and to lubricate machines of mass production. The advent of steam powered ships and exploding harpoons put further pressure on maritime populations, pushing whales and other species towards the brink of extinction. This chapter explores the globally entangled history of the earth's largest animals with their human counterparts, and it highlights the destructive potential of modern technology. 'From farm to table: Industrialized animals and food production' looks at rivalling regimes of meat procurement and explores the rise of industrialized farming in fascist, socialist and capitalist states. In doing so, it shows the changing role of animals in agriculture through technological progress and automatization. The processing of pigs and cattle into protein puts a spotlight on the ongoing disputes about ethical and sustainable food production that avoids depleting natural resources in an age of ready availability in Western societies and an excessive increase in caloric intake.

With a strong nod to science and technology studies, 'Space monkeys and Pavlovian dogs: Animals in science and technology' diverts attention to the role of animals in modern science from laboratory testing to space exploration. It focuses on questions of standardization, on ethical disputes in everyday experiments and on competing visions of progress – not least in the context of the Cold War. As stand-ins for their human counterparts, the borders between 'humans' and 'animals' were constantly renegotiated. Thus, apes, canines and other species became involuntary trailblazers in the name of social advancement, making 'giant leaps' such as space travel and the settling of new worlds possible. 'Breaking free: Circuses, zoos and animal liberation' then shows how animals serve as spectacles across the world. Following ideas of entertainment and leisure as they gained popularity during the nineteenth century through travelling animal tamers and the opening of hitherto inaccessible aristocratic menageries to the public, activists' voices became louder that asked for animals to be freed from captivity or at least for a more 'humane' treatment. Not only does this reconnect to the ethical issues at the heart of human–animal relations presented at the beginning of the book, but it also confronts us with varying, often-problematic degrees of anthropomorphization on all sides of the debate. The perspectives presented throughout the book will be brought together in the 'Conclusion and outlook' while neglected topics and possible avenues for the further development of the field are sketched. A bibliography that collects the cited works along with selected further reading and an index will round off the presentation.

2

Wilderness and civilization: Animals at the nature–culture divide

Wolves have reappeared in Central Europe. What may be hardly newsworthy to societies around the world that have been living with the animal for centuries has sparked notable concern among people in countries like France, Germany and Poland. Seemingly, wilderness has returned to everyone's backyard. This provides strong fodder for fear and hysteria.[1] With the help of EU funding, shepherds are putting up fences to protect their flocks while right-wing populists peddle the narrative of wild beasts that hail from supposedly less civilized regions and thus somehow pose a threat to national culture. So-called wolf stones marking their last sightings usually during the nineteenth century are rediscovered and compared to today's migration routes.[2] As Örjan Kardell and Anna Dahlström remind us:

> The conflict between wolves and humans is as old as the advent of agriculture. This process simultaneously included the domestication of the ancestors of our farm animals, the dog (*Canis lupus familiaris*) excluded. Sedentary mixed farming communities and nomadic herding societies, which developed as a result of this initial domestication, have long seen

---

[1] On the emotional dimension of human–animal interaction in Germany, see Thorsten Gieser, *Living with Wolves. Affects, Feelings and Sentiments in Human-Wolf-Coexistence* (Bielefeld: transcript, 2024). A broader continental perspective is presented in Michaela Fenske and Bernhard Tschofen (eds), *Managing the Return of the Wild. Human Encounters with Wolves in Europe* (London and New York: Routledge, 2022).

[2] Patrick Masius and Jana Sprenger, 'Reconstructing the Extermination of Wolves in Germany. Case Studies from Brandenburg and Rhineland-Palatinate', in Patrick Masius and Jana Sprenger (eds), *A Fairytale in Question. Historical Interactions Between Humans and Wolves* (Knapwell: White Horse Press, 2015), pp. 119–40.

wolves as fierce competitors for their livestock. In Europe, Christian dogma has also branded the wolf as inherently evil, a fact which has made wolf control a worthy cause in its own right.[3]

There is a lot to unpack here. Apart from the looming economic losses through wolf attacks, there is a much deeper dimension to humanity's uneasiness around lupine creatures. This is reflected in folklore, fairy tales and religious prose in such figures as the *Big Bad Wolf* who devoured Little Red Riding Hood's grandmother, the proverbial *Wolf in Sheep's Clothing* referring to evil in innocent disguise or the monstrous *Fenrir* that brings about the end of days in Norse mythology. This symbolism of great strength and voracity goes back to ancient times, as it is also presented in a more positive light in such foundational stories like that of the twins Romulus and Remus who were suckled by a she-wolf.[4] As Kardell and Dahlström underline, modern approaches to wolf management would benefit greatly from reasonably weighed historical experience. In this, they are in line with biologists and ethologists who warn us of human–wildlife conflicts as a result of an increasing rivalry for resources that entail violent backlashes which have already led to the animal's decline.[5]

With this in mind, the chapter aims at relaying how the history of wolves was written – or rather, how wolves were written into human history. For this, two historiographical works will be treated as central case studies, *The Lost Wolves of Japan* by Brett Walker and *That Savage Gaze* by Ian Helfant, before delving deeper into the meaning of the nature–culture divide through the, at times philosophical, musings of William Cronon, Roderick Nash and Philippe Descola. Naturally, this selection can be disputed, as there exists a huge treasure of books on these creatures. Most of them, however, cannot be considered animal history in the sense of this introduction. One popular example would be *American Wolf* by Nate Blakeslee. While the author, a journalist by trade, presents us with valuable insights into the often-times still unknown nature of lupine behaviour in Yellowstone National Park through the example of the female grey wolf 'O-Six', it is lacking on a more abstract level. In other words: we learn less about the animals' complex place in our cultural environment, and more about the intricacies of wolf watching and the

---

[3]Örjan Kardell and Anna Dahlström, 'Wolves in the Early Nineteenth-Century County of Jönköping, Sweden', *Environment and History* 19 (2013), pp. 339–70, here p. 344.
[4]On the many variations of 'lupophilia' see Garry Marvin, *Wolf* (London: Reaktion Books, 2012), pp. 119–71.
[5]Ellen de Wolf, 'The Return of the Wolf in Europe' *WWF* (30 September 2021), https://www.worldwildlife.org/stories/the-return-of-the-wolf-in-europe [accessed on 24 April 2024]; see also Eva M. Gross, Nilanga Jayasinghe, Ashley Brooks, Gert Polet, Rohan Wadhwa and Femke Hilderink-Koopmans, *A Future for All. The Need for Human-Wildlife Coexistence* (Gland: WWF, 2021).

legal ramifications of their protection. The book does, however, highlight the possibilities and limits of writing the history of animals from an anthropocentric viewpoint: eventually, we can only speculate about the true intentions of such protagonists like 'O-Six'. And we must be wary of projecting too much of our own ideas onto them. In parts, the book is set up rather like a novel than a work of nonfiction. Yet for some readers, it was this capturing accessibility that helped spark a discussion about wolf protection in and around US national parks – much in the vein of environmentalist Farley Mowat's popular book *Never Cry Wolf*, which was published in 1963 and made into a Disney movie twenty years later about a wildlife biologist's whimsical encounter with the animal.

Karen Jones duly reminds us about the sharp criticism such works faced from the scientific community: replacing the negative connotations of the Big Bad Wolf with the opposite that is framed as an anthropomorphized ideal of strength and freedom 'did the species a disservice'. How was the wolf as 'a creature representative of our fears and our idealisations of wilderness' to be truly understood through such superficial literary approaches that lacked a deeper scientific understanding of wolf behaviour?[6] As the author of *American Wolf* puts it with a romanticizing undertone: 'The professionals [i.e. the Wolf Project biologists] recorded their subjects' ages and weights, their ranges and diets, their fertility and longevity. But the watchers knew their stories.'[7] Yet we do have to ask us: which stories about wolves did these onlookers perceive through their human eyes and minds? It is our job as animal historians to question this time and again.

The Lost Wolves of Japan

Brett Walker, an environmental historian living in Montana, was acquainted not only with the sober arguments but also with the emotional side of the discussions surrounding wolves in Yellowstone when he wrote his book: '[S]cience, the reality of wolf ecology, and the economy of ranching always surrender to anger, anxiety, fear, and passion. I've never met a person who, when asked for his or her opinions about wolf recovery, responded with indifference.'[8] In Japan, similar conflicts could be witnessed as a result of

---

[6]Karen Jones, 'Writing the Wolf: Canine Tales and North American Environmental-Literary Tradition', *Environment and History* 17 (2011), pp. 201–28, quotes pp. 218, 201.
[7]Nate Blakeslee, *American Wolf. A True Story of Survival and Obsession in the West* (New York: Broadway Books, 2018), p. 65.
[8]Brett L. Walker, *The Lost Wolves of Japan* (Seattle: University of Washington Press, 2005), p. xvi.

industrialization when the natural realm was subdued to human control. Animals once revered as gods became seen as a nuisance, and the last wolf was killed in 1905. What is interesting about Walker's study is his point of departure: rather than pondering the loss of wilderness, he starts out with Charles Darwin's 1872 treatise *The Expression of the Emotions in Man and Animals*. Here, Darwin expanded his works on evolutionary theory as he had noted strong similarities in sentimental behaviour across the species like showing one's teeth in rage or the bristling of hair under terror.[9] Thus, 'In the expression of emotions, in other words, humans and wolves share similar means of articulation, creating a common emotional space for human and nonhuman animals', Walker argues.[10] He concludes that these animals must also have a history.

Consequently, Walker starts out by defining what the Japanese Wolf (*Nihon ōkami*) actually was. As a zoological category, it came to be commonly accepted by scientists only at the turn of the twentieth century as 'a product of the twin historical forces of the birth of the modern Japanese nation and the development of its own zoological sciences'. This connects to his observation that agricultural civilizations and hunting societies like those of Japan cared less about a strict distinction between wolves and dogs than those relying on animal husbandry did.[11] Thus, two words are repeatedly used somewhat interchangeably in Japanese to denote wild canine creatures, hybrids included: *yamainu* (mountain dog) and *ōkami* (wolf). Not only does this challenge a clear division between nature and culture, but it also expands into a religious dimension that materializes in Shinto shrines and Buddhist temples where wolves are revered as sacred beings. They were considered divine messengers, and their appearance was linked to talismans that protected from misfortune – including wild boar attacks and deer devastating the grain fields of agrarian communities. Wolf hunts were respectful ceremonial endeavours.

While reports of encounters with wolves in Japan date back to the eighth century, it was more than one thousand years later that they were commonly perceived as a nuisance and hunted down systematically. At the time, horse ranchers in southern and northeastern Japan saw their trade in jeopardy and asked for firearms to defend themselves, the use of which had been restricted by the Edo shogunate military government (1603–1867/8).[12] Professional wolf

---

[9]For some, this work does even mark one of the founding texts of psychology, as in Paul Ekman, 'Darwin's contributions to our understanding of emotional expressions' *Philosophical Transactions of the Royal Society of London. Series B, Biological Sciences* 364(1535) (2009), pp. 3449–51.
[10]Walker, *Lost Wolves*, p. 12.
[11]Walker, *Lost Wolves*, pp. 27, 31.
[12]Walker, *Lost Wolves*, p. 103.

hunters were now called to scenes of carnage to bring down the culprits. For this, they relied not only on guns, but also on poisons, often used on carcasses to attract wolves, and on traps. In the early eighteenth century, bounties were introduced to boost motivation. As Walker argues, the initial goal was not to eradicate but to control wild canine populations that posed a threat to livestock. Yet it was the spread of a new disease since the 1730s that changed this: reports about what became known as 'rabies' brought about the image of the 'mad wolf' as 'the high number of canines afflicted (…) translated into a frightening number of wolf attacks' by the 1750s.[13] This beastly madness rendered established modes of cohabitation between humans and animals obsolete.

The Meiji Restoration of 1868, named after the new emperor of Japan, was accompanied by administrative centralization and an opening of the country to Western influence, not least in agriculture. In this new socioeconomic context, wolves were not to be considered guardian creatures anymore, but categorized as 'noxious animals' that stood in ecological competition with humans and had to be exterminated as part of a civilizing mission. 'By the 1870s and 1880s', Walker writes, 'after Japan's appropriation and refashioning of newly imported Western assumptions about predators through the agency of [the American adviser Edwin] Dun and others, a new greeting for wolves was created: shoot them, sever their ears or legs, bring these to a municipal office, and collect a lucrative bounty.'[14] One rather problematic connection as to the origin of such policies is drawn here by Walker himself. Based on his experience with naturally occurring wolf kills of other wild animals in Yellowstone National Park he suggests that this violent sight might have sparked a lust for revenge in humans that was in its results just as gory as the observed example:

Indeed, the culture of wolf killing might be a product of feelings of anxiety evoked at wolf kill sites around the world, which led me to believe that, staring at this dead elk along Antelope Creek, I had come to the birthplace of the Western obsession with wolf killing, the very one transported to Japan in the Meiji years by Dun and others.

Especially ranchers that just lost one of their animals must have been left 'full of hatred and rage'.[15] From this, he spins the argument that stories, narratives and symbols were created that framed the wolf in a deeply negative way.

---

[13] Walker, *Lost Wolves*, p. 115.
[14] Walker, *Lost Wolves*, p. 132.
[15] Walker, *Lost Wolves*, p. 136.

When this met the interest of a modernizing economy that favoured control over wilderness, the wolf's days were numbered. Following the American example, they were to be eradicated with strychnine in a cost-effective way.[16] Meanwhile, industrialized cattle rearing, slaughtering and processing changed the diet of the people through the ready availability of beef that would provide workers and soldiers alike.[17] Such endeavours did also present new opportunities to wolves and feral dogs who sought out horse ranches and pastures as the perfect killing grounds.

Human mastery over nature as a pillar of the ideology of modernization was to be realized through 'The American Model' which resulted from the practices of British colonists who 'carried the pathology of wolf eradication across the Atlantic Ocean' – thus, according to Walker, 'killing wolves became part of reshaping the New World into a Neo-European landscape'.[18] Meiji modernizers adopted this practice, refashioning Japan's environment accordingly. As a result, not only did human economies change, but also those of wolves, Walker continues:

> What this means is that historical watersheds, though often political, social, and economic in nature, reverberate throughout the natural world as well, often in ways that modify the behavior of all living things; because wolves adapt to their surrounding ecologies, in a sense they too experience history and they too can modernize.[19]

Though wolves are classically considered hemerophobic, i.e. they suffer from anthropogenic changes in the land and try to avoid proximity to humans, they are nonetheless affected by them.[20] Discussions on their role in the natural environment were spurred by the teachings of the German zoologist Ernst Haeckel (1834–1919), a follower of Darwinism who popularized a broad

---

[16]Walker does elaborate that the use of strychnine did not originate in the United States but in Europe and early modern Japan to eradicate predators and pesky birds such as magpies and crows. Yet it was the wolfers of the American prairie that reportedly perfected the practice by lacing every carcass with it – Walker, Lost Wolves, pp. 152–3.

[17]On the industrialization of agriculture and livestock rearing, see Chapter 6.

[18]Walker, Lost Wolves, p. 166. The author highlights that wolves were eradicated in England around 1500, in Scotland by 1743, and in Ireland in the 1770s.

[19]Walker, Lost Wolves, p. 177.

[20]In truth, this discussion is a lot more complex. Newer studies underline the fact that wolves do adapt quickly to human behaviour and can be considered hemerophiles in spatially more constricted conditions as we would find them in Central Europe. A cruel, if rather telling, example would be the stories of wolves following armies into battle, to feed on the fallen soldiers – see, e.g. Sander Govaerts, 'Wolves and Warfare in the History of the Low Countries, 1000–1800' Low Countries Historical Review 137(1) (2022), pp. 4–27.

understanding of the word 'ecology' as 'the body of knowledge concerning the economy of nature – the investigation of the total relations of the animal both to its inorganic and to its organic environments'. Japanese scholars largely adapted Haeckel's understanding, although it was contested by the concept of 'ethology' as a science that was more focused on animal behaviour itself.[21] According to Walker, however, it was ethnologists who were the first to become academically inclined into researching the disappearance of the wolf in Japan, linking it to rural development and the destruction of habitats. This transformation broke apart pack structures and created dangerous loners that at times started to live rather like dogs and were prone to attacking humans.[22] Thus, the loss of wilderness meant also the hybridization and ultimately the loss of the wolf as a wild animal at the turn of the century.

In his book, Walker weaves together a variety of sources, ranging from library and archival findings to scientific texts, works of literature, religious poetry, oral-history interviews with descendants and personal experience in both Japan and the United States. From the point of view of environmental history, such place-based research done with both feet on the ground is highly laudable as it makes for a more colourful description that adds an air of authenticity.[23] Yet this panache does also invite criticism about the consistency of the author's emotional stance in the face of lupine violence that is absolutely natural animal behaviour. In another text, which became part of a much-lauded handbook of environmental history, Walker relates the story of a mining-engineering student who became prey to wolves. The in part unnecessarily gruesome details that follow are to underline his argument that animals do have historical agency – be it as the domesticated and wild dogs, hybrids and wolves of Japan or the seemingly much less threatening but equally active species of the human microbiome. Animals, he concludes, 'are not separate from humanity, but rather an intimate partner in humankind's biological and historical transcendence', a term he uses to denote the crossing of species boundaries through acts of cooperation or exploitation to secure their persistence. This, according to Walker, 'is the principal lesson on writings on animals in environmental history'.[24] As a

---

[21]Walker, *Lost Wolves*, pp. 184–6.

[22]Walker, *Lost Wolves*, pp. 196–8.

[23]On this approach, see also the edited volume David Moon, Nicholas B. Breyfogle and Alexandra Bekasova (eds), *Place and Nature. Essays in Russian Environmental History* (Cambridgeshire: White Horse Press, 2021).

[24]Brett L. Walker, 'Animals and the Intimacy of History', in Andew C. Isenberg (ed.), *The Oxford Handbook of Environmental History* (New York: Oxford University Press, 2014), pp. 52–75, quote p. 71.

consequence, the fluid distinctions between nature and culture, humans and animals are continuously redrawn.

That Savage Gaze

Ian Helfant's book starts with a bold statement: 'Wolves are becoming a public pestilence, a national scourge: they run into the cities and even the capitals in broad daylight, and in the villages they approach herds and throttle livestock without fear or danger.' The author of these words, written in 1880, is Leonid Pavlovich Sabaneev (1844–98), a zoologist and one of the most prominent publicists on hunting in late-nineteenth-century imperial Russia. 'Our peasants', he continues, 'have once again fallen into servitude – only this time not to people, but rather to a predatory beast.'[25] Reports of such vile animals that brutally attacked people were legion, and contemporaries spoke of a veritable wolf plague in the tsarist empire.[26] What made matters worse was the associated spread of rabies. Consequently, Helfant unboxes the stereotypes and preconceived notions regarding wolves in Russia. Similar to Japan, wolf populations would be brought under control in the European part of the country through the introduction of cartridge-fired guns and the use of strychnine by the turn of the century. The central theme of his work is the complex interrelationship between humans and wolves, as symbolized by the titular 'savage gaze' that potentially emanates from both parties through their violent behaviour towards each other. For this, Helfant takes an ecocritical perspective that – much in the vein of Brett Walker's *The Lost Wolves of Japan* – combines works of the arts and the sciences ranging from the belles lettres to pamphlets that either aim at exterminating the animal or seek mercy on it.

In his first chapter, Helfant tackles one of Russian literature's greats head-on, with a scene from Lev Tolstoi's *War and Peace* that gives us a detailed account of an aristocratic hunt in the early nineteenth century during the time of the Napoleonic Wars (*c*.1800–1815). Worlds collide as a terrified wolf is held down by a borzoi dog under the cheerful eyes of the hunting party after a brutal chase. The wild animal, succumbing and fearing for its life, is reduced to a spectacle. Helfant attests a 'deep and symbolic significance' of such events

---

[25]Ian M. Helfant, *That Savage Gaze. Wolves in the Nineteenth-Century Russian Imagination* (Boston: Academic Studies Press, 2018), p. vi.
[26]Helfant, *That Savage Gaze*, pp. 41–2.

in tsarist gentry culture: 'Wolf hunting with borzois provided Russian hunters with a visceral yet mediated opportunity to confront a fierce predator that embodied the threat and challenge of Russi[a]'s remaining wilderness.'[27] This coincided with a representation of masculine prowess, not least in the figure of the patriarch, that showed notable similarities to bear hunts.[28] Throughout the nineteenth century, Russia remained a country with a strong lupine population, unlike parts of Central Europe where the animal was increasingly eradicated, as shown above. Also, Russian protagonists were depicted as being much more engaged in the actual violence of the kill, in contrast to fox hunters in England, for example, with its 'tamed landscapes and manicured parks'.[29] Dozens of wolfhounds were employed in these grand hunts with borzois and horses, according to Helfant, situated as skilful mediators between nature and culture that, thanks to their heightened senses, 'amplify and intensify the hunters' own perceptions'.[30]

In all this, the tsarist empire was framed as an example of a less-civilized, supposedly wilder and – with regard to the ideals of Enlightenment – backward society. Here, serfdom was only abolished in 1861. Until then, it was considered a peasant's duty to support such luxurious aristocratic hunts, often for several weeks a year which meant serving as a beater, catering for a large hunting party and seeing fields along with their crops trampled during the chase. This, of course, created tensions and fostered discontent as it endangered the livelihood of peasants. The decline of these lavish hunts as a result of the wide-ranging social reforms in the 1860s brought to the fore discussions about how to ensure effective predator control, which had been propagated as a service to society by noble protagonists. Especially since the 1870s, a rise in wolf populations was reported and ardently discussed by members of newly founded hunting societies that had a high social prestige due to their prominent aristocratic members, also of the tsar's family. It fell unto them to find ways to reduce the numbers of predatory animals – either through exclusive driven hunts geared towards well-paying members as in the case of the elitist Moscow Hunting Society (*Moskovskoe obshchestvo okhoty*, created in 1862), or a more systematic approach as suggested by the Imperial Society for the Promotion of Game and Wildlife of Economic Significance and Proper Hunting (*Imperatorskoe obshchestvo razmnozheniia*

---

[27]Helfant, *That Savage Gaze*, p. 2.
[28]See also Timm Schönfelder, 'Constructing Masculinities: Bear Hunting in Tsarist Russia Toward the Fin de Siècle', in Laura Beck and Maurice Saß (eds), *Hunting Troubles: Gender and Its Intersections in the Cultural History of the Hunt* (Cham: Palgrave, 2024), pp. 259–74. Worth mentioning here is the often-ignored role of Indigenous guides and helpers that not only made these kills possible but also secured the survival of the wealthy yet at times inexperienced participants.
[29]Helfant, *That Savage Gaze*, p. 7.
[30]Helfant, *That Savage Gaze*, p. 10.

okhotnich'ikh i promyslovykh zhivotnykh i pravil'noi okhoty, since 1872) that favoured the use of strychnine as a reliable measure. The latter understood itself as being grounded in science and fulfilling an educational mission on good hunting practices, hence the reference to 'proper hunting' (*pravil'naia okhota*) in their title. This found its way into the society's publications like the monthly journal *Nature and Hunting* (*Priroda i okhota*) which appeared between 1878 and 1912. It spanned a variety of themes, combining literary texts, professional discussions and personal memoirs for a broad readership. Thus, it is an excellent source for the debates of the time that Helfant makes good use of.

A strong voice that called for the extensive use of poison was the controversial government-sponsored work *On the Destruction of Domestic Livestock and Wild Game by Wolves and on the Eradication of Wolves*, completed in 1876 by privy councillor Vasilii Matveevich Lazarevskii (1817–90). Dubbed the *Lazarevskii report*, it was based on statistical data from the Russian regions west of the Urals. The direct economic losses he calculated were in the millions of roubles annually. Lazarevskii speculated that the value of all wildlife falling prey to wolves in European Russia added up to a staggering 50 million roubles.[31] Furthermore, he included difficult to verify and often-sensationalist (and selective) accounts of lethal wolf attacks on humans in rural regions which he set at 125 persons per year between 1849 and 1851, i.e. even before the perceived disorder following the curtailing of aristocratic hunting rights in the wake of the liberation of the serfs. Although leading members of the Imperial Hunting Society considered these numbers to be exaggerated, they shared Lazarevskii's conclusions that wolf killings of livestock and game had increased notably after the 1861 emancipation. This posed a threat to subsistence agriculture throughout Russia. The use of strychnine in a controlled manner appeared rational, cost-efficient and humane.[32]

The above-mentioned Sabaneev, who was also editor-in-chief of *Nature and Hunting*, went so far as to classify wolves as 'the most bitter enemy of our well-being' and 'to declare ruthless, implacable war on the predator'. According to Helfant, Sabaneev understood the decrease in wolf populations as an important indicator of civilization. Their allegedly rising numbers in Russia posed a conundrum that was to be done away with – 'but Russian society had not yet developed socioeconomically and politically to the point of organizing and mobilizing to defend itself effectively', Sabaneev lamented.[33] In effect, his was a modernizing mission, and he saw Russia in a catch-up development with

---

[31]Helfant, *That Savage Gaze*, pp. 41–2.
[32]Helfant, *That Savage Gaze*, p. 47.
[33]Quotes: Helfant, *That Savage Gaze*, p. 48.

the more advanced Western Europe. This also meant dispelling preconceived notions, superstitions and outdated science on wolf behaviour. In a range of publications, Sabaneev demystified anthropomorphic traits ascribed to wolves and underlined their strong social bonds. At the same time, a revision of hunting regulations was on the way in Russia that aimed at scientifically based predator control. This culminated in the first comprehensive hunting law as it was passed in 1892. It clearly differentiated two categories of wild animals according to their economic utility: predatory and non-predatory. While the latter enjoyed closed season and special protection (the bison, for example, became subject to wildlife conservation), the hunting of predators knew practically no limits: threats to agriculture and forestry including sparrows, crows, magpies and ground squirrels were to be exterminated.[34]

One driving motivation for the control of predatory animals was, just as in the case of Japan, the spread of rabies. The disease could only be treated after the invention of a vaccine by the French chemist and microbiologist Louis Pasteur in 1885 which was administered after the fact. Rabies stations were established throughout the Russian Empire and in other parts of the world following the realization that time was of the essence for a successful treatment. As Helfant shows through the broad contextualization of two literary works which were both first published in 1886 – Anton Pavlovich Chekhov's 'Hydrophobia' (*Vodoboiazn'*) and Tatiana Andreevna Kuzminskaia's 'The Rabid Wolf' (*Beshenyi volk*) – there had been a predominant fear of wolf bites, especially among the rural population, as they were considered more lethal than dog bites (a view that was upheld by Pasteur due to the brutality of the attacks). This connected with folklore on vampires and werewolves that 'conflates the demoniacal with the bestial and the sexual, emphasizing above all the savage ferocity of those suffering from the disease'.[35] While Chekhov, who was a physician by training, describes human traits in the suffering of a rabid wolf, Kuzminskaia stresses the mistreatment of the victims by their peers and the harsh reaction of the authorities who admit them to an asylum. Taken together, the two stories highlight compassion for the wild animal on the one hand, but also scepticism of modern developments on the other.

The first aspect was addressed by early forms of animal activism: in 1865, the Russian Society for the Protection of Animals (*Rossiiskoe obshchestvo pokrovitel'stva zhyvotnym*) had been founded (see also Chapter 8). They condemned wolf hounding and other forms of animal-on-animal violence

---

[34]Ekaterina Pravilova, *A Public Empire. Property and the Quest for the Common Good in Imperial Russia* (Princeton: Princeton University Press, 2014), pp. 70–1.

[35]Helfant, *That Savage Gaze*, pp. 75–6.

along with snaring and the use of leg-hold traps. There were also much less civilized means, as told in an 1893 article in the ROPZh's bulletin:

> this method had been employed by the peasants of the Novgorod province from ancient times to the present. Hearing the howls of wolf pups from mid-June to mid-July, they would locate the den. The most intrepid among the villagers would then approach when the adults were away, pull out the pups, bind them with ropes, and take them to the nearest river. There they would nail them by their paws to round rafts, which they set afloat down the river. The yelping of the crazed pups was intended to cause the older wolves to pursue them along the river banks. The rafts, being round, would typically float a good distance, clearing the countryside around the den for some time if the method worked.[36]

The author stressed that wolves were simply following their instincts while human violence was premeditated, intentional (what is more, the communities living downstream were hardly happy about this kind of cargo). Anton Chekhov voiced similar criticism in 1882 about noble coursing competitions that were often held on horse-racing tracks where borzois – just as in Tolstoi's *War and Peace* – were let loose on unsuspecting wolves: 'No joking, humanity has disgraced itself before wolves in contriving this quasi-hunt! … It's another matter to hunt in the steppe, in the forest, where humans' bloodthirstiness can be excused by the possibility of an equal struggle, where the wolf can defend itself, run.'[37] The agony of these captive animals provoked unease and disgust – not least concerning the effect it must have had on the children in the audience. To Chekhov, this was a clear symbol of Russia's backwardness.

Helfant closes his account with a look across the ocean. The US-American nature writer Aldo Leopold (1887–1948), considered a pioneer in wildlife ecology and conservation, participated in government-sponsored wolf-eradication programmes as a forest ranger during the 1910s and 1920s. Similar to Chekhov's stories, he describes the 'fierce green fire' in the eyes of a dying she-wolf that triggers compassion and a deeper understanding for its nature in him.[38] Helfant notes strong parallels in the changing attitudes towards wolves and wilderness in the nineteenth and early twentieth centuries 'during an era when modern scientific approaches were gaining ascendancy but before the genesis of contemporary ecology and our concomitant recognition of the crucial importance of apex predators in well-functioning ecosystems'.[39] The

---

[36]As paraphrased in Helfant, *That Savage Gaze*, p. 105.
[37]'At the Wolf Hounding', as quoted in Helfant, *That Savage Gaze*, p. 109.
[38]From 'Thinking Like a Mountain', as quoted in Helfant, *That Savage Gaze*, p. 132.
[39]Helfant, *That Savage Gaze*, p. 136.

treatment of these animals was seen as indicative for progress towards a modern society. Here, however, Helfant highlights a problem of the sources, as the accounts he based his work on are usually not those of 'simple folk' (since they hardly left any documents due to illiteracy or a lack of prestige that would have made their voices heard), but of aristocrats and the bourgeoisie who considered them 'untrustworthy', 'uneducated', naïve and superstitious. Thus, they create a contrast between what they define as civilization and backwardness, providing 'a culture's sense of itself'.[40] But how can one conceptualize wilderness as it is symbolized by wolves in the works of Walker and Helfant?

Delineating wilderness

Wildness is, to say the least, a fickle concept. A popular and intuitive understanding revolves around the question of an individual's autonomy, the non-fiction writer Emma Marris argues:

> If an animal is free to make its own choices – even in a world shaped by humanity – then it is wild. If its life is controlled by another organism, then it is not wild. Under this definition, pets, farm animals and zoo animals are not wild. Neither is an aphid that is farmed for honeydew by a colony of ants. Humanness is not central to this definition (…) Wildness is freedom.[41]

The environmental historian William Cronon, in turn, reminds us that the notion of wilderness as a place of wildness is 'quite profoundly a human creation'.[42] During the nineteenth century he sees a change in semantics from barren, unproductive land to something that is worth being protected. Thus, in 1864 Yosemite became the first wildland park in the United States 'upon the express conditions that the premises shall be held for public use, resort, and recreation', as stipulated in the Yosemite Grant Act signed by President Abraham Lincoln.[43] It was followed by Yellowstone being declared the first federally protected national park in 1872.[44] This made territory that was read

---

[40]Helfant, *That Savage Gaze*, p. 138.

[41]Emma Marris, 'New York Is Wilder Than You Think' *The New York Times* (15 March 2024), https://www.nytimes.com/2024/03/15/opinion/free-new-york-wild.html [accessed on 30 July 2024].

[42]William Cronon, 'The Trouble with Wilderness or, Getting Back to the Wrong Nature' *Environmental History* 1(1) (1996), pp. 7–28, quote p. 7.

[43]Today in History – June 30. Yosemite, *Library of Congress*, https://www.loc.gov/item/today-in-history/june-30 [accessed on 30 April 2024].

[44]Act Establishing Yellowstone National Park (1872), *National Archives*, https://www.archives.gov/milestone-documents/act-establishing-yellowstone-national-park [accessed on 30 April 2024].

as 'wild' and 'untouched' a desired destination for tourism, echoing romantic notions of a return to a sublime nature. Another, typically American reading of this was the idea of the *frontier* as formulated by Frederick Jackson Turner in 1893:

> As Turner described the process, easterners and European immigrants, in moving to the wild unsettled lands of the frontier, shed the trappings of civilization, rediscovered their primitive racial energies, reinvented direct democratic institutions, and thereby reinfused themselves with a vigor, an independence, and a creativity that were the source of American democracy and national character. Seen in this way, wild country became a place not just of religious redemption but of national renewal, the quintessential location for experiencing what it meant to be an American.[45]

Cronon argues that this origin myth of the already vanishing frontier was to be preserved in the imagined wilderness of the new national parks. Here, projections of city dwellers and urban tourists onto nature birthed an ideal of wilderness that mirrored their civilizational background and was therefore alienated from actual practices on the ground. This nostalgia has an even more problematic downside in the repression, displacement and extinction of Indigenous people who had worked the land for millennia. Thus, the wilderness of the frontier was never truly wild and untouched, and – in consequence – the national park system can be seen as an expression of cultural imperialism. What is more, humans do not exist alongside nature but are a part of it. Our actions extend far into what is viewed as out of reach, and the effects of global warming are only the most obvious example of this. 'Instead, we need to embrace the full continuum of a natural landscape that is also cultural, in which the city, the suburb, the pastoral, and the wild each has its proper place, which we permit ourselves to celebrate without needlessly denigrating the others', Cronon concludes.[46]

What happens if humans do not adhere to this ideal was relayed by Roderick Nash's study *Wilderness and the American Mind* which first published in 1967 saw its fifth edition in 2014: 'early American colonists harbored a preternatural fear of wilderness, a fear that impelled generations of settlers to raze forests and destroy wildlife', Andrew Isenberg résumés.[47] But what is this boundary

---

[45]Cronon, 'The Trouble with Wilderness', p. 13.
[46]Cronon, 'The Trouble with Wilderness', p. 24.
[47]Andew C. Isenberg, 'From the Periphery to the Center: North American Environmental History' *Global Environment* 12 (2013), pp. 80–101, here p. 88.

that environmental historians refer to? According to Nash's repeatedly uttered – if highly dubious and ultimately untenable – ad hoc etymology of 'wild' as a contraction of 'willed', 'wilderness' is 'self-willed land'. In this understanding, it is merely a perceived reality, a state of mind, a cultural construct, a product of civilization that gained positive momentum as a reaction to urbanization. 'Appreciation of wilderness began in the cities', Nash posits at the outset of his third chapter on 'The Romantic Wilderness'. 'The literary gentleman wielding a pen, not the pioneer with his axe, made the first gestures of resistance against the strong currents of antipathy.'[48] It was the imagination of intellectuals that saw in wilderness 'the sublime in nature was linked with God's grandeur'.[49] Ultimately, this glorifying strand that experienced nature through the distorted prism of a modernizing world fed into the conservationist ideals of the national parks movement in the United States as it was sketched at the beginning of this chapter. 'In the 1960s and 1970s', Nash argues, '"environment" and "ecology" became household words', and humans were 'rediscovered as being part of nature'.[50] The first step in reconnecting the physical and the cultural as already hinted in his book would be to overcome anthropocentrism – even if wilderness, for Nash, remains 'a concept that exists solely in the human mind'.[51] This point of contention became an important theme that was further fleshed out in the years that followed.

Overcoming the nature–culture divide

A less associative and much more theoretically elaborated contribution to our understanding of boundary-making was made by the French anthropologist Philippe Descola. In 'Beyond Nature and Culture', which was first published in French in 2005, he questions the binarism of 'human' and 'non-human' in what he labelled an 'anthropology of nature'. Knowing that his musings can be a demanding read, he was invited to give a lecture at the National Institute of Agricultural Research (INRA) in Paris in 2007. This provided him with the opportunity to frame his ideas about 'the role of nature in shaping

[48]Roderick Frazier Nash, *Wilderness and the American Mind* (New Haven: Yale University Press, [5]2014; first published in 1967), p. 44.
[49]Nash, *Wilderness*, p. 54.
[50]Nash, *Wilderness*, p. 254.
[51]'Finally some preservationists have attempted to defend wilderness based on nonanthropocentric reasons. They have argued that wilderness has a right to exist for its own sake, independent of whether mankind values it or not (...) There are several problems with this approach to defending wilderness. For one thing, as explained earlier, wilderness is an entirely human concept, an invention of civilized man' – Nash, *Wilderness*, p. 270.

human destiny' in a manner that is more accessible to people without a background in the social sciences or the humanities; it formed the basis for a rather theory-laden essay.[52] Nonetheless, Descola's text is a consequent call for transdisciplinary approaches as it is typical for his specialty. Anthropology, he writes, 'first constituted itself, around the end of the nineteenth century, as a science of interface between nature and culture'.[53] This statement is all the more notable, considering Descola's academic background. As a student of Claude Lévi-Strauss (1908–2009), he was heavily influenced by the ideas of structuralism which preferred binary oppositions to understand the world through difference and contrast. Such was the distinction of *nature* as a biological being from *culture* as the social individual. According to Descola, this dualism had evolved with European modernity and found its culmination point towards the end of the nineteenth century.[54]

His doctoral studies in the Amazon in the 1970s together with his wife Anne-Christine Taylor sensitized Descola to the underlying Eurocentric bias of this dualistic idea, since Indigenous communities differ greatly in their perception of nature: for the people of the Achuar in Peru and Ecuador, for example, nature does not exist – at least not as something that is clearly detached from humans. In their animist worldview, living beings are deeply connected with their environment.[55] Descola goes on to argue that the question where nature stops and culture begins ultimately does not make any sense in an age of global interconnectedness when we consider such phenomena like climate change or the use of stem cells in medicine.[56] As we have seen in the example of *The Lost Wolves of Japan*, this predominantly European and North American model of thought spread around the world through Western colonization and modernization. This brings us back to the issue outlined at the beginning of this chapter: how can a modern society reacquaint itself with wilderness?

Almost ironically, Japan is reportedly among the few countries that would decidedly favour the reintroduction of wolves due to its large number of agriculturalists and foresters. As the anthropologist Garry Marvin explains:

---

[52]Philippe Descola, *The Ecology of Others* (Chicago: Prickly Paradigm Press, 2013), p. ii.
[53]Descola, *The Ecology of Others*, p. 6.
[54]Descola, *The Ecology of Others*, p. 31. He highlights, however, that the oeuvre of Claude Lévi-Strauss was not limited to such 'simple-minded' dualisms and 'binary oppositions that are as abstract as they are unverifiable'. In Descola's view, this was rather an issue with ethnologists and historians who were influenced by Lévi-Strauss but adhered to a more superficial understanding of structuralism – pp. 23–4.
[55]Philippe Descola, *In the Society of Nature. A Native Ecology in Amazonia* (Cambridge: Cambridge University Press, 1994); further elaborated in *Beyond Nature and Culture* (Chicago: The University of Chicago Press, 2014) which was first published in French in 2005, as noted above.
[56]Descola, *The Ecology of Others*, p. 82.

Both groups must put a great deal of effort into keeping these crop-raiding animals [wild boar and monkeys] at bay and it is argued that the wolf would be a powerful weapon to control their numbers and impact. Beyond any utilitarian benefit, the possible reintroduction of wolves to Japan is also discussed in terms of a symbolic process of atonement for the sins of the destruction of wild environments in the pursuit of progress, the eradication of wolves because of human wrong-doing and deviation from traditional ways of engaging with the natural world.[57]

The biggest challenge in rewilding, of course, is finding the right balance of many conflicting economic interests and reconciling them with cultural preconceptions. Communities that have lived in close proximity to wolves for generations hold a lot of knowledge and advice which is slowly being rediscovered by scholars and scientists alike. From an idealistic standpoint. it is a historian's duty to keep these experiences alive in order to inform future endeavours – and to avoid the repetition of mistakes due to a reduced or lost understanding of our place in the world. Though wolves remained wild animals and did not become human companions, they came to play an increasingly important role in nature management as indispensable mediators along the nature–culture divide.

---

[57]Marvin, *Wolf*, p. 179.

3

Coevolution and domestication: Companion species in everyday interaction

While the preceding chapter was concerned with boundary-making to delineate 'nature' and 'culture' or 'wilderness' and 'civilization', we will now focus our attention on the result of millennia of coevolution and selection: 'human's best friend', the dog. Such a companion is Cayenne Pepper, trained to compete in the discipline of agility by Donna Haraway, herself one of the most provocative thinkers of the past decades and a notable trailblazer for more-than-human theory. This is followed by established studies on animals in urban environments, including Harriet Ritvo's *The Animal Estate* on Victorian England, Chris Pearson's *Dogopolis* on canines in New York, London and Paris as well as *The Horse in the City* by Clay McShane and Joel Tarr. Not only do practices of everyday interaction with companion species make us reflect on the question how urban spaces are created at their interplay, but they also force us to re-evaluate the controversial status of emotions in historiography.

Such emotions are a strong descriptive building block of Donna Haraway's account of her close, at times seemingly romantic, relationship with her dogs. The essay starts out with her crossing more than just boundaries of taste, as she describes the exchange of saliva, with her dog's 'darter-tongue kisses' being 'irresistible':

Her red merle Australian Shepherd's quick and lithe tongue has swabbed the tissues of my tonsils, with all their eager immune system receptors (...) We have had forbidden conversation; we have had oral intercourse; we are bound in telling story upon story with nothing but the facts. We are training each other in acts of communication we barely understand. We are, constitutively, companion species.[1]

In her 'Companion Species Manifesto', Haraway aims at overcoming binary distinctions in what she calls 'natureculture' as an affectionate bond between various species: 'we signify in the flesh a nasty developmental infection called love. This love is an historical aberration and a naturalcultural legacy'.[2] In doing so, she connects *technobiopolitics* to feminist theory. *Technobiopolitics*, as presented in Haraway's earlier work *A Cyborg Manifesto* (1985), is a framework that questions a clear-cut nature–culture divide by illuminating the intersections of humans, machines and life itself.[3] Her texts are a mixture of provocation and associative analysis delivered at a feverish pace that borders the nonsensical – inspiring yet at times difficult to handle.[4]

The Companion Species Manifesto sets out to test the limits of our understanding of the human–animal bond: 'A bestiary of agencies, kinds of relatings, and scores of time trump the imaginings of even the most baroque cosmologists.'[5] Haraway's musings are based on a relational understanding of the world around us: connections are being constantly remade, nothing is static and ever-lasting. Her manifesto is an intellectual earthquake that shakes preconceived notions of agency, interaction and cross-species partnership. The parallels to feminist criticism regarding the hierarchies of the latter, partnership, become obvious as she breaks down the conventional understanding of (co-)evolution: 'Man took the (free) wolf and made the (servant) dog and so made civilization possible.'[6] But what about the changes that humans themselves underwent in this reciprocal endeavour (hence the prefix in *co-evolution*) over a timespan of thousands of years? It becomes clearer now why Haraway started out with the provocation of her becoming one with her dogs, exchanging bacteria and pathogens.

This, however, is not comradery based on unconditional love, an idea she labels 'a rarely excusable neurotic fantasy'.[7] Haraway is also highly sceptical of other common perceptions of human–animal kinship: 'To regard a dog as

---

[1] Donna Haraway, *The Companion Species Manifesto. Dogs, People, and Significant Otherness* (Chicago: Prickly Paradigm Press, 2003), pp. 1–3.

[2] Haraway, *The Companion Species Manifesto*, p. 3.

[3] For a more recent introduction, see Benjamin Lipp and Sabine Maasen, 'Techno-bio-politics. On Interfacing Life with and Through Technology' *Nanoethics* 16 (2022), pp. 133–50.

[4] The author herself probably would not dispute this, as she states: 'The accounts I offer are idiosyncratic and indicative rather than systematic, tendentious more than judicious, and rooted in contingent foundations rather than clear and distinct premises' – Haraway, *The Companion Species Manifesto*, pp. 23–4.

[5] Haraway, *The Companion Species Manifesto*, p. 6.

[6] Haraway, *The Companion Species Manifesto*, p. 27.

[7] Haraway, *The Companion Species Manifesto*, p. 34.

a furry child, even metaphorically, demeans dogs and children – and sets up children to be bitten and dogs to be killed.'[8] Her critics, in turn, have expressed doubt regarding the overly positive interpretation of 'the freedom to live safely in multi-species, urban and sub-urban environments with very little physical restraint and no corporal punishment while getting to play a demanding sport with every evidence of self-actualizing motivation'.[9] Haraway's discipline of choice in that regard which occupies a central place in her manifesto – *agility* – was first presented to the public at the prestigious 1978 Crufts dog show in London as entertainment during breaks between competitions. It was inspired, as she explains, by equestrianism and took some of its cues from police and military dog training as it had developed during the twentieth century.[10] Yet authors like Boria Sax and Rebecca Cassidy deem such dog training 'a symbolic affirmation of human dominance over the natural world', labelling it potentially 'hierarchical and patriarchal'.[11] An obvious issue that both sides of the debate are susceptible to is the pitfall of anthropomorphizing their canine companions – either by claiming they enjoy activities in the same way as their human counterpart or in demanding equal consideration of their rights within today's societies (a controversial issue also among scholars of human–animal relations).

Towards the end of her text Haraway puts a historical focus on two breeds she has the most experience with: Great Pyrenees as guardian dogs for livestock and Australian Shepherds, which are highly suitable for agility. The former are presented as a recurring success story for US-ranchers as they protect their 'xenobiological cattle and sheep' (brought from the 'Old World', as will be explained in a later chapter) after they had for a time been displaced by the use of specialized poisons against predators (reminiscent of the discussions on wolves in the preceding chapter).[12] For Haraway – much in the vein of this introduction – animal history is closely connected to the human stories we tell 'about immigration, indigenous worlds, work, hope love, play, and the possibility of co-habitation'.[13] Aptly, the sociologist Joanna Latimer writes in her appraisal of the manifesto:

Haraway's huge move here is to show us in companion species how kinship and inheritance is not linear-up and down a chronological tree of life – with each species having a different tree. But also lateral. The who and what we

---

[8]Haraway, *The Companion Species Manifesto*, p. 36.

[9]Haraway, *The Companion Species Manifesto*, p. 45.

[10]Haraway, *The Companion Species Manifesto*, p. 57.

[11]Chris Vanderwees, 'Companion Species under Fire: A Defense of Donna Haraway's *The Companion Species Manifesto*' *Nebula* 6(2) (2009), pp. 73–81, here p. 77.

[12]Haraway, *The Companion Species Manifesto*, quote p. 75.

[13]Haraway, *The Companion Species Manifesto*, p. 80.

live with, and the worlds we make together with these whos and these whats, make us up as both fleshy and virtual beings.[14]

The author herself summarizes that the making of companion species is like creating a family that is 'made up in the belly of the monster of inherited histories that have to be inhabited to be transformed'. In her very own rebellious style, she adds: 'I always knew that if I turned up pregnant, I wanted the being in my womb to be a member of another species; maybe that turns out to be the general condition.'[15] While Haraway succeeds at delivering important impulses, animal history has to go beyond such provocations through an empirically based analysis of human–animal interaction – not least if it aspires to connect with other disciplines and speak to policymakers as well as interested laypeople. Such an analytical and historical depth characterizes the more informative works on companion species.

Summoning the estates

It is no exaggeration to count Harriet Ritvo's book among the pathbreaking works of animal history. Published in 1987, it appeared at a time when environmental history was still in its infancy, and non-human histories were wrongly relegated to the esoteric fringes of academia by many. *The Animal Estate* proves the critics wrong by presenting a sociocultural panorama of Victorian England. Ritvo carefully introduces her readers to the world of the nineteenth century when animals became objects possessed by humans. As property they could no longer be brought to court for their misdeeds – a practice often ascribed to less enlightened medieval and early modern times.[16] In contrast, the Victorian Era is commonly perceived as a time of scientific, technological and industrial development. Yet people showed a strong interest in the natural world: illustrated books and journals on zoology were printed in large numbers, and natural history exhibitions which soon turned into museums were sure to draw a crowd. 'Natural history elaborated

---

[14]Joanna Latimer, 'Review: Donna Haraway, "Manifestly Haraway"' *Theory, Culture & Society* (26 June 2016), https://www.theoryculturesociety.org/blog/review-donna-haraway-manifestly-haraway [accessed on 11 September 2024].

[15]Haraway, *The Companion Species Manifesto*, p. 94.

[16]Cf. Peter Dinzelbacher, 'Animal Trials: A Multidisciplinary Approach' *The Journal of Interdisciplinary History* 32(3) (2002), pp. 405–21 who underlines 'that animal trials took place only under extremely unusual circumstances in order to help the local community cope with an otherwise recalcitrant threat – not because they were proven to work but because they created the impression that the authorities were assiduously maintaining law and order in a cooperative and decided manner, even if the delinquents were not human beings' (p. 406).

a hierarchical vision of creation, with humanity at the apex', she observes. 'The more naturalists discovered about exotic animals in distant places, the less they doubted that human dominance was divinely ordained.'[17] This translated not only into the daily use of animals, but also into violent colonial policies that extracted resources with utter disregard for the suffering of the local Indigenous population (a theme that will be the focus of Chapters 4 and 5): 'The dichotomy between domesticated animals and wild animals was frequently compared to that between civilized and savage human societies.'[18]

The prime example of such a 'most sagacious' companion was, of course, the dog with its 'ingenious loyalty' to its human masters.[19] Selective breeding – a practice that began at the turn of the eighteenth century with thoroughbred horses and gained a serious following with cattle and pigs in the ensuing decades – translated also into the canine world: 'Although dog breeding was not apt to be a profitable hobby, it did not require either great wealth or broad acres.'[20] Much to the dismay of aristocratic actors, the lower social ranks also took a liking to creating pedigrees of prize pets as a pastime. While the underlying human–animal bonds date back millennia, they gained a new quality during the Victorian Age as creatures were kept not to work but rather 'for companionship and amusement'.[21] Soon, the judging of these animals became institutionalized through contests and dog shows that followed intricate point systems. This marked a qualitative change in perception as earlier classifications were generally 'based on function rather than physical appearance (...) Any large dog would have been called a mastiff, any lapdog a spaniel-gentle'.[22] Now, a myriad of new breeds made it to the market and left their imprint on popular leisure culture:

The advent of modern dog shows purged dog fancying of an earlier, less savory reputation as suitable only for country squires, who needed

---

[17]Harriet Ritvo, *The Animal Estate. The English and Other Creatures in the Victorian Age* (Cambridge: Harvard University Press, 1987), p. 14. For another excellent introduction, see Keith Thomas, *Man and the Natural World. Changing Attitudes in England 1500–1800* (London: Allen Lane, 1983).

[18]Ritvo, *The Animal Estate*, p. 16.

[19]Ritvo, *The Animal Estate*, p. 37.

[20]Ritvo, *The Animal Estate*, pp. 60, 85 For more detail on the transfer of ideas from livestock to dog breeding and its cultural implications, see Michael Worboys, Julie-Marie Strange and Neil Pemberton, *The Invention of the Modern Dog: Breed and Blood in Victorian Britain* (Baltimore: The Johns Hopkins University Press, 2018).

[21]Ritvo, *The Animal Estate*, p. 85. For the preceding centuries, see also Edmund Russell, *Greyhound Nation: A Coevolutionary History of England, 1200–1900* (Cambridge: Cambridge University Press, 2018), Ingrid H. Tague, *Animal Companions. Pets and Social Change in Eighteenth-Century Britain* (University Park: Penn State University Press, 2015), and Erica Fudge, *Quick Cattle and Dying Wishes. People and Their Animals in Early Modern England* (Ithaca: Cornell University Press, 2018).

[22]Ritvo, *The Animal Estate*, p. 94.

foxhounds and shooting dogs, and for the rough urban types who liked to bet on bulldog matches and greyhound races. Show prizes were awarded for elegance and breeding, rather than brute strength and speed.[23]

In 1859, the first such dog show was organized in Newcastle (its precursors had usually been held in public houses with a more 'convivial' setting). They soon gained a broad audience: by the end of the century, Ritvo counts 380 events in a single year, predominantly on a small-town and regional level. A fact that reconnects nicely to Donna Haraway's work above is the increasing role women occupied through organizations like the Ladies' Kennel Association, which was founded in 1895. Starting with the Kennel Club in 1873, these organizations tried to secure good sportsmanship in the face of the widespread fraudulent dealings during these competitions. One year later, the *Stud Book* was first published, listing 'excellent and well-bred' prized dogs that had been exhibited since 1859 and laying down a code of ground rules. Thus, pedigree was codified that in turn not only determined breed standards but also opened ways for people to distinguish themselves from others through the status of their animals: 'It had become a respectable and well-regulated pastime, a reflection of the carefully calibrated human social order.' As Ritvo continues to argue, this catered to 'the desire of predominantly middle-class fanciers for a relatively prestigious and readily identifiable position within a stable, hierarchical society'. Consequently, dogs used in aristocratic hunting practices like greyhounds, foxhounds and shooting dogs 'were judged not in the artificial environment of shows but by their performance in the field'.[24] This marked a notable contrast to the arbitrary standards set for pets that served rather to distinguish than to have real-world application. Thus, former working canines like bulldogs and collies lost many of the features that enabled them to perform their original tasks. The 'physical malleability' of these animals, Ritvo concludes, was self-referential of the breeders, indicating their 'paradoxical willingness aggressively to reconceive and refashion the social order in which they coveted a stable place'.[25]

---

[23]Ritvo, *The Animal Estate*, p. 97.
[24]Ritvo, *The Animal Estate*, pp. 98–105, quotes pp. 104–5; see also 'The Ladies' Kennel Association – 100 not out!' *Our Dogs*, https://www.ourdogs.co.uk/News/2004/November2004/News261104/lka.htm [accessed on 17 September 2024].
[25]Ritvo, *The Animal Estate*, p. 115. Naturally, this proved much more difficult with cat breeding (the first show was held in 1871) due to an 'inherent resistance of the species to subdivision and genetic manipulation' (p. 116). See also Jonathan B. Losos, *The Age of Cats. From the Savannah to Your Sofa* (London: William Collins, 2023).

Beastly city dwellers

While Ritvo's book has laid out more of the core themes for animal history, this chapter will stay focused on companion species in urban contexts for now. Curiously enough, the role of animals in the development of these spaces had remained largely neglected for decades, notwithstanding the many rich examples, as Dorothee Brantz argues:

> Despite this wealth of sources, urban historians were not particularly interested in how animals affected the development of cities because cities were commonly regarded as 'man-made' spaces created solely through human intentions and for human purposes.[26]

Especially through cultural studies, animals found their way back into the history of modern settlements. One outstanding example that goes beyond the borders of Great Br tain is Chris Pearson's *Dogopolis*. The author describes how the cities of London, New York and Paris evolved as places of cohabitation during the nineteenth century. Following the example of Harriet Ritvo, he attests a 'veneration of domesticity that fetishized pet dogs' as a constituting element of dogopolis surrounding 'the middle-class emotional experiences of urbanization'.[27] Unfortunately, Pearson does not further define what exactly he considers 'middle-class'. This issue must be addressed not only due to the socioeconomic differences between Great Britain, the United States and France, but also because its composition changed notably during the time span under scrutiny from the early 1800s to the 1930s, i.e. from a time marked by the aftermath of the American War of Independence (1775–83) and a rise of the bourgeoisie following the French Revolution of 1789, through the pinnacle of British colonialism in the 'Global South', to the post-war depression of the 1920s. This period's protagonists saw the intensifying industrialization of production and a globalization of trade that remade urban infrastructures along with waves of societal unrest and social reform that were often followed by phases of more reactionary policies across Europe. What is deemed 'bourgeois' in French and English or 'bürgerlich' in German does not automatically correspond to the idea of an urban 'middle-class' that is situated somewhere between workers and nobles. A translation into the seemingly less rigid American social system, where aristocracy is out of the

---

[26]Dorothee Brantz, 'Animals in Urban-Environmental History', in Sebastian Haumann, Martin Knoll and Detlev Mares (eds), *Concepts of Urban-Environmental History* (Bielefeld: transcript, 2020) pp. 191–201, here p. 192.
[27]Chris Pearson, *Dogopolis. How Dogs and Humans Made Modern New York, London, and Paris* (Chicago and London: The University of Chicago Press, 2021), p. 5.

picture and a strong business elite develops not least through upward mobility in line with the myth of the 'American Dream', proves equally difficult.[28] As one scholar aptly put it referring to the historian Reinhart Koselleck: 'In many respects, nineteenth century bourgeois society was a "transitional society" on the threshold between the persistent estatist past and the challenges posed by democracy.' Accordingly, the bourgeois middle classes as they evolved in Western societies form a complex amalgamation of political, economic and cultural factors. It is through common value systems and interests that their *socialization* (i.e. their functional societal integration) ultimately succeeds.[29]

Such shared values and ideas are presented by Pearson in the discourses on street dogs and their connection to the 'lower classes'. Both were identified with 'disease, dirt, and disorder', as it was also mirrored in the term *canaille*, taken from the Italian *canaglia* ('pack of dogs'), meaning 'rabble' or 'riffraff'. Not least in the case of New York, this was permeated with strong racist undertones. As the author observes, 'stray dogs joined prostitutes, manual laborers, beggars, and hawkers as unwelcome and physical obstacles to wealthy metropolitan lifestyles (...) they had become dislocated from civilized human society'. He considers the campaigns to remove them from urban life 'early building blocks of dogopolis'.[30] As such, New York started to employ dogcatchers in 1811 to round up and kill them. Citizens were allowed to participate in this as well. A municipal pound where strays were held and culled if not claimed in time had been created in Paris at least by 1791 while one in New York can be dated back to 1647 (a dedicated dog pound was only created in 1851, however). Great Britain ultimately experienced a pinnacle of anxiety in 1830 in connection with outbreaks of rabies. In all cases, the introduction of taxes on pets and bounties on their heads made little difference in managing stray animals. What is more, public opinion was divided about the violent means employed which led to protests and altercations with dogcatchers in the streets and at the pounds. 'In coming between dogs and their owners', Pearson notes, 'the unscrupulous dogcatchers were human-canine bond breakers and perpetrators of emotional distress'.[31] At the same time, strays were thought to lack the 'capacity for emotional refinement' of pedigree dogs; this 'distanced them from the middle-

[28]Cf. Christof Dejung, David Motadel and Jürgen Osterhammel (eds), *The Global Bourgeoisie. The Rise of the Middle Classes in the Age of Empire* (Princeton: Princeton University Press, 2019).
[29]Manfred Hettling, 'Bürger, Bürgertum, Bürgerlichkeit (English Version)' *Docupedia-Zeitgeschichte* (8 June 2016), http://docupedia.de/zg/hettling_buerger_v1_en_2016 [accessed on 21 September 2024].
[30]Pearson, *Dogopolis*, pp. 15–17.
[31]Pearson, *Dogopolis*, p. 23.

class veneration', allowing them 'to be killed in the vivisectionist laboratory and in lethal chambers' (see also Chapter 8).[32]

It is a pity we do not learn more about the fledgling field of the history of emotions from the author at the beginning of his work, given that fear and compassion play such a central role in his story.[33] A more analytical focus would have helped Pearson structure his impressionistic retelling of events that follows broad thematic strokes without investing lasting attention into locally specific developments as he breaks with chronology quite often.[34] Before looking at the remaining chapters of his *Dogopolis* – *Biting*, *Suffering*, *Thinking*, and *Defecating* – we will divert our curiosity to what some colleagues have deemed the 'emotional turn'. This includes a long-standing debate on the question how exactly 'emotions are the result [of] our values and our assessments'.[35] To understand the above-described fierce reactions regarding the treatment of animals one must not only ask about the origins of supposed 'middle-class norms of cleanliness, respectability, and domesticity'[36] – and if they can truly be delineated from those of upper-class citizens, an operation Pearson sadly ignores. One must also try and understand the makeup of such urban emotional communities not least as a result of religious beliefs, traditions and a shared knowledge of the world. Dealing with emotions in history is not supposed to be an isolated field of its own, as Barbara Rosenwein underlines. Ideally, it is about integrating it into what she calls 'regular history' as it has already happened with questions of sex and gender.[37]

In his commendable multi-perspective introduction, Jan Plamper highlights that defining emotions creates issues similar to the distinction between nature and culture. Thus, it is still debated whether emotions are universal constants or rather social phenomena representative of their respective time and place.[38] Historians can both facilitate our understanding of the past by establishing abstract categories that are apt for comparison and complicate

---

[32] Pearson, *Dogopolis*, p. 33.

[33] His concise 'Reflections on Animals, History, and Emotions' are hidden as an appendix on pp. 187–91. They present more of a literature review of corresponding anthropological and historiographical studies, underlining the necessity of a history of emotions to refocus on human–animal relatedness and emotional responses to it.

[34] To amend this, he offers a timeline on pp. 193–6.

[35] Jan Plamper, 'The History of Emotions: An Interview with William Reddy, Barbara Rosenwein, and Peter Stearns' *History and Theory* 49(2) (May 2010), pp. 237–65, here p. 251.

[36] Pearson, *Dogopolis*, p. 180.

[37] Plamper, 'An Interview', p. 260.

[38] Jan Plamper, *The History of Emotions. An Introduction* (Oxford: Oxford University Press, 2015; first published in German as *Geschichte und Gefühl. Grundlagen der Emotionsgeschichte* in 2012), pp. 6–7.

the picture by describing specific cultural codes in emotional communities, e.g. by looking at bourgeois pet keepers in nineteenth-century Paris. Each case study must elaborate its own working definition to understand emotional practices in their sociocultural environment.[39] In the case of 'dogopolis', this means that to understand the unease and disgust of the witnesses to the state of the pounds and their fear about rabies is to re-create their worldview. While the reader sure does feel a degree of compassion with the victims, as in the story of six-year-old New Yorker John Clark who dies of 'hydrophobia' after being bitten by a German Shepherd in 1878, it is difficult to reimagine the widespread anxiety today that persisted even after the discovery of a rabies vaccine by Louis Pasteur in 1885. Pearson's observation that '[c]anine aggression toward humans challenged the assumption that domestication had tamed the wild beast within dogs, perhaps reviving fears of wolves and other wild animals' is a great starting point to understand the popular nineteenth-century assumption 'that disturbing emotions and images could create rabid symptoms in susceptible individuals'. Interestingly, this was also thought to extend to non-humans: 'Certain dogs were on an emotional knife-edge and could easily become rabid', which would be triggered by sexual frustration, anger and fear.[40] The strong moralistic undertones of such a belief in emotional vulnerability parallels the liminality of both stray dogs and the 'dangerous classes' in urban environments as dehumanized vagrant poor on the verge of wildness in a purgatorial state.[41] Since they did not fit in with society, they were prone to sickness and, in the cases of dogs caught in the streets, marked for death unless it was shown that they actually belonged to a respectable owner. 'Humane slaughter, rather than social reform or emigration, was the agreed response to the canine underclass', Pearson describes a common fin de siècle-sentiment.[42]

---

[39]Cf. Monique Scheer, 'Are Emotions a Kind of Practice (and Is That What Makes Them Have a History)? A Bourdieuan Approach to Understanding Emotion' *History and Theory* 51(2) (2012), pp. 193–220. Here, Scheer emphasizes 'the mutual embeddedness of minds, bodies, and social relations in order to historicize the body and its contributions to the learned experience of emotion' (p. 199) in accordance with a praxeological approach. See also Plamper, *History of Emotions*, pp. 265–70.

[40]Pearson, *Dogopolis*, pp. 47–56, quotes pp. 49–50, 53, 54.

[41]Philip Howell, 'Between Wild and Domestic, Animal and Human, Life and Death: The Problem of the Stray in the Victorian City', in Clemens Wischermann, Aline Steinbrecher and Philip Howell (eds), *Animal History in the Modern City. Exploring Liminality* (London et al.: Bloomsbury, 2019), pp. 145–60, and Philip Howell, *At Home and Astray. The Domestic Dog in Victorian Britain* (Charlottesville: University of Virginia Press, 2015).

[42]Pearson, *Dogopolis*, p. 111. See also the chapter 'Cave Canem' in Ritvo, *The Animal Estate*, pp. 167–202. Ritvo stresses that the fear of rabies was rather exaggerated: 'the average English citizen of the later nineteenth century was more than ten times as likely to be murdered as to die of hydrophobia' (pp. 169–70).

Motivating compassion

Animal protectionists soon joined the voices that underlined mistreatment as a possible cause of rabies. Due to 'their heightened capacity to feel and their close bond with humans', they argued that dogs 'deserved the most sympathy'. They also wanted to avoid the brutalization of fellow citizens through excessive cruelty. 'Emotion acted as the glue that bonded civilized people together and ensured the smooth operation of modern societies', Pearson observes.[43] Harriet Ritvo underlines the long rocky road in developing a public consciousness from early-nineteenth-century attempts to ban bull baiting in Great Britain – a blood sport where hounds were set to attack and kill these creatures – and early legislation like the Cruel Treatment of Cattle Act of 1822 (also called Martin's Act after the responsible member of parliament) to the more encompassing Cruelty to Animals Acts of 1835 and 1849, as it was supported by the efforts of the Society for the Prevention of Cruelty to Animals (SPCA), created in 1824. In France, this evolution was mirrored in the Grammont Law of 1850 against the public display of violence on domestic animals and in the activities of the Société Protectrice des Animaux (SPA) since 1845. In the United States, it was the American Society for the Prevention of Cruelty to Animals (ASPCA), founded in 1866. While the SPCA was granted royal patronage by Queen Victoria in 1840 as a sign of recognition and support, its activities remained geared towards the interests of the upper class: 'Many of the society's most distinguished members were also, for example, enthusiastic fox hunters or grouse shooters and perceived no incongruity between their humane and their sporting avocations', Ritvo reminds us. Cruelty was identified 'as a lower-class propensity', and the now Royal Society for the Prevention of Cruelty to Animals (RSPCA) 'continued to reserve its systematic surveillance for cruelties that threatened to disrupt, rather than to sustain, the orderly hierarchy of Victorian society' in line with this bias.[44] This resulted in an overall less critical stance on animal experiments and vivisection.

Towards the end of the century, female pet owners in London protested the muzzling of their companions to fight the spread of rabies in contrast to the hunting dogs of wealthy men which were exempt from this measure: 'They likened muzzles to earlier male attempts to restrict female freedom and voices', Pearson notes.[45] The occurrence of rabies in foxhounds that used to symbolize 'the easy sway the gentry and aristocracy held over Victorian rural

---

[43]Pearson, Dogopolis, pp. 83–4.
[44]Ritvo, The Animal Estate, pp. 134–5, 165. See also: Hilda Kean, Animal Rights. Political and Social Change in Britain since 1800 (London: Reaktion Books, 1998).
[45]Pearson, Dogopolis, p. 77.

society' put this elitist claim to dominance into serious question, however.[46] As Kathleen Kete argues, pet keeping had become 'the way bourgeois talked about themselves'. The categorization of working and luxury dogs in Paris for the purpose of taxation (since 1856) proved a contentious issue: 'To bureaucrats, only working dogs were useful. For bourgeois pet owners, affect and defense against the onslaughts of modern life were essential functions of the dog.'[47] A new method 'to reshape the human-canine bond' that followed such utilitarian ideals was the training for police duty, Pearson writes:

> This was specialized canine labor that gave a select handful of dogs social purpose within the emerging dogopolis. It stood in contrast to the use of relatively unskilled dogs to pull, say, New York ragpickers' carts, the sort of canine labor animal protectionists associated with working-class cruelty and rabies and succeeded in banishing (...) Police dogs might become part of the modern police force, which was integral to the rise of 'bourgeois civilization' based on liberalism, capitalism, and the protection of private property.[48]

In this almost ironic turn of events as Pearson relates it, despised creatures of the streets had become pillars of a modern society. This upended long-standing prejudices about the dumb and unthinking companion which had famously been formulated by the early modern French mathematician and philosopher René Descartes (1596–1650) who characterized animals as 'natural automata' and 'self-moving machines' bereft of reason.[49] Criminologists arguing in the spirit of Darwinist evolutionary theory like the Italian Cesare Lombroso (1835–1909) believed that straying dogs (who lacked a purpose in society) were prone to fall back into a state of wildness: 'Domestication and civilization were traits that could be reversed in certain environments.' Projected on humans, inebriation, injury, heat and rabies were considered to be possible triggers for innate (i.e. biologically determined) savage and criminal behaviour.[50] The

---

[46]Ritvo, The Animal Estate, p. 182.
[47]Kathleen Kete, The Beast in the Boudoir. Petkeeping in Nineteenth-Century Paris (Berkeley and Los Angeles: University of California Press, 1994), pp. 40, 46.
[48]Pearson, Dogopolis, pp. 115–16.
[49]Deborah J. Brown, 'Animal Souls and Beast Machines: Descartes's Mechanical Biology', in Peter Adamson and G. Fay Edwards (eds), Animals. A History (New York: Oxford University Press, 2018), pp. 187–210, here p. 203. Brown underlines the overall laudable stance Descartes took in trying to formulate scientific explanations for natural phenomena.
[50]Pearson, Dogopolis, p. 121. Cesare Lombroso's main work Criminal Man, which was first published in 1876, became especially notorious for the figure of the 'atavistic born criminal', though newer editions tended to focus more strongly on the influence of environmental factors in shaping such personalities, as Pearson highlights.

resulting discipline of criminal anthropology, while prominent in the United States, played a lesser role in Great Britain. 'Nonetheless, some British criminologists depicted criminals as animal-like savages unable to control their violent urges', Pearson reminds us.[51] Natural, animalistic instinct and deviant behaviour seemed closely linked.

Canine instincts and intuition were to be harnessed to solving crime. In the case of the serial killer known as Jack the Ripper who roamed London in the late 1880s, two bloodhounds were set on his trail – yet to no avail.[52] In less spectacular fashion, and in line with the convictions of criminal anthropology that offenders were discernible by their smell, the use of such dogs in New York was also considered and they were ultimately deployed by the Long Island Railroad. It soon became clear, however, that '[m]odern urban infrastructure would confuse bloodhound noses'.[53] What might have worked in the countryside – not least to track down runaway slaves which was a cause for ethical concern – proved no match for a sprawling metropolis. For these reasons, law enforcement started to focus on more versatile (and less historically burdened) breeds. Paris, for this matter, never used bloodhounds following the British example – France promoted multi-purpose canines instead like the Belgian and the German Shepherd at the beginning of the new century. These companions were to make up for the loss of bodily strength and sensory acuity the urban middle-class population had allegedly experienced. Following its creation in 1910, the Union of Guard and Police Dog Enthusiasts in France organized their own pedigree shows.[54] On both sides of the Atlantic, their introduction into service was by no means a straightforward affair, however: 'It was only in the postwar period that permanent police canine units were established in all three cities, and police dogs became enduring features of dogopolis.'[55]

Modernization on horseback

Another key representative of charismatic fauna in urban environments was the horse.[56] This 'living machine' had become indispensable as a working animal in the cities of the nineteenth century where 'the climax of human

---

[51]Pearson, *Dogopolis*, p. 122.
[52]Pearson, *Dogopolis*, p. 126.
[53]Pearson, *Dogopolis*, p. 128.
[54]Pearson, *Dogopolis*, pp. 129–31.
[55]Pearson, *Dogopolis*, p. 146.
[56]For an overview on arguably less charismatic creatures, see Dawn Day Biehler, *Pests in the City. Flies, Bedbugs, Cockroaches, and Rats* (Seattle and London: University of Washington Press, 2013).

exploitation of horse power' was reached, according to Clay McShane and Joel A. Tarr.[57] Equine companions were indispensable for transport, to propel industrial machinery, water pumps or even ferries. Newer research also revisits their role in warfare, revealing 'the blurring of boundaries between humans and animals in the status of mobilized creatures', as Oksana Nagornaia writes.[58] In the cities, they were only slowly replaced by increasingly thrifty steam engines and electric motors. Lacking their own breed of working horses, Americans predominantly imported Percheron stallions from France since the mid-nineteenth century for their stamina and pulling force. 'In the 1880s, more than 40,000 horses came to the United States from Europe each year', McShane and Tarr show.[59] Yet breeding was successful, and imports were soon superseded by exports, even to Japan. Chicago became the largest horse market in the world with around 100,000 animals shipped annually at the turn of the century, reaching the extreme of 180,000 animals during the First World War.[60] The authors underline, however, that horses did not attain the same level of companionship as dogs or other pets:

Nineteenth-century animal owners valued horses almost exclusively for their productive utility. In other words, horses became living machines to be bought and sold like commodities, valued only rarely as natural beings. The willingness of horse owners to end the life of animals that had become even slightly lame – that is, lost their productive value – is a powerful measure of this outlook. Presumably, if horses were companion animals like modern pets or were living in nature, they would have been allowed to graze out their lives to the extent that their disability allowed. The killing of injured but live horses occurred not just because hauling, carrying, and lifting were the only economic functions of horses but also because their carcasses carried considerable economic value, generating income for tanners and renderers, among others. Even the wastes of

---

[57]Clay McShane and Joel A. Tarr, *The Horse in the City. Living Machines in the Nineteenth Century* (Baltimore: The Johns Hopkins University Press, 2007), p. 1 – reiterated on p. 17: 'For most of the century, the horse was indispensable as a living machine, to the point that we can label the nineteenth century as the golden age of the horse'.
[58]Oksana Nagornaia, 'Animal Fighters, Animal Victims: the Animal Dimension on the Russian-Austrian Front of the First World War', in Kerstin S. Jobst, Oksana Nagornaia and Kerstin von Lingen (eds), *The Great War and the Anthropocene. Empire and Environment, Soldiers and Civilians on the Eastern Front* (Leiden and Boston: Brill, 2024), pp. 127–44, here p. 143. See also Earl J. Hess, 'The Animal-Human Relationship in War. Cavalry Horses and Their Riders in the American Civil War' *Animal History* 1(1) (2025), pp. 71–90.
[59]McShane and Tarr, *The Horse in the City*, p. 11.
[60]McShane and Tarr, *The Horse in the City*, p. 23.

horses generated income for their human masters, since manure was a valued fertilizer in urban hinterlands.[61]

As we can gather from the discussion on working animals above, this argument appears to be rather one-sided. Yet it makes a valuable point about the importance of rationalization in the Victorian Age and how this extended to basically all living creatures, especially in a dense urban environment where space was scarce and people tried to find a footing. Consequently, horses were part of a complex economic network. This is already seen in the manure trade with farmers in the countryside which was an important source of income for stable owners until it was replaced by cheaper chemical fertilizers. The same, of course, could not be said of dog droppings which were commonly considered a public health issue – although they had been collected and sold in Paris and London to tannery workers who used it on sheep, goat and calf: 'The excrement removed moisture from the skins, making the leather destined for book covers and other uses smell nicer,' Pearson writes.[62] With human waste disappearing from the streets thanks to elaborated sewer systems and horses being replaced by new modes of transportation, canine faeces remained as a prominent reminder of less civil times.

Apart from police officers and veterinarians, it was often the humane societies that took care of unproductive working horses: 'Between 1887 and 1897, New York's ASPCA, the city's leading killer of animals, shot between eighteen hundred and seven thousand horses a year', McShane and Tarr highlight. Owners could then validate insurance claims.[63] In places where horsemeat was consumed, animals that were past their prime were brought to slaughterhouses. Dead horses had to be removed swiftly from the streets, ideally before rigor mortis set in to make use of the corpses' full economic potential. Meanwhile, swaths of harness makers, blacksmiths, wheelwrights, hay dealers and others serviced the still functioning animals and their wagons. In New York, the ASPCA tried to rein in cruelty against animals on public streets with their own agents as deputy sheriffs. Yet it was accused of playing favourites with prominent representatives of New York's social elite who had invested in transportation firms with their own large herds and were themselves members of the ASPCA or served as directors of similar humane organizations. As a result, not all classes were prosecuted equally.[64]

The role of the horse as a driving force of progress became most obvious in its use for transit. Here, the advent of the omnibus that offered space for

---

[61] McShane and Tarr, *The Horse in the City*, p. 18.

[62] Pearson, *Dogopolis*, pp. 149–77, here p. 159.

[63] McShane and Tarr, *The Horse in the City*, p. 27.

[64] McShane and Tarr, *The Horse in the City*, pp. 47–50.

more than a dozen passengers at once marked the beginning of a transport revolution. It stimulated urban growth by establishing fixed lines and regular timetables that connected designated residential and business districts. This vehicle had first appeared in the streets of Nantes, Bordeaux and Lyon in the 1820s before being legalized in the French capital in 1828 – 'Parisian police had initially resisted the innovation because they feared that omnibuses would create public safety issues by mixing various classes and would also obstruct narrow streets', McShane and Tarr explain. London received Parliament approval in 1832, and US-American cities followed suit.[65] This was succeeded by the horse-drawn railed streetcar which offered a smoother ride, had three times the capacity, and charged less than half of an omnibus (steam locomotives, which were still in their infancy, were prohibited in the streets of New York's city centre due to the danger they posed to pedestrians and passengers; downtown London and Paris did not authorize horse railways in the first place). 'In 1857 the new horsecar lines carried more than 23 million Manhattanites, the great mass of the riding public.'[66] While racial segregation remained an issue across the United States that carried over into the times of the 'Jim Crow' laws, members of the working class took to the cars 'in much the same way' as the middle-class for shopping and recreation, especially on the weekends – if not with the same frequency. 'More highly paid working people', in turn, 'used the cars to access work or perhaps occasionally to avoid exposure to foul weather'.[67] Just as the Parisian law enforcement had feared, this was not without social conflict. Meanwhile, the wealthy elite paraded their own coaches around Central Park and organized horse racing competitions – much to the entertainment also of lower-class onlookers.[68] Thus, McShane and Tarr remain positive in their conclusion:

> as one attempts to estimate the effects of the horsecar on the city, it should be viewed as a path-breaking technology, setting in motion far-reaching changes in urban spatial structure. The horse retained its animal nature, but in its relationship to the streetcar it had become a machine and a critical source of transforming power.[69]

---

[65]McShane and Tarr, *The Horse in the City*, pp. 57–9, quote p. 58.
[66]McShane and Tarr, *The Horse in the City*, p. 64. 'By 1880, New York horsecar ridership had expanded to 160,952,832 passengers, with 11,760 horses and mules pulling 1,493 cars over 136 miles of track' (pp. 64–5). Elevated railroads were built in New York starting in the 1870s – p. 171.
[67]McShane and Tarr, *The Horse in the City*, p. 82.
[68]McShane and Tarr, *The Horse in the City*, pp. 92–5. See also Simon Dixon, 'Horse-Racing in Nineteenth-Century Russia' *Slavonic and East European Review* 98(3) (2020), pp. 464–503 for an encompassing account.
[69]McShane and Tarr, *The Horse in the City*, p. 83.

This is closely reflected in the way horses shaped urban ecological patterns in their image, as these 'reflected the city's dependence on horses primarily in the character of street paving, the distribution of retail and wholesale markets selling provisions for horses, and the location and construction of stables'.[70] It was through the rise of steam and electric engines, however, that the horse became 'mostly a companion animal, even a domestic pet'.[71] The infrastructure it helped create served as a basis for the automobile in the decades that followed.[72]

Inside four walls

Much in the bourgeois spirit, we will now leave the bustling city streets of New York, London and Paris to return to the private where animal companionship was of a much more intimate nature. Predating the eerily erotic undertones of Donna Haraway's relationship with her dogs, the anthrozoologist James Serpell delved into the historical depths of the human–animal bond in the mid-1980s. He was interested in the purpose of petkeeping and the role of animals as social companions from an ethical perspective, as he noted a strong contradiction in the way we treat different animals: why are some considered partners while others can be killed and consumed? (As we have seen with the example of horses, boundaries are fluid, of course.) The most important takeaway for this chapter is his ideas on our 'four-legged friends' that tackle the question why respective cultures chose only a certain (at times differing) handful of them. According to Serpell, 'right from the outset, wolves and wildcats possessed particular qualities which made them especially suitable and desirable as animal companions'. They remain in our vicinity without being forced, become attached, develop social bonds (in the case of wolves, as seen in Chapter 2, also among each other), they are 'relatively hygienic', active and ready to interact during the day, and their bodies are of a manageable size, keeping in mind that they are predators. 'They are large enough for us to view them as recognizable individuals and treat them, so to speak, as small people. But they are also small enough so that the majority do not pose a serious threat.'[73] Serpell continues to identify a mutual non-verbal understanding as

---

[70]McShane and Tarr, *The Horse in the City*, p. 103.
[71]McShane and Tarr, *The Horse in the City*, p. 177.
[72]For further reading on the evolution of the urban sphere through non-human involvement, see Andrew A. Robichaud, *Animal City: The Domestication of America* (Cambridge and London: Harvard University Press, 2019).
[73]James Serpell, *In the Company of Animals. A Study of Human-Animal Relationships* (Cambridge: Cambridge University Press, ²1996; first published in 1986), pp. 126–7.

the central reason for the selection of human–animal bonds, which – unlike human relationships – bear no risk of betrayal. Here, the way he highlights the deep emotional connection of humans and animals seems fitting also with Victorian times:

> Like small children, cats and dogs are uninhibited in their demands for physical attention and comfort, and pet-owners, like parents, respond to these spontaneous demands by relaxing and becoming less physically inhibited themselves. Living as we do in a society where physical intimacy between adults is strongly repressed, at least in public, pets provide us with a valuable and socially acceptable outlet for the expression of intimate behaviour.[74]

Telling insights into the culture of pet-keeping can be gained by looking at care books which became ever more popular during the nineteenth century. As Kathleen Kete has observed, the act of training dogs was understood as 'the manufacture, from any breed, of a *chien de fantasie*'.[75] Results were presented while in good company, ideally after dinner. Central themes revolve around the infantilization of animals, projecting either human or toy-like qualities which extended to special clothes for dogs that went along with fitting hairstyles and luxurious ornaments like silver or golden collars. 'The Parisian dog in its idealized elaboration was feminized', Kete continues:

> Duplicating the costumes for middle-class women was a proliferation of canine outfits for many occasions that could be coordinated with their mistresses' clothing (…) The fashionable dog had a costume for afternoon visits, for the evening, for travel, and for the beach. Some authors recommended canine underwear (…) dogs functioned as signatures for human nature. Clothes marked off bourgeois from beast; but more than that, the clothed pet was a double, a doppelgänger, a personalized expression of control. Canine clothing was clearly as restricting of movement, as denaturing, as that of contemporary women's fashion.[76]

As studies on the cultural history of fashion suggest, this can be understood as a response to changing gender roles in consumer culture and the rise of

---

74 Serpell, *In the Company of Animals*, p. 132.
75 Kete, *The Beast in the Boudoir*, p. 83.
76 Kete, *The Beast in the Boudoir*, p. 85.

the feminist movement towards the turn of the century, which was perceived by many as a 'crisis of masculinity'.[77] 'Gender stereotypes played a major role in mobilizing customers at the turn of the century. Ideas and ideals of beauty were displayed and cultivated in the newly opened department stores that soon spread all across Europe and the New World.'[78] Bourgeois normativity also affected the diet of pets, not least in an attempt to control their sexuality. Reducing meat, exercise and cold baths, Kete writes, were to counter 'satyriasis' in male dogs and 'nymphomania' with bitches in heat (also considered a prophylaxis against rabies believed to stem from sexual desire, as seen above).[79] 'The physical presence of animals in the home was shaped to bourgeois expectations of self', with 'deanimalization, feminization, and control' going hand in hand.[80]

Arguably, bourgeois ideals of coziness found their most paradoxical expression in the keeping of cats. Feline companions were historically considered to be wild, untameable, free-spirited, unfaithful or devious even by some commentators – much unlike the loyal dog. 'The cat was linked rather with bohemia, a social space only indirectly concerned with class: intellectuals were elitist, and their affiliation was to the ancien régime's republic of letters rather than to a supposedly Philistine class (...) The companionship of a like-minded animal became a trope of intellectuals, the cat a sign for the literary life, a signature' which was 'constitutionally difficult to shape to utilitarian ends'.[81] Nonetheless, its popularity only grew, as evidenced by cat shows with new breeds from distant lands that 'testifie[d] to the impulse to introduce the safely exotic into everyday life, a belated echo of canine structures in catkeeping practice' that followed the British example. Adding to this exoticism in a time of germophobia (seen in the rabies scare) was the cat's natural cleanliness, its 'obsessive self-care'.[82] In a prejudiced way, this contrasted working-class life with the tacitly adopted remains of aristocratic culture.

---

[77]Venita Datta, *Heroes and Legends of Fin-de-Siècle France. Gender, Politics, and National Identity* (New York: Cambridge University Press, 2011), pp. 227–8. For an overview: Helen Louise Cowie, *Victims of Fashion. Animal Commodities in Victorian Britain* (Cambridge and New York: Cambridge University Press, 2022).

[78]Timm Schönfelder, 'Fur Trade in Turmoil: Pelt Commodification in Leipzig from Fin de Siècle to Sovietization', in Magdalena Eriksröd-Burger, Heidi Hein-Kircher and Julia Malitska (eds), *Consumption and Advertising in Eastern Europe and Russia in the Twentieth Century* (Cham: Palgrave, 2023), pp. 113–34, here p. 117.

[79]Kete, *The Beast in the Boudoir*, p. 93. As she states in the following chapter in line with her colleagues, the panic was exaggerated: 'Rabies is a fatal disease but, as the most superficial investigation will reveal, its rate of incidence is woefully inadequate to account for pre-Pasteurian fears' (p. 97).

[80]Kete, *The Beast in the Boudoir*, pp. 95, 79.

[81]Kete, *The Beast in the Boudoir*, pp. 123–5.

[82]Kete, *The Beast in the Boudoir*, p. 132.

According to Frederick Brown, the paradigm was a much more utilitarian one in Seattle at the beginning of the twentieth century where 'cats and dogs bridged human distinctions between pets and livestock'. They were, he continues, considered both servants and pals that had a working role in the household.[83] Cats defended against mice and rats while dogs scared off burglars and thieves; 'bird dogs', in turn, served as hunting companions. In a more intimate setting, pets were either ersatz-children (as underlined by James Serpell) or playmates for the offspring. Just as in Great Britain, a market for pets developed in the United States; animals became commodities that were bred and traded. With horses disappearing from the streets, pets were the main focus of animal protection societies.[84] For safety concerns, dogs were confined to the home instead of being allowed to roam the streets freely. Calls to spay or neuter pets to control populations (which exploded after the Second World War) rather than euthanize them intensified. 'Concern about pet populations emerged at the same time that many Americans, especially those in the nascent environmental movement, worried that accelerating human population growth would bring a crisis of famines and unrest', Brown explains.[85] While members of the charismatic fauna thus lost their liberty of movement in urban environments, they became an integral – and often pampered – part of the domestic sphere.

---

[83]Frederick L. Brown, *The City Is More Than Human. An Animal History of Seattle* (Seattle and London: University of Washington Press, 2016), p. 151.
[84]Brown, *The City Is More Than Human*, p. 161.
[85]Brown, *The City Is More Than Human*, p. 181.

4

Global exchanges: Species transfer and the making of new worlds

During the past millennia, horses have proven to be the most important vehicle for conquest. Prominent examples include the Mongol invasion of Rus' that resulted in the siege of Kyiv in 1240 and the Spanish expansion into the 'New World' 250 years later. Though it had become extinct in North America, whence it originally evolved, and in large parts of Europe after the last ice age ended some 11,700 years ago, the horse successfully made its comeback from the steppes of today's Ukraine and Central Asia thanks to its domestication around 4000 BC. 'By 4,000 years ago, horses were once again common in archaeological sites from West Asia to the British Isles', according to science writer Stephen Budiansky.[1] As in the case of dogs, selective breeding and coevolution created sturdy and reliable companions. Soon after they had made their voyage across the Atlantic, they spread throughout the new colonies. By the end of the eighteenth century, a growing population of semi-feral mustangs had migrated across the Great Plains and reached Canada. They adapted so well that they were soon considered a pest and a nuisance: 'When the gold rush began in 1849, there were so many wild horses that ate so much of the grass that livestockmen with an eye for the

[1]Stephen Budiansky, *The Nature of Horses. Their Evolution, Intelligence and Behaviour* (London: Weidenfeld & Nicolson, 1997), pp. 33–5, quote p. 35. While his book serves well as a popular introduction into equine natural history and behaviour, Budiansky's utilitarian views on coevolution and animal behaviour (which he considers to be in the service of humans) have generally been criticized.

profit that other stock could make out of the same grass drove the horses off the cliffs at Santa Barbara by the thousands.'[2]

One of the most discussed syntheses of the past half century that captures this expansion of species was Alfred W. Crosby's 1972 book *The Columbian Exchange* which, as the subtitle underlines, deals with the ecological ramifications of the conquest of the Americas – and to a smaller degree Australasia – since the late fifteenth century.[3] He achieved this by integrating scientific insights into a sweeping historiographical framework. Though criticized by many of his professional peers for his approach, it became 'one of the foundational texts for the field of environmental history', as John R. McNeill rightly observes in his foreword to the thirtieth anniversary edition. The laudator continues to highlight that it was neither the first nor the last such exchange of 'seeds, spores, and germs' if we consider the trade across the Silk Road from the second century BC ('Cherries, and perhaps smallpox and measles, came to the Roman world; China acquired grapes, alfalfa, donkeys, camels, and also perhaps smallpox and measles, among other items'), or Captain James Cook's explorations of Oceania during the second half of the eighteenth century:

> uniting previously separate ecosystems with dramatic results that paralleled the Columbian Exchange. The antipodes had no equivalent of the potato or maize to give to the world (eucalyptus trees are perhaps their most successful biological export), but for the peoples and ecosystems of Australia, New Zealand, or Tahiti, the Cook Exchange, as it might be called, proved jarring in the extreme.[4]

Crosby labelled his approach 'biohistory', and large parts of his book are about so-called virgin soil epidemics, which describe the contraction of diseases by populations that lack basic immunity – probably due to prolonged isolation on the global agora of pandemics. In explaining how the conquistadors brought

---

[2]Alfred W. Crosby, *Ecological Imperialism. The Biological Expansion of Europe, 900–1900* (Cambridge: Cambridge University Press, ²2004; first published in 1986), p. 183. On the symbolic re-enactment of the taming of wild horses, see Susan Nance, *Rodeo. An Animal History* (Norman: University of Oklahoma Press, 2020).

[3]For a state-of-the-art overview, see first two volumes of the series *Handbook of the Anthropocene in Latin America*: Olaf Kaltmeier, María Fernanda López Sandoval, José Augusto Pádua and Adrián Gustavo Zarrilli (eds), *Land Use. Handbook of the Anthropocene in Latin America I* (Bielefeld: Bielefeld University Press, 2024); and Olaf Kaltmeier, Antoine Acker, León Enrique Ávila Romero and Regina Horta Duarte (eds), *Biodiversity. Handbook of the Anthropocene in Latin America II* (Bielefeld: Bielefeld University Press, 2024).

[4]See his foreword in Alfred W. Crosby, *The Columbian Exchange. Biological and Cultural Consequences of 1492. 30th Anniversary Edition* (Westport and London: Praeger, 2003; first published in 1972) [e-book].

measles, smallpox and influenza to the Indigenous people they encountered, it is a strong precursor to the recently identified 'microbial turn'.[5] But also from the perspective of animal history it is worth taking a closer look at the 'tidal wave of people and their non-human accompaniments' that 'surged across the globe' and reached its pinnacle in the nineteenth century.[6] As Crosby notes, this resulted in a Europeanization of local flora and fauna with pigs, sheep and cattle following the conquerors on horseback.[7] This laid the groundwork for meat, leather and wool industries with an irreversible impact on the Indigenous environments. Centring animals in Latin American History – to borrow the title of an edited volume that explores a less human-oriented perspective through a variety of interactions ranging from animist beliefs to zoophilia – reminds us that 'the classic distinction between Nature and Culture cannot be assumed to describe domains internal to non-Western cosmologies' (as we have already seen through the work of Philippe Descola in Chapter 2). 'Animals are not passive recipients of human agency, but are active in shaping our culture', writes the anthropologist Neil L. Whitehead. 'Loving, being, and killing animals (.) dissolves the binaries of nature-culture, human-animal, lover-pet, and through a deictic perspectivism opens the possibility for corporeal transformation as spirits (subjectivities, identities) occupy variant material forms.'[8]

In order to understand these changes, the observer has to take a step back from the exhausting details of microhistory. Just as in evolution, transformation is much better visible in the long run – though, of course, this increases the risk of forgetting about the alternative avenues a process could have taken in hindsight. Crosby's studies, just as many works in environmental history, are deeply influenced by the fundamental ideas of the French historians Marc Bloch (1886–1944) and Lucien Febvre (1878–1956). Since 1929, they edited the journal *Annales* that underlined a multidisciplinary, international and transepochal approach with the goal to overcome 'pointless disciplinary schisms' and achieve 'methodological innovation'. Their colleague Fernand Braudel (1902–85) focused explicitly on the influence of environmental

[5]Cf. Stefan Herbrechter, 'Microbes', in Lynn Turner, Undine Sellbach and Ron Broglio (eds), *The Edinburgh Companion to Animal Studies* (Edinburgh: Edinburgh University Press, 2018), pp. 354–66 who recapitulates that 'microbes might be seen as the real "heroes" of evolution, as the ancestors of non-human and human animals and "the origin of sociable life" in general' – p. 356.

[6]Jodi Frawley and Iain McCalman, 'Invasion Ecologies. The Nature/Culture Challenge', in Jodi Frawley and Iain McCalman (eds), *Rethinking Invasion Ecologies from the Environmental Humanities* (London and New York: Routledge, 2014), pp. 3–14, here p. 5.

[7]See the chapter on 'Old World Plants and Animals in the New World' in Crosby, *The Columbian Exchange*.

[8]Neil L. Whitehead, 'Conclusion: Loving, Being, Killing Animals', in Martha Few and Zeb Tortorici (eds), *Centering Animals in Latin American History* (New York: Duke University Press, 2013), pp. 329–45, quotes pp. 333, 337, 335, respectively.

conditions in his monumental *The Mediterranean and the Mediterranean World in the Age of Philip II* (1949). Of central importance became the perspective of the so-called *longue durée*: '*Annales* historians were convinced that the key to historical explanations could be found in an integrated analysis of structures and developments over decades or centuries', Matthias Middell writes.[9] For this, the conquest of the Americas and the ensuing exchange of people, flora and fauna serve as prime examples.

Neozoa in a New World

'While plants travelled two ways and many American crops became staples of the European diet, animals followed a one-way route from Europe into the New World', Miguel de Asúa and Roger French generalize at the outset of their collaborative work.[10] The reliance on these animals for transport and nourishment in exploration, however, did not diminish the wonder and fascination the conquistadors felt when faced with these fabulously exotic beasts. The authors thus focus their attention on the perception of fauna in travel reports, diary entries, letters and chronicles during the first two centuries after the arrival of Columbus which were based on both observation and native lore about animals. In the spirit of classical authors like Pliny and Aristotle, early writers laid the groundwork for the new genre of 'natural and moral histories of the New World' which informed encyclopaedias of Renaissance Europe. During translation, however, they experienced a 'gradual "purification" of the Western interpretation of the fauna of the New World from all the indigenous material which had been incorporated in it'.[11] Especially in the beginning, rather prosaic concerns came to the fore, like in a letter by the Sevillian physician Dr Diego Álvarez Chanca who took part in Columbus's second voyage (1493–6), addressed to the municipal council of his hometown:

> Chanca's remark about the edibility of the animal which has been identified as a *hutia* (the *Capromys* which Columbus thought were the Pharaoh's rat mentioned by Marco Polo) is telling of what constituted a basic and

---

[9]Matthias Middell, 'The *Annales*', in Stefan Berger, Heiko Feldner and Kevin Passmore (eds), *Writing History. Theory and Practice* (London: Bloomsbury Academic, ³2021; first published in 2020), pp. 113–27, quotes pp. 115, 120. For further reading, see Peter Burke, *The French Historical Revolution. The* Annales *School, 1929–2014* (Cambridge: Polity Press, ²2015; first published in 1999).
[10]Miguel de Asúa and Roger French, *A New World of Animals. Early Modern Europeans on the Creatures of Iberian America* (London and New York: Routledge, 2016; first published in 2005), p. xiii.
[11]de Asúa and French, *A New World of Animals*, p. 232.

primary concern for all those who travelled to the Indies at this early stage when the availability of domestic European animals was almost nil: native animals were, first and foremost, food. And much of the talk about animals in the early chronicles is, in the end, talk about food, hunting and cooking. Seldom is a new animal described without mentioning the way the Indians cook it or without comparing its flavour with that of a similar dish at home.[12]

Parrots, toucans, monkeys, armadillos and guinea pigs were commodified as luxury goods to be sold at the markets of Western Europe (nuancing the authors' generalization above), and the pearl-fisheries on the islands of Margarita and Cubagua provided items of unusual size and quality. Also, the red dyestuff cochineal, which was made from the pulverized bodies of cactus-eating insects, turned out to be a sought-after trading good. Bezoars ('stomach stones') were a popular medicinal product, along with a wide range of even more obscure treatments processed from armadillo tails or skunk dung.[13] The notable profits notwithstanding, native species were considered 'grotesque and outlandish creatures, essentially different from those of the Old World' by many. As de Asúa and French continue to elaborate, the 'Eurocentric devaluation of New World animals and the more general thesis of the inferiority of American nature' became an influential notion during the eighteenth century which stood in stark contrast to the idea of the 'luxuriant nature of the New World' that served as 'a screen of gigantic proportions upon which the dreams and fears of the Old were projected'.[14] As ever so often with human perceptions of wilderness, these contradictions remained unresolved.

Rather than adapting to what the local fauna had to offer, Europeans introduced the animals they knew best to thrive on the rich resources of the American ecosystems. As Elinor G. K. Melville has shown in her work on the introduction of sheep, this brought about 'a profound shift in the modes of production from horticulture to some form of agropastoralism':

It has long been argued that the development of pastoralism in the New World was a major factor in the evolution of the distinctive colonial regimes; in this study I explore the idea that the expansion of pastoralism enabled

---

[12]de Asúa and French, *A New World of Animals*, p. 8, for similar descriptions, see p. 31.

[13]de Asúa and French, *A New World of Animals*, pp. 91–2, 103. 'It is difficult to exaggerate the economic importance of the spice and drug trade in the sixteenth century', the authors write, 'a sizeable part of which took the form of monopolistic ventures in the hands of the great bankers' like the Fuggers or the Welsers – p. 104.

[14]de Asúa and French, *A New World of Animals*, pp. 161, 231. On the creation and dissemination of knowledge in the field of natural history within the context of colonial exploitation, see Helen Cowie, *Conquering Nature in Spain and Its empire, 1750–1850* (Manchester: Manchester University Press, 2011).

the conquest of the indigenous populations and the domination of vast areas of rural space, as well as the corollary to this idea – that the evolution of colonial society itself constituted the conquest.

Melville builds explicitly on the argument made by Crosby about an ecological imperialism of the Europeans. She underlines, however, that by far not all ecosystems could be conquered by their 'portmanteau biota': 'the tropics are still, after all, dominated by New World peoples, flora, and fauna'.[15] Ungulate conquest was no easy endeavour. Flora and fauna reconfigured reciprocally in a process called 'irruptive oscillation' through phases of overpopulation due to an abundance of forage, food scarcity (an ovine and bovine *tragedy of the commons*, if you will), population decline, recovery of plants and animals, and, ultimately, a 'new biological regime (...) in a radically changed landscape' with lower population densities. 'Animal and plant communities will oscillate around this level of accommodation unless there is some radical change in the conditions of plant growth leading to a marked increase in the carrying capacity, at which time the whole process will begin again.'[16]

Usually, nature finds a new balance as long as there is no external interference – were it not for pastoralism with humans as its driving force. They put entire ecosystems at risk by tightly controlling animals and changing nature in accordance with their economic interests. Melville shows this in the example of the Valle del Mezquital in highland central Mexico that had been inhabited by the Otomí people for centuries:

> When Europeans first entered these wide, flat valleys and plains they saw a landscape that had been shaped by centuries of human occupation. It was a fertile, densely populated, and complex agricultural mosaic composed of extensive croplands, woodlands, and native grasslands; of irrigation canals, dams, terraces, and limestone quarries. Oak and pine forests covered the hills, and springs and streams supplied extensive irrigation systems.[17]

Its landscape experienced a shift from human-centred intensive irrigation agriculture to animal-centred extensive pastoralism:

---

[15]Elinor G. K. Melville, *A Plague of Sheep. Environmental Consequences of the Conquest of Mexico* (Cambridge: Cambridge University Press, ²1997; first published in 1994), pp. xi, 2. Melville refers to Crosby, *Ecological Imperialism*, pp. 132–44 on the lack of success in these humid climates as well as in regions that were densely populated by Indigenous peoples.

[16]Melville, *A Plague of Sheep*, p. 7. See also pp. 47–8 for a technical explanation, and pp. 49–54 for the case of the Valle del Mezquital. Melville takes a comparative look at the well-documented and more recent 'Australian experience' on pp. 60–77.

[17]Melville, *A Plague of Sheep*, p. 31.

By the end of the sixteenth century, only eight decades after the Spaniards arrived, the picture had changed. The Indian populations were decimated and their fields reduced. The once fertile flatlands were covered in a dense growth of mesquite dominated desert scrub, the high, steep-sided hills were treeless, and the piedmont was eroded and gullied. Sheep grazing, not agriculture, took precedence in regional production. Sheep, not men, dominated the ecosystems of the Valle del Mezquital and shaped its landscapes.[18]

'The sixteenth-century transformation of the water regime of this region prejudiced future exploitation. The Valle del Mezquital received increasingly arid forms of land use', Melville continues. Sheep were followed by goats and cattle before they made way for the cultivation of agave.[19] New colonial administrative structures were created on the local and regional levels not least in the form of towns, and the local population was subjected to laws, regulations and customs they were not acquainted with:

> The Indians had no knowledge of pastoralism, no experience in dealing with grazing animals, and were faced with a legal system that was based in an alien culture and organized according to unfamiliar principles. The Indians' lack of knowledge and their status as conquered peoples meant that they were unable to provide an informed and effective counterbalance to the actions of the Spanish pastoralists in the early years of the colony.[20]

In the process, Indigenous populations were displaced and marginalized, turning them into 'an impoverished peasantry in a new political economy' – if they had not yet succumbed to diseases like the Cocoliztli ('pestilence') epidemics that killed millions of people within mere decades.[21] Unlike in Spain and other parts of Europe, pastoralism competed with agriculture instead of complementing it, and 'long-term interests were sacrificed for short-term gain'.[22] For this, Melville presents meticulously elaborated statistics on land

---

[18]Melville, *A Plague of Sheep*, quote p. 39; on the epidemic, see p. 52.

[19]Melville, *A Plague of Sheep*, p. 115.

[20]Melville, *A Plague of Sheep*, p. 120.

[21]Melville, *A Plague of Sheep*, p. 44. It stands to argue that such displacement is referred to when Indigenous protagonists spoke of the Spaniards 'converting people into cattle' – *cf.* León García Garagarza, 'The Year the People Turned into Cattle. The End of the World in New Spain, 1558', in Martha Few and Zeb Tortorici (eds), *Centering Animals in Latin American History* (New York: Duke University Press, 2013), pp. 32–61, quote p. 32.

[22]Melville, *A Plague of Sheep*, p. 162. For comparison, see Vincent Clément, 'Spanish Wood Pasture: Origin and Durability of an Historical Wooded Landscape in Mediterranean Europe', in Sarah Johnson (ed.), *Farming. Themes in Environmental History 6* (Knapwell: White Horse Press, 2016), pp. 57–76.

use (including animal population numbers and grazing rates) throughout her book that she compiled from archival information and secondary sources. While her work falls short in the description of everyday interaction, it is a testament to the possibilities of a transdisciplinary approach in environmental history and animal studies by incorporating methods from economic history. Thus, she fills the abstract model of 'irruptive oscillation' with life by looking at how a concrete ecosystem evolved after the introduction of a non-native species. Here, the events in Mexico's Valle del Mezquital serve as a blueprint for many more acts of ecological imperialism.

Fostering conflict

The history of the pandemonium of species that participated in the Columbian Exchange is continued in the English settlement of North America from the seventeenth century onward. In this, Virginia DeJohn Anderson goes one step further than her precursors by asking more explicitly not only about 'changes in the land but also in the hearts and minds and behavior of the peoples'. Consequently, she opens her book with a most curious monument in Duxbury, Massachusetts not far from Plymouth where the Mayflower landed in 1620. Here, a granite slab commemorates the erection of a palisade in 1634 as 'a high fence to prevent cattle from straying and probably to keep the Indians out'.[23] The interaction of the three groups that are implicated here – Indians, settlers and livestock – is at the centre of Anderson's interest, as 'nothing brought Indians and colonists into contact more frequently than livestock'.[24]

> By bringing livestock across the Atlantic, colonists believed that they provided the means to realize America's potential, pursuing a goal that Indians who lacked domestic animals had failed to accomplish (...) Indians who learned how to keep livestock, colonists asserted, would grow in prosperity, advance along the path toward civility, and eventually convert to a Christian faith that considered human dominion over animals to be divinely ordained.[25]

'Colonists born and raised in England never questioned the indispensability of livestock for all sorts of human endeavors', Anderson ensures.[26] Goats, pigs

---

[23]Virginia DeJohn Anderson, *Creatures of Empire. How Domestic Animals Transformed Early America* (New York: Oxford University Press, 2004), quotes pp. 5 and 1, respectively.
[24]Anderson, *Creatures of Empire*, p. 177.
[25]Anderson, *Creatures of Empire*, pp. 8–9.
[26]Anderson, *Creatures of Empire*, p. 84.

and chickens were shipped to Plymouth from England starting in 1623, soon to be followed by cattle and horses Sheep, in turn, probably arrived in the 1640s. 'By 1650, English animals of all sorts outnumbered English colonists.'[27] These animals proved difficult to control, however, and the lack of human resources to watch them meant that they were often left to roam free, damaging the belongings of Indigenous people in the process which provoked escalating conflicts. Through the example of New England and the Chesapeake Colonies, the author thus tells an archetypal story of expansion, colonization and the displacement of the autochthonous people.

Notable here are the different perceptions of animals which are reminiscent of the discourse about the inexistent nature–culture divide in non-Europeans' worldviews as mentioned above. Anderson assumes that the Indigenous communities in her regions of interest only referred to distinct species when talking about non-human creatures. The lack of words to denote them in a generic manner, she continues her argument, suggests 'that Indians did not conceive of the natural world in terms of a strict human-animal dichotomy but rather as a place characterized by a diversity of living beings'. In accordance with animist beliefs, they also transcended the physical plane of existence. 'Failing to understand this world view, colonists often mistakenly reported that Indians thought that animals were gods', Anderson notes.[28] Their proximity to the animal world was mirrored in clothing, ornaments and body modification as respective signs of tribal culture. This could serve to pay respect to *manitou* (an omnipresent 'spirit' or 'spiritual power' in the Algonquian languages), or to mimic animal behaviour during hunts.[29] While colonists usually held their own set of folklorist beliefs and superstitions about animals, e.g. to foretell the weather through certain behaviour, they rather identified animal spirits with animal familiars as accomplices of witches: 'Anxiety about witchcraft shaped the colonists' evaluation of Indian comments about animal spirits and manitous. The tendency to draw such a parallel reflected a prevalent assumption among colonists that Indians were devil-worshipers anyway.'[30]

In contrast to more densely settled regions, the Eastern Algonquians had little incentive to domesticate animals (except for hawks and dogs) and to keep livestock, as they 'enjoyed a varied diet of wild and cultivated plant foods along with abundant game and fish'.[31] As a result, their first encounters with free-roaming swine and cattle did not suggest to them that these were, in fact, domesticated species: 'Living much of the time in the forest, Chesapeake

---

[27]Anderson, *Creatures of Empire*, pp. 98, 104 (quote).
[28]Anderson, *Creatures of Empire*, p. 18.
[29]Anderson, *Creatures of Empire*, p. 29.
[30]Anderson, *Creatures of Empire*, p. 50.
[31]Anderson, *Creatures of Empire*, p. 33.

livestock appeared to have become part of the forest. Other than the fact of their Old World origins, it seemed that little remained to distinguish them from American fauna.'[32] These were not considered property by the Indigenous people, but free for anyone's taking:

> Drawing an analogy between livestock and New World fauna implied that English creatures could be hunted so long as the proper rituals were discovered and then followed. The Indians' strategy for integrating livestock into their world thus had the effect of redefining English property as fair game. For colonists, however, livestock differed from wild animals precisely because they were property, a status intrinsic to their identity as domesticated creatures. The Indians could not have known that a distinction that had little or no meaning in their culture would loom so large in the colonists' minds. Yet for English settlers, this was a distinction that made all the difference.[33]

Of course, there were not only conflicts with the native people. Colonists who stole or preyed on other people's livestock had to expect draconian punishment, especially in the beginning when these animals were still scarce and populations unstable. 'Property became the slender thread by which dominion was preserved in an agricultural regime that otherwise appeared to liberate animals from their masters', Anderson underlines. In New England, this system was highly dependent on livestock, as European crops like wheat and barley did not deliver the necessary yields. Corn cultivation as done by the Indigenous population fared better, even if it took up slowly among settlers. With time, commercial networks grew among the colonies, and livestock became a staple good of New England's agrarian economy.[34]

With the animals came invasive English grasses that replaced native plants.[35] Agriculture was expansive at its core: new land was cleared when soil quality decreased. Manure was used to improve soils, and livestock was kept from the fields by movable split-rail fences. 'Pooling their labor, inhabitants generally erected one fence around the common and one around each large planting field instead of enclosing individual holdings', Anderson notes.[36]

---

[32]Anderson, *Creatures of Empire*, p. 123.

[33]Anderson, *Creatures of Empire*, p. 42. These discussions on property regimes and their effect on the natural landscape of the region are highly reminiscent of the classical study by William Cronon, *Changes in the Land. Indians, Colonists, and the Ecology of New England. 20th-Anniversary Edition* (New York: Hill and Wang, 2003; first published in 1983), e.g. on pp. 128–31.

[34]Anderson, *Creatures of Empire*, pp. 124, 140 (quote), 144, 152.

[35]For more detail about such invasive Eurasian flora like bluegrass and white clover that was well adapted to the 'harsh requirements of pastoralism' and soon became 'so common that they were regarded as native', see Cronon, *Changes in the Land*, pp. 142–4, quotes p. 142.

[36]Anderson, *Creatures of Empire*, p. 159.

Much of the territory claimed by colonists during the seventeenth century remained uncleared and unfenced, the domain of free-ranging animals and not sedentary settlers. Colonists in effect appropriated Indian common lands to serve as their own commons. Indians would be puzzled by this turn of events, wondering how the colonists' use of the land created rights superior to native claims.[37]

Livestock held in free-range husbandry was repeatedly killed – either as a premeditated form of resistance, in spontaneous defence, or accidentally after it had strayed into native hunting grounds. In any case, William Cronon writes, it 'interfered with native subsistence practices in ways that could neither be ignored nor easily remedied'. What made matters worse was that these animals may have exacerbated the epidemiological crises that smallpox and other diseases brought upon native communities: 'Once villages were attacked by a new pathogen, they often missed key phases in their annual subsistence cycles – the corn planting, say, or the fall hunt – and so were weakened when the next infection arrived', which could prove lethal for whole communities, Cronon continues.[38] In the end, 'English animals, along with the people who brought them, reconfigured the Indians' world into a very different place from what it had been before the newcomers arrived', Anderson observes.[39] This meant that they had to adapt not only through diplomacy and agreements, but also by copying techniques like the construction of fences. In some cases, they even received compensation for damages.[40] More often, however, the plight of the Indigenous population was ignored by the authorities and their harsh colonial regime in the hope that 'thoroughly frustrated by persistent trespass problems [they] might simply move away'.[41] Yet to the surprise of many colonists, native people proved to be very resourceful in obtaining their own livestock, especially pigs, which they used in their trade with the new settlements.

That numerous Indian communities acquired their own livestock, turning the colonists' rationale against them in a futile attempt to preserve native control over land, bespeaks both the irony and the tragedy of the story. An adaptation that colonists had encouraged, and ought thus to have applauded, instead produced friction when it became obvious that Indians intended to pick and choose among the items on the English agenda for

[37]Anderson, *Creatures of Empire*, p. 171. See also p. 195 on the 'well-established tradition of common use rights to uncultivated territory' in native communities.
[38]Cronon, *Changes in the Land*, pp. 87–90, here p. 88.
[39]Anderson, *Creatures of Empire*, p. 184.
[40]Anderson, *Creatures of Empire*, pp. 192–3.
[41]Anderson, *Creatures of Empire*, p. 224.

native cultural transformation. Owning cows did not make them Christians, much less apprentice Englishmen.[42]

Native cultural practices gave way first to free-range husbandry, and later to agriculture on a larger scale when plantations became the modus operandi fuelled by the labour of slaves from Africa in the 1700s. The 'cattle frontier' moved ahead of new settlements.[43] 'Wherever labor was harder to find than land, animals occupied territory on their own account and their owners dealt with the consequences much as the first English colonists had.' Eventually, 'Indians found room in their world for livestock, but the colonists and their descendants could find no room in theirs for Indians', Anderson concludes.[44]

Staking claims, destroying habitats

European conquest and settlement continued in the centuries that followed. Since the mid-1800s, the westward movement of the 'American pioneers' was accompanied by the idea of 'Manifest Destiny' which described a supposedly God-given right to acquire land. Connecting to the work of Cronon and Anderson above, Andrea L. Smalley tracks this trajectory from seventeenth-century Chesapeake to the postbellum southern plains with a focus on the role of the Indigenous fauna that 'acted as obstacles to colonization because their wildness was at odds with Anglo-American legal assertions of possession'.[45] Smalley identifies three partly overlapping key phases of subjugation starting with 'English colonizing, concentrating on extraction and extermination', marked by 'efforts to domesticate the faunal environment and to channel Indian-produced animal commodities into new economic streams'. This was followed by an 'American turn, aimed at settlers' direct use of indigenous creatures as a natural resource pool to support independent proprietorship and to feed a developing market society'. In the late nineteenth century, 'a third form of colonizing emerged that focused on the creation of bounded pockets of wildness within which America's animal heritage might be preserved'. Under the guise of the conservation movement (as mentioned in Chapter 2) 'wild beasts were transformed into wildlife' and 'protected within a legal framework that regulated access and use' as US state property.[46]

---

[42]Anderson, *Creatures of Empire*, p. 211.
[43]See Crosby, *Ecological Imperialism*, p. 179.
[44]Anderson, *Creatures of Empire*, p. 245.
[45]Andrea L. Smalley, *Wild by Nature. North American Animals Confront Colonization* (Baltimore: Johns Hopkins University Press, 2017), p. 3.
[46]Smalley, *Wild by Nature*, p. 4.

According to Smalley, the perception of New World animals changed over time. Sixteenth-century Spanish explorers – while fascinated by their exotic appeal – were rather interested in acquiring silver and gold: 'American animals, though astonishing and abundant, remained wild and therefore marginal to the larger story of Spanish colonization.' In New France, this predilection for precious metals was replaced by 'animal wealth in the form of fish and furs'. This is reflected in the narratives of first-encounters that show a strong interest in Indigenous activities: 'Explorers and missionaries focused on the interplay between animal habits and native social practices. They devoted long passages of their reports to detailed descriptions of Indian hunting methods and explications of indigenous environmental knowledge.' While this laid the groundwork for a commercial empire, the 'English colonial imagination' perceived New World animals 'as potential aids to settlements' that had to be brought to 'productive use', she states: 'In a colonial vision centered on the planting of agrarian settlements, access to wild animals represented not a route to fabulous riches but a path to competency.'[47]

A source of such riches was fur-bearing animals that proved to be invaluable to trade and commerce: beaver pelts – usually procured by Indigenous trappers – were used to make hats (which were en vogue in Europe from the mid-sixteenth to the mid-nineteenth century) and other articles of clothing; they became a major driver in the exploration and settlement of today's Canada and Alaska. Organizations like the Hudson's Bay Company (HBC), founded in London in 1670, established networks of trading posts and held monopolies in certain areas which was also expressed in its own currency of 'made beaver' that reflected the worth of a grown animal's pelt.[48] Greed had fuelled conflict since the beginning, as Smalley shows:

The market in furs turned English colonies and individual colonists against each other in a short-sighted, frenzied, cut-throat competition for Indian trading partners and profits. Though the animal itself remained an abstraction for adventurers and traders who encountered mainly dead pelts rather than live creatures, the beaver nonetheless played key roles in the English colonizing process [49]

---

[47]Smalley, *Wild by Nature*, pp. 16–17.

[48]For further reading, see Eric Jay Dolin, *Fur, Fortune, and Empire. The Epic History of the Fur Trade in America* (New York: W. W. Norton & Company, 2010). There were, of course, other important uses for beavers as well: their meat was edible, their organs, blood and bones were ascribed medicinal effects, and their musky gland excretions (*castoreum*) were used to make perfume – cf. Smalley, *Wild by Nature*, p. 46.

[49]Smalley, *Wild by Nature*, pp. 43–4.

This competition extended among Indigenous protagonists, while colonists aimed at bringing the market under their control as they 'saw the expansion of an Indian-dominated extractive empire as an obstacle to English settler colonialism'.[50] The situation was further complicated by issues of sustainability: overexploitation of animal populations motivated the movement to territories hitherto uninhabited by Europeans. This gave way to new forms of land use, as we have seen above in the example of livestock farming in New England, or through a switch to large-scale agriculture as in the tobacco plantations of Virginia that created a vast range of environmental issues like soil exhaustion.[51] According to Smalley, predators formed another group of antagonists to colonization with the wolf as their leading representative. As seen in Chapter 2, a 'war of extermination' ensued that was 'carried out over centuries on different wild-animal frontiers' while colonists continued their westward move.[52]

Beginning in the eighteenth century, European settlers made it across the Appalachians and later the Rocky Mountains. In the wake of the American Revolution, the idea to cast natural resources as property (a discussion that hails back to the English east coast colonies, as seen above) was increasingly understood as a 'reward for doing the transformative work of settlement', which Smalley elaborates at length through the example of fishing rights.[53] These liberties extended to hunting game (for its imperial dimension, see Chapter 5), and the market for deerskins grew notably as European populations were depleted in many regions – a fate that soon threatened New World animals as well; repeated regional hunting bans tried to mitigate the effects.[54] In the Great Plains, which once marked the northern frontier of the Viceroyalty of New Spain,[55] conquistadors considered the bison 'akin to domestic livestock' due to their great importance to Indigenous economies.[56] Still roaming the land in sizeable groups and largely untroubled by humans, they made for easy prey in the beginning of European settlement. 'The wealth of buffalo on the plains reenergized colonizing impulses and led Anglo-American colonizers

---

[50]Smalley, *Wild by Nature*, p. 76.

[51]See also Carolyn Merchant, *The Columbia Guide to American Environmental History* (New York: Columbia University Press, 2005), pp. 39–58 and David Silkenat, *Scars on the Land: An Environmental History of Slavery in the American South* (New York: Oxford University Press, 2022).

[52]Smalley, *Wild by Nature*, p. 84.

[53]Smalley, *Wild by Nature*, pp. 119–54, quote p. 154.

[54]Smalley, *Wild by Nature*, pp. 155–88, here p. 163.

[55]Cf. Ralph H. Vigil, Frances W. Kaye and John R. Wunder (eds), *Spain and the Plains. Myths and Realities of Spanish Exploration and Settlement on the Great Plains* (Niwot: University of Colorado Press, 1994) and David J. Weber, *The Spanish Frontier in North America* (New Haven: Yale University Press, 1992).

[56]Smalley, *Wild by Nature*, p. 192.

to imagine new narratives of possession for the western landscape', as was reflected in the 1803 Louisiana Purchase from France.[57]

During the second half of the eighteenth century, durable bison leather became an important commodity for industrialization. Thanks to new methods for processing animal hides, it could be used for belts that powered large machines, but also for more refined attire. Professional hunting outfits that were made up of a handful of men covered a lot of prairie ground: 'An average hunter could kill about fifty bison a day, and an average skinner could remove about thirty to forty hides.' Their meat fed the construction crews of the transcontinental railroad, which was completed in 1869, and 'Buffalo Bill' Cody alone claimed to have killed around 4,280 animals in Kansas to this end. This marked a notable departure from the hitherto rather sustainable dynamics, which only worsened after the Kansas Pacific Railway was built: 'Bison disappeared first along the railway routes that provided easy access to the herds and easy transportation for their hides.'[58] This encroached upon Indigenous communities whose right to occupancy had been conditioned on the presence of bison in treaties that were concluded after the end of the American Civil War (1861–5). Thus, as Smalley observes, 'the buffalo became a party to the treaties and a player in US-Indian policy'.[59]

To break resistance against colonization, frontier militias and US military forces attacked and killed native men, women and children along with their livestock, burning their camps and villages to the ground.[60] The introduction of European cattle – as seen above – exacerbated the problems, not least since cows carried brucellosis and other pathogens that proved a great danger to the bison. As Andrew C. Isenberg shows in his authoritative work *The Destruction of the Bison*, the overall picture is much more complex, however. Already the introduction of horses from Europe (which competed with the bison for forage) had strongly affected the way native communities hunted, and the eventual drive to save the species through conservation efforts also catered to fears of a decline in masculine virtues: 'The installation of bison in managed preserves in the early twentieth century by the American Bison Society', Isenberg argues, served 'as a reminder of frontier manliness'.[61]

---

[57]Smalley, *Wild by Nature*, p. 196.
[58]Smalley, *Wild by Nature*, quotes pp. 205, 207, 208, respectively.
[59]Smalley, *Wild by Nature*, p. 214.
[60]Smalley, *Wild by Nature*, p. 215.
[61]Andrew C. Isenberg, *The Destruction of the Bison. An Environmental History, 1750–1920* (Cambridge: Cambridge University Press, 2000) [now available as the twentieth-anniversary edition, ibid. ²2020], p. 5. On the bison's fate and its connection to the conservation movement, see also Smalley, *Wild by Nature*, pp. 231–8. On the photographic documentation of its extermination, see Joshua Schuster, *What Is Extinction? A Natural and Cultural History of Last Animals* (New York: Fordham University Press, 2023), pp. 43–68.

What attracted professional criticism was his portrayal of the Indigenous hunters' share in the extinction of these creatures of the plains. Yet it is important to underline, as Isenberg does, the long-standing interaction of all humans with their environment:

> In the last 10,000 years, the Great Plains have never been without human influences; the very dominance of the bison in the eighteenth and nineteenth centuries owed itself, in part, to the hunters who, at the end of the last Ice Age, helped to kill off giant herbivores and thereby opened a niche for the bison. For as long as they have existed, people have inhabited, altered, and been affected by the nonhuman natural world. Even such precapitalist societies as the equestrian bison hunters of the Great Plains were sometimes given to waste and degradation of the resources upon which they depended. To assume an unchanging, harmonious relationship between Indians and the Great Plains environment classes both Indian culture and nature as static.[62]

This *longue durée* view (as presented in the beginning of this chapter) is now commonplace in environmental history, which 'properly understood is the story of the interaction of dynamic forces, with both nature and human society contributing to change'.[63] Without such a long-term perspective, one will always run the risk of delivering rather one-sided elaborations on victimhood and guilt – and lack understanding of the changes to the grassland biome.

> The near-extinction of the species cannot be understood simply as the result of hunting. It was surely also the consequence of less direct human alteration of the bison's habitat: displacement of bison from river valleys by Indians' horses and the livestock of Euroamerican emigrants; and the introduction of cattle to the bison's range. More important, however, the volatile plains environment itself contributed to the near-extinction of the herds. The pressures of drought, fires, blizzards, and other animals chronically depressed the bison's numbers (...) Human hunters pressured the bison in combination with these unpredictable environmental forces.[64]

As Isenberg elaborates, this happened as a result of the Columbian Exchange: native people were driven to the Great Plains by war and famine. There, a nomadic lifestyle proved to be more resilient to epidemics like smallpox,

---

[62] Isenberg, *The Destruction of the Bison*, p. 12.
[63] Isenberg, *The Destruction of the Bison*, p. 12.
[64] Isenberg, *The Destruction of the Bison*, p. 30.

which spread from Mexico in 1780. They tamed horses and acquired guns by trading pelts with the British and the French. 'In response to the European ecological and economic invasion of North America, the Sioux, Cheyenne, and others created a new social organization and resource strategy based on the exploitation of the bison.'[65] Arguably, this prepared the field for the animal's extinction by European hunters.

This, of course, shall not serve to bluntly shift the blame solely on Indigenous communities. The story of the bison's near extermination from the Great Plains is well documented, along with the insight that the extinction of the species was cynically anticipated by those who made a profit from its hides, meat and bones – and by those who wished for its disappearance along with the native population to claim space for Euroamerican settlement and livestock, which in their minds marked a 'triumph of civilization'.[66] Isenberg's study shows well how cultural, economic and environmental change went hand in hand. It reminds us that we have to be critical of meta-narratives as they are mirrored in the teleological description of the encounter between Indigenous actors ('a people presumed to possess a higher ecological consciousness than Europeans and their descendants') and colonists: supposedly akin to the biblical *fall from grace* when Adam and Eve were cast out of Eden, a *locus amoenus* where humans and animals lived in harmony was destroyed when 'the Indians of the western plains (...) were seduced into the bison robe trade in the 1830s'. Such a paradisiacal place, however, did not exist. Therefore, this simplified narrative is highly problematic:

It idealizes Indians, at one end of the story, and preservationists, at the other, while demonizing commercial hunters in the middle. It contextualizes neither Indian nor Euroamerican use of the bison; it does not recognize that bison hunters and conservationists, whether Indian or Euroamerican, were entangled in a host of social and economic concerns. Nor does it recognize that, from the perspective of the bison, there were striking similarities between the nomads and the Euroamericans. Both were newcomers to the plains in the eighteenth century. Both employed new technologies and adopted new modes of production to hunt the bison. Both sacrificed bison to meet social demands of integration, prestige, or conquest. Both increasingly adapted to capitalism in the eighteenth and nineteenth centuries. In the end, that adaptation was fatal to millions of bison (...) The peculiar tragedy of the slaughter of the bison is that both Indians and

---

[65] Isenberg, *The Destruction of the Bison*, p. 61.
[66] For more on the economic implications, see Isenberg, *The Destruction of the Bison*, pp. 123–63; quote p. 162.

Euroamericans had the opportunity to regulate commercial hunters and, until the end of the nineteenth century, declined to do so.[67]

Ending on this uncompromising note, Isenberg's study ties together the themes elaborated in this chapter about the introduction of invasive species into an unprepared environment along with its uneasy and multi-layered consequences that defy simple explanations. After all, there is no innocence in ecological interaction.

---

[67]Isenberg, *The Destruction of the Bison*, pp. 196–7.

5

Killing game: Hunting and the legacy of colonialism

Hunters are ambivalent figures. A prominent characterization of their craft was given by Matt Cartmill, an anthropologist who set out to fathom how deeply engrained brutality is in human sociocultural evolution:

> We define hunting [as] the deliberate, direct, violent killing of unrestrained wild animals; and we define wild animals in this context as those that shun or attack human beings. The hunt is (...) an armed confrontation between humanness and wildness, between culture and nature. Because it involves confrontational, premeditated, and violent killing, it represents something like a war waged by humanity against the wilderness (...) Hunting is an end in itself for the hunter, and he wants the beasts he kills to be endlessly replaced so that his sportive battle with the wilderness can go on indefinitely (...) Hunters, then, are not simply fighters on the side of humanity against the wilderness. Their loyalties are divided. Because hunting takes place at the boundary between the human domain and the wilderness, the hunter stands with one foot on each side of the boundary, and swears no perpetual allegiance to either side. He is a liminal and ambiguous figure, who can be seen either as a fighter against wildness or as a half-animal participant in it.[1]

Though this already seems like a lot, hunting can still be more than that: it represents strength, status, maturity, even sexual prowess – but also a

---

[1] Matt Cartmill, *A View to a Death in the Morning. Hunting and Nature Through History* (Cambridge and London: Harvard University Press, 1993), pp. 30–1. Cartmill's work continued in the spirit of heated debate as it had been triggered by the writer and trained anthropologist Robert Ardrey's *The Hunting Hypothesis. A Personal Conclusion Concerning the Evolutionary Nature of Man* (New York: Atheneum, 1976). For a feminist reading of the debate, see Mary Zeiss Stange, *Woman the Hunter* (Boston: Beacon Press, 1997).

talent for reading and understanding nature and its non-human inhabitants. Consequently, hunters often present themselves as the 'true conservationists' and 'animal ethicists' (as hinted at in Chapters 2 and 3). It is no surprise that their overbearing image of self has repeatedly been an object of scorn and ridicule due to the seemingly obvious contradictions in their claims between a pleasure to kill and the need for sustainable access to animals as resources for bloodsport, as Cartmill highlights. Due to all this, hunting serves as a telling prism of society, not least in the way it refracts the idealized understandings of human–nature interactions. It also provides a helpful focus when studying colonial rule.

While 'British tiger hunting represented imperial domination not just of India's politics but also of its natural environment', as Joseph Sramek summarizes, these pretensions met their limits already in the reliance on guides like the *shikari* as '"professional experts" who taught British hunters how to hunt tigers successfully and safely'.[2] This story is part and parcel of the imperial experience – and a fact that is commonly downplayed or completely ignored in the self-aggrandizing reports of Western protagonists across imperial boundaries. Although Indigenous hunters were revered for their abilities and keen senses, this was often done in a way that either underlined their societal backwardness or even their beastly nature which according to the onlookers made such traits possible in the first place. Treating the question how Indigenous people orient themselves, for example, Russian author Aleksandr Cherkasov (1834–95) writes in his *Notes of an East Siberian Hunter* from 1884:

> The reader may ask how the returning Orochon found his yurt in the forest, which had been moved without him by his wife to a third place? – Very simple: the Orochon is a forest animal (*lesnoi zver'*) that has the shape of a man; he is able to track a squirrel in the forest in summer, not just a yurt that has been moved in the snow.[3]

In his now-classic study of imperialism, John MacKenzie highlights the importance of animal resources in conquest for sustenance, as means of control, and objects of leisure that brought about their own kind of symbolism which is mirrored in the pursuit of trophies. This reflects the cultural mindset

[2]Joseph Sramek, '"Face Him like a Briton": Tiger Hunting, Imperialism, and British Masculinity in Colonial India, 1800–1875' *Victorian Studies* 48(4) (2006), pp. 659–80, quotes pp. 661, 676.
[3]Quoted in Timm Schönfelder, 'Constructing Masculinities: Bear Hunting in Tsarist Russia Toward the Fin de Siècle', in Laura Beck and Maurice Saß (eds), *Hunting Troubles: Gender and Its Intersections in the Cultural History of the Hunt* (Cham: Palgrave, 2024), pp. 259–74, p. 262.

of British imperialism, he argues. MacKenzie's observation that 'in the high noon of empire hunting became a ritualised and occasionally spectacular display of white dominance' when 'European world supremacy coincided with the peak of the hunting and shooting craze' goes beyond the insight that animals along colonial frontiers 'contributed to the expansionist urge', as it was shown in Chapter 4 through the example of bison or cattle.[4] Not only had the perceived primacy been deeply rooted in Western culture since antiquity, but it also reflected the nineteenth-century understanding of a hierarchical order in nature. This idea was popularized through natural history which formed 'an important part of the downward percolation of elite values and ideals' and was 'characteristic of the time'.[5] Racist notions were reflected in the visual arts, sporting magazines and literature for adolescents, museum exhibitions, circuses and zoos (see Chapter 9) which were either inspired or directly supplied by prominent imperial hunters.

In her description of the hunter's image, Harriet Ritvo sees a 'direct and obvious' connection 'between triumphing over a dangerous animal and subduing unwilling natives' – thus, 'the hunter emerged as both the ideal and the definitive type of the empire builder'.[6] Ritvo relays examples of their scolding criticism towards supposedly lazy, incapable, cowardly or even insubordinate Indigenous guides and helpers as it was commonplace in accounts of the time on hunting outings in Africa, India and other parts of the world that were regarded as exotic. This questionable self-perception was twisted into a colonial saviour complex with big game hunting as an imperial duty: 'When natives were threatened by wild animals, especially by man-eating predators, business and pleasure overlapped.'[7] Hunters were also employed by the British government of India to clear large areas of game 'in order to make them available for cultivation'[8] – rearranging not only local ecosystems but also Indigenous economies in the process. In the African colonies, meanwhile, there appeared to be a continuously moving frontier that divided 'civilization' from an impoverished 'wilderness' where the discovery of 'virgin hunting grounds' was increasingly difficult. European diseases like rinderpest or the cattle plague 'decimated indigenous bovines, deer, and antelope' in both Africa and India.[9]

---

[4]John M. MacKenzie, *The Empire of Nature. Hunting, Conservation and British Imperialism* (Manchester: Manchester University Press, 1988), p. 7.

[5]MacKenzie, *Empire of Nature*, p. 37.

[6]Harriet Ritvo, *The Animal Estate. The English and Other Creatures in the Victorian Age* (Cambridge: Harvard University Press, 1987), p. 254.

[7]Ritvo, *The Animal Estate*, p. 275.

[8]Ritvo, *The Animal Estate*, p. 282.

[9]Ritvo, *The Animal Estate*, p. 286. See also MacKenzie, *Empire of Nature*, p. 172.

Subverting subsistence

In his chapter on hunting and African societies, MacKenzie underlines its wide acceptance as a cultural practice in southern, central and eastern Africa that fulfilled an array of functions in local subsistence, trade and religion. When this pragmatism collided with colonial economies and resulted in the killing of domestic stock like sheep, horses and cattle, Indigenous hunters became the hunted. Compared to 'slaughter in cold blood' by the British General Officer Commanding of the Cape Colony in 1870, they along with their families were 'hunted like game' in retribution.[10] Eventually, they were forced to adapt to Western practices, and to the 'ideological superstructure of "sportsmanship" clearly derived from European ideas'.[11] Local traditions were subverted and branded 'poaching' in the process. The resulting frictions are well described in Edward Steinhart's aptly named study 'Black Poachers, White Hunters'. Based on local archival research and field studies conducted as oral history, the author focuses on hunting as a social activity that created strong, in his reading almost binary distinctions. Although his account has been criticized as untimely in the way it ignores newer avenues of research like environmental history and fails to deliver a more nuanced understanding of local societal structures that highlights the pragmatic self-interest of native communities (Steinhart had conducted his interviews in the late 1980s and early 1990s), it nonetheless gives a useful first impression of the narratives one encounters when studying the effects of colonial rule.[12] Appealing simplicity should never be taken at face value – a caveat that is to be uttered about many works on colonial history, in fact.[13] Yet Steinhart does a more convincing job than the critics let on in delineating the socioeconomic interests of the Indigenous population without paying homage to a romanticized version of the 'noble savage': not only were they motivated by survival in the face of devastating drought and famine, but hunting was also an expression of deeply rooted local customs and culture that, at times, culminated in greed for profit.

---

[10]MacKenzie, *Empire of Nature*, p. 60.

[11]MacKenzie, *Empire of Nature*, p. 62.

[12]Cf. Jane Carruthers, 'Review of Black Poachers, White Hunters: A History of Hunting in Colonial Kenya' *African Studies Review* 49(3) (2006), pp. 102–4. Another, more recent work that focuses on the interplay of colonial and indigenous actors in the example of hunting expeditions, highlighting the strong interconnectedness of practices and knowledge, is Angela Thompsell, *Hunting Africa. British Sport, African Knowledge and the Nature of Empire* (New York: Palgrave Macmillan, 2015).

[13]For an in-depth discussion, see Rochona Majumdar, *Writing Postcolonial History* (London and New York: Bloomsbury Academic, 2010).

The 'sportsman's paradise' of Kenya, where Indigenous and later Western hunters roamed the grounds largely undisturbed until a government ban on their activities was declared in 1977 due to 'a poaching crisis that was spreading across the African continent', was the birthplace of the 'big game safari'. According to Steinhart, it combined 'African commercial caravan organization and leadership with European ideas of the Hunt' as a cross-cultural creation and reached its pinnacle during the 1920s and 1930s. African hunters, whose intimate knowledge was tapped and labour force exploited by their European counterparts, were 'demeaned in the process'.[14] The way Kenya was framed by European observers as a bucolic, paradisiacal place catered to colonial tropes of backwardness and inferiority.

> By laying claim to the 'hunting safari' as a cultural attribute of the rich and powerful, the great white hunters would also complete the alienation of Africans from their traditional and visible practices of hunting, silencing their independent voices and turning them increasingly and tragically into the 'black poachers' of colonial imagination.[15]

This incriminating characterization continued to be employed by wildlife conservationists, Steinhart underlines. What is strongly reminiscent of cultural appropriation was a much more complicated and delicate process that he sets out to delineate in his book. Kenya, the author argues, serves as a prime example for a study on class-consciousness and conflict since it attracted 'the wealthy and highborn' and offered 'a corps of professional hunters and guides' while lacking 'an independent local dynamic towards conservation'.[16]

Hunting in the region of today's Kenya can be traced back millennia. It was part of a lively ivory trade in antiquity and home to a range of venatic practices revolving around trapping and the use of bows and spears. These rich and long-standing traditions, however, were largely ignored by European settlers who in accordance with the laws of their countries of origin identified hunting as an elite endeavour reserved for the upper echelons of society. This was accompanied by a prejudiced stance against farmers and peasants who were excluded from participation.[17] As a result, clandestine forms developed not only for subsistence, but also in rites of passage as important steps in

---

[14]Edward I. Steinhart, *Black Poachers, White Hunters: A Social History of Hunting in Colonial Kenya* (Oxford: James Currey, 2006), p. 2.
[15]Steinhart, *Black Poachers, White Hunters*, p. 3.
[16]Steinhart, *Black Poachers, White Hunters*, p. 11.
[17]For an overview, see Emma Griffin, *Blood Sport. Hunting in Britain since 1066* (New Haven and London: Yale University Press, 2007).

the socialization of adolescents.[18] With the notable expansion of trade that linked up with long-distance Arab-Swahili networks in the 1800s, commercial specialists entered the scene as entrepreneurs 'who derived legitimacy and experience from their roles as hunting leaders'.[19] Ivory was exchanged for oriental craft goods and Western industrial products like cloth, but also for cattle and small stock, Steinhart continues. As a response to the rising demand, ivory hunting (which included the scavenging for tusks of animals that had died of natural causes) was transformed in eastern Kenya during the second half of the nineteenth century: 'instead of small groups of from three to perhaps a dozen experienced hunters travelling together in pursuit of elephant herds, expeditions of several score, often upwards of a hundred and more hunters, had become common.'[20]

Intensified commodification and professional specialization resulted in the creation of a commercial elite that concentrated power and wealth. This helped leading figures obtain the status of a regional chieftain or – as Steinhart prefers to call it – of a 'hunting leader' that 'accommodate[d] new sources of power within old paradigms of authority' (rather than marking the transition from a kinship-based to a modern society as classical works preferred to suggest).[21] As he shows throughout his study, elephant hunting was highly ritualized and at times even informed by cultural practices that he translates as the 'bewitching' of animals and labels 'witchcraft'. This prejudice served as a welcome excuse for colonial forces to take a stance against Indigenous activities which were outlawed in their drive to monopolize the ivory trade towards the end of the century.[22] This went hand in hand with the discovery and exploitation of East African hunting grounds by European sportsmen who tried to escape the 'embourgeoisement of European culture' which had made the unchecked killing of game ever more difficult.[23] Their accounts convey a

---

[18]Steinhart, *Black Poachers, White Hunters*, p. 20. A flawed collection of articles dealing with the performance of manliness in bloodsport as a preparation for war (lat. *praeludium belli*) is J. A. Mangan and Callum McKenzie, *Militarism, Hunting, Imperialism. 'Blooding' The Martial Male* (London: Routledge, 2010). For well-founded criticism, see John M. MacKenzie, 'Militarism, Hunting, Imperialism: "Blooding" the Martial Male' *The Journal of Imperial and Commonwealth History* 38(1) (2010), pp. 160–2.
[19]Steinhart, *Black Poachers, White Hunters*, p. 43.
[20]Steinhart, *Black Poachers, White Hunters*, p. 50.
[21]Steinhart, *Black Poachers, White Hunters*, p. 49. On p. 48, he underlines that this kind of chieftaincy as it was attributed to 'the most successful of these entrepreneurs in the 1830s and 1840s (...) the premier ivory trader in Kitui' Kivoi Mwendwa (1790s–c. 1851) was 'only instituted a half-century later by the colonial administration'.
[22]See, e.g., Steinhart, *Black Poachers, White Hunters*, pp. 50–5. For a general description of traditional hunting techniques across Africa, cf. MacKenzie, *Empire of Nature*, pp. 54–84, as highlighted above.
[23]Steinhart, *Black Poachers, White Hunters*, p. 67.

degrading image of Indigenous guides and trackers as either 'happy go lucky savages' or as unskilled hunters without 'true sporting feeling': 'If Africans do not love animals and their pursuit, it is because they lack true human affections' is still one of the milder accusations.[24] Colonial police officers and soldiers were also involved in hunting activities, and were expected to turn a blind eye to these gentlemen's at times illicit exploits – and to those of their brothers in arms.[25]

Such favouritism notwithstanding, the roots of conservation lay in these same administrative structures, Steinhart argues. Its advocates were caught in the paradox of 'being at times the leading settler defenders of animals and game conservation and the leading destroyers of wildlife and habitat in the name of progress'.[26] Their harmful practices included not only venatic pursuits, but also the fencing of habitats, slash-and-burn agriculture and the active involvement in trading game products.[27] Yet these settlers did observe Indigenous techniques that informed their otherwise-fruitless pursuits, especially when it came to finding and tracking animals. Consequently, Steinhart postulates a combination of 'black' and 'white' practices in safari hunting, which was popularized not least through the ample press coverage of the 1909/10 Smithsonian-Roosevelt African expedition with the participation of the 26th president of the United States, Theodore Roosevelt (1858–1919). The term 'safari' ('journey') can be traced back to the Arab-Swahili commercial networks mentioned above, denoting their caravan-like character which at times involved hundreds of porters or beasts of burden and the necessity to hunt for the party's sustenance.

The efforts to 'whiten' the safari, to see its inventors and developers as the European pioneers of African exploration and settlement, were begun early in the history of the transition from trade to hunting, as colonial officials, white settlers, and local resident hunters replaced the coastal caravan leadership and organization with their own (...) The safari, I will contend was the central arena in which European and African ideas about hunting met and merged to create a truly Euro-African synthesis by the 1930s. We can see clearly, in the various meanings with which the idea of safari has been inscribed, the workings of what Mary Louise Pratt has described as

---

[24]Steinhart, *Black Poachers, White Hunters*, p. 76.
[25]Steinhart, *Black Poachers, White Hunters*, pp. 81–90.
[26]Steinhart, *Black Poachers, White Hunters*, p. 93.
[27]Steinhart, *Black Poachers, White Hunters*, p. 99.

transculturation 'in the contact zone' between Western imperialism and indigenous ideas.[28]

As the mentioning of the Smithsonian Institution underlines, which had been founded in 1846 with a clear educational mission, much of the killing was done under the guise of science and research. This was followed by what Steinhart calls 'royal' and 'literary safaris' that attracted aristocrats like members of the British royal family and writers like Ernest Hemingway during the times leading to the 'glamorous crescendo' of the imperial hunting safari in the mid-1930s.[29] Professional hunters' associations that projected ideas of 'white supremacy over blacks' accompanied this development,[30] and Steinhart does not tire to underline the limited respect these indispensable local companions received:

> despite the Olympian perspective assumed by the great white hunters, from Roosevelt to Hemingway to [novelist Robert] Ruark, they were in fact standing on the shoulders of the thousands of Africans who had gone before them historically, as well as literally, as guides and trackers. They would seldom acknowledge their debt to their 'dark companions' and predecessors, preferring to cast themselves as the active agents and their Africans as both subordinate and without initiative. Even when they praise their loyalty and courage, they deny to their African colleagues any capacity for independence of thought or purpose and agendas of their own. Only occasionally can we see the veil slip in the travel, hunting, and safari literature to allow an African to take an initiative.[31]

The considerable value of ivory as an export good that made up about half of tax revenues in the early twentieth century along with its blooming illegal trade, and the fact that sportsmen rather than scientists headed Kenya's Game Department arguably hampered more decisive conservation efforts.[32] This is also the origin of the paradoxical utilitarian policies on game preservation that allow certain animals to be killed for the supposed overall benefit of their populations as they have been harshly criticized by activists – not least since they continue to propel a form of colonialism for affluent actors rather than facilitating an 'Africanization of the conservation movement' that may fight

---

[28]Steinhart, *Black Poachers, White Hunters*, pp. 113–14. Here, he refers to Pratt's 1992 work *Imperial Eyes. Travel Writing and Transculturation*. Her concept of the 'contact zone' can be especially helpful when looking at the exchange of cultural practices as it is not limited by political-administrative boundaries.
[29]Steinhart, *Black Poachers, White Hunters*, p. 125.
[30]Steinhart, *Black Poachers, White Hunters*, p. 132.
[31]Steinhart, *Black Poachers, White Hunters*, p. 137.
[32]Steinhart, *Black Poachers, White Hunters*, pp. 150–1.

poverty and dependence more convincingly.[33] Nonetheless, in the decades after the First World War a system of national parks developed from the general idea to preserve game for hunting. Both the international conservation movement and local endeavours in Kenya followed two presumptions, according to Steinhart:

> The first is that the best guardians of nature were the imperial and colonial ruling classes, the great aristocratic hunters of the previous generation, now transformed and reincarnated as champions of game preservation. The second is that the best instrument for preservation lay in the creation of nature and wildlife sanctuaries modelled on the aristocratic hunting parks of eighteenth-century Britain and their ideological progeny, the new national parks, such as Yellowstone Park, in the United States.[34]

Milestones like the 1933 Convention Relative to the Preservation of Fauna and Flora in their Natural State that resulted from the International Conference for the Protection of the Fauna and Flora of Africa in London in the same year furthered this development, even though it was interrupted by yet another global conflict, the Second World War, and the localized Mau Mau Rebellion which marked Kenya's struggle for independence from the early 1950s to 1963. With time, the hunting safari was read as a stereotypical example of colonial rule, and its classical form opened up to the replacement of carriers by motorcars and sharpshooting rifles by large-lens cameras – a commercialization that was widely marketed as catering to the spirit of protecting wildlife. 'In the end', Steinhart summarizes, 'it was the conservationists who ended all three of Kenya's hunting traditions – African subsistence, imperial, and safari hunting – and made every hunter a poacher'.[35]

Colonialism at play

While Steinhart focused on the intersections of hunting practices, Bernhard Gissibl is much more interested in the intricacies of colonial administrations

---

[33]See the critical overview by Sian Sullivan, '"Hunting Africa": Trophy Hunting, Neocolonialism and Land' *The Land* 31 (2022), pp. 22–7, 58 (references and footnotes) – quote p. 24.

[34]Steinhart, *Black Poachers, White Hunters*, p. 174. Worth mentioning in this context would be the activities of the Society for the Preservation of the Fauna of the Empire, see p. 98. For a comparison with developments in the United States, see Louis S. Warren, *The Hunter's Game. Poachers and Conservationists in Twentieth-Century America* (New Haven and London: Yale University Press, 1997).

[35]Steinhart, *Black Poachers, White Hunters*, p. 213. For a similar conclusion also with regard to India, see MacKenzie, *Empire of Nature* pp. 298–9.

and their ecological fallout. As the highly metaphoric cover of his book on *The Nature of German Imperialism* illustrates, where a zebra ridden by a man in colonial attire clears what looks like an obstacle made for horse jumping that is held by two locals, the will to subdue obviously extended to the native fauna. This is symbolic for the colonists' claim to power and their self-imposed entitlement to rule over human and non-human bodies alike.[36] Gissibl focuses on the parts of German East Africa (*Deutsch-Ostafrika*) that were ultimately referred to by the portmanteau of Tanzania with the unification of Tanganyika and Zanzibar in 1964 after independence from Britain. In the spirit of political ecology, he contextualizes environmental issues within a socio-economic framework, asking 'how wild animals and elephants in particular have shaped the culture and geography of colonial rule, and how conservation policies evolved in a stuttering and highly uneven quest for a more sustainable utilization of the wildlife resource'.[37] While the terms *conservation* and *preservation* are often seen as two sides of the same coin and are therefore employed interchangeably without much concern – as the above example of Steinhart shows – Gissibl aims to keep them apart:

'Conservation' and 'preservation' are used according to their established understanding in international environmental history, that is, with conservation denoting measures of nature protection that allowed for management and sustainable utilization to ensure the continued use of animals through humans, as opposed to preservation as noninterventionist forms of protection predicated upon assumptions of ecological integrity and natural balance.[38]

The author is rightfully cautious about the colonial bias of his archival material which extends to ethnographic works and personal memoirs. 'Hunting tales are a genre underlying their own plots of dramatization culminating in the final kill (...) presenting an eternal contest between man and the brute', Gissibl

---

[36]On boundary-making and transgressions in whaling, the slave trade, conservation, zoological gardens or the exhibition of humans, see Winfried Speitkamp and Stephanie Zehnle (eds), *Afrikanische Tierräume. Historische Verortungen* (Köln: Rüdiger Köppe Verlag, 2014). Sandra Swart, *Riding High. Horses, Humans and History in South Africa* (Johannesburg: Wits University Press, 2010) meanwhile looks at the complex relationship between Indigenous people, European colonizers and equine creatures to the south of the continent.

[37]Bernhard Gissibl, *The Nature of German Imperialism. Conservation and the Politics of Wildlife in Colonial East Africa* (New York and Oxford: Berghahn, 2016), p. 9. See also MacKenzie, *Empire of Nature*, pp. 250–4.

[38]Gissibl, *The Nature of German Imperialism*, p. 23. For a useful, if slightly outdated, bibliography see Adam Rome, 'Conservation, Preservation, and Environmental Activism: A Survey of the Historical Literature' *National Park Service* (16 January 2003), https://www.nps.gov/parkhistory/hisnps/NPSThinking/nps-oah.htm [accessed on 17 December 2024].

reminds us.[39] Consequently, he expanded his already rich source base not only by looking at specialized hunting periodicals, but also by including daily local newspapers and scientific works in such related fields like veterinary medicine. This creates a plurality of voices and opinions that many works on colonial history are missing.

Two of the most striking corrections to existing research that Gissibl postulates in his first chapters are that 'the idea that ivory trade and hunting advanced along a linear frontier, and the assumption that elephants in Tanzania were close to extinction by the onset of colonial rule' cannot be maintained with regard to late-nineteenth-century Tanganyika.[40] This does not mean that wild animal populations did not come under pressure, nor that colonization did not create something akin to a moving frontier as it was highlighted by Harriet Ritvo above.

> The notion of an ivory frontier is especially misleading for it conflates a commercial with an ecological frontier. It does not distinguish between ivory trade and ivory hunting, and suggests that the frontier of trade followed hard on the heel of the exhaustion of elephant stocks. But the price of tusks did not rest upon a simple translation of biological scarcity into economic value. Rather value was determined by a whole set of political, social, economic, and ecological factors. Even more than the increasing scarcity of elephants, economic rationales motivated the ever further intrusion of Zanzibari traders into the interior.[41]

Another aspect that sets Gissibl apart is the explicit statement of animal agency:

> Observations by hunters, explorers, and colonial officials suggest that elephants reacted to hunting pressure by migration and learned to be wary. Their disappearance from one area could easily lead to their reappearance in another area where trade might have already deemed to be no longer lucrative.[42]

As these quotes show, Gissibl focuses rather on refining an often overly dramatized discourse of crisis and threat that overshadows existing regimes of relatively sustainable resource use which had evolved over generations within Indigenous populations. As already seen in Steinhart's work, colonists

---

[39]Gissibl, *The Nature of German Imperialism*, p. 19.
[40]Gissibl, *The Nature of German Imperialism*, p. 44.
[41]Gissibl, *The Nature of German Imperialism*, p. 47.
[42]Gissibl, *The Nature of German Imperialism*, p. 47.

adopted many of their practices in adapting to local environments that were hitherto unknown to them. It remains an important task of colonial history to try and resurface these voices for a more qualified assessment that may ultimately even reveal alternative paths of relevance to us today. Another aspect of this history, which was critically remarked in *Black Poachers, White Hunters* as noted above, however, was the economic self-interest of local communities. Here, Gissibl notes that elephant hunting contributed to the rise of East Africa's so-called entrepreneurial kings in the second half of the nineteenth century:

Mirambo [in the historical region of Unyamwezi], for example, claimed the complete monopoly over all ivory procured in his territories. So did other chiefs and big men who were in power when Germany's expeditionary forces strove to impose European ideas of statehood upon Eastern Africa. The struggle over power after the middle of the 1880s, long held to be a struggle between a modern bureaucratic state and traditional tribal chiefs, essentially played out as a struggle over ivory.[43]

This paints a fairly complex picture where the protagonists' motivations are not always easy to discern. As a result, there is no straightforward answer to the question how conservation evolved in the African colonies, as sketched above in Steinhart's book. The rather apologetic argument with regard to the colonial system that it was the economic interests and animist worldviews of the autochthonous population who did not conceive of species as potentially endangered which hindered the implementation of protection measures has to be contrasted with the practices of big-game hunting as 'a multidimensional and multifunctional, ritualized performance of power over nature'.[44] Based in Central European traditions, German hunters liked to present themselves as overly considerate, since they followed their own honour codex of *Weidgerechtigkeit* which loosely corresponds to the Anglophone idea of fair chase.

It comprised, among others, an ethical responsibility and an attitude of respect of the hunter toward the game, the exertion of hunting with restraint, and the observation of a number of rules such as the sparing of feeding [especially meaning lactating] females, the quick and painless infliction of death and the avoidance of unnecessary suffering, and the overall responsibility for the sustainable management of game. In the colonial context, *Weidgerechtigkeit* was relevant not so much as an actual

[43]Gissibl, *The Nature of German Imperialism*, p. 56.
[44]Gissibl, *The Nature of German Imperialism*, p. 74.

practice but as a language of distinction that could be invoked and mobilized against those that should, for various reasons, be excluded from the Hunt.[45]

In effect, this collection of written and unwritten rules and regulations served to assure the hunters of their own superiority, in spite of their heavy reliance on local guides and helpers. As Gissibl underlines, '*Weidgerechtigkeit* was not only a language to express environmental chauvinism and prescribe certain codes of behavior to potentially subversive whites. Hunting also provided an idiom in which more material interests could be framed and negotiated.'[46] Thus, it informed early attempts at hunting ordinances towards the late nineteenth century that established the first game reserves. 'Although usually entitled *Jagdverordnung*, such regulations effectively did more than just regulate hunting,' he argues. 'They are biopolitical classifications that define human–animal relationships and determine how wild animals can and should be treated.' As a result, ''Western utilitarian and conservationist values' coexisted and mixed with African spiritual concepts, the author continues, and with local patterns of maintaining authority as in the organization of an ivory tribute tax system to chiefs and the colonial administration.[47] Ordinances that followed in the spirit of the 1900 Convention on the Preservation of Wild Animals, Birds, and Fish in Africa (which was signed in London and presented an important precursor to the above-mentioned 1933 International Conference for the Protection of the Fauna and Flora of Africa) aimed to abolish the native tribute system; elephant hunting was monopolized.[48] As it was typical of the hunting legislation of the time, the London Convention differentiated 'pests' from 'useful' species worth being protected by creating reserves for rare and endangered wild animals. Although it was not ratified by most of its signatories and thus never became legally binding, it nonetheless inspired conservation measures.[49] The exclusion of indigenous hunters, however, along with the strain agricultural development put on local economies, led to the frustration and resistance that fed into the Maji Maji Rebellion in German East Africa between 1905 and 1907 which cost the lives of tens of thousands of people at least, mainly due to the resulting famine.

---

[45]Gissibl, *The Nature of German Imperialism*, p. 75.
[46]Gissibl, *The Nature of German Imperialism*, p. 147.
[47]Gissibl, *The Nature of German Imperialism*, pp. 87, 96.
[48]Gissibl, *The Nature of German Imperialism*, pp. 114, 123. On the historical trajectory from preservation to conservation, see MacKenzie, *Empire of Nature*, pp. 200–224, and on its international impact, pp. 261–94.
[49]For an overview on its further evolution, see *An Introduction to the African Convention on the Conservation of Nature and Natural Resources* (Gland and Cambridge: IUCN, 2004), here p. 3.

Correlating conservation

The example of Kenya's tourism with its expensive game licenses for the wealthy proved to be an inspiring – if ultimately unattainable – model for the German colonies.[50] Aristocratic and military protagonists were among the most avid hunters in the region. In elitist views on wilderness and wildness 'mediated by the presence of large animals', we see an idealized reflection on the nature–culture divide as it was already discussed in the preceding chapters:

> the megafauna of the East African savanna provided an ideal canvas for exoticist imaginations of a primeval and wild paradise that could be charged with a rich heritage of European cultural meaning (…) Such reading of the savanna as paradise, Eden, and wilderness inscribed a timeless primeval originality into African space, which not only erased any previous human history of these places, but also current human ecologies (…) once declared as the spatial and temporal opposite of Europe – pristine, wild, uncultivated, and devoid of people – conservationists disposed with East African lands at their will.[51]

According to Gissibl, it was a number of factors that motivated and facilitated the creation of wildlife reserves: along with the romanticized understanding of wilderness and an expansion of agriculture that called for a solution to the spread of diseases transmitted by wild animals, it was also the experience of species extinction elsewhere like in the case of the American bison (*cf.* Chapter 4) that pressed protagonists into action.[52] Adding to this was the interest in access to and authority over natural resources. In a cynical turn of events, the devastating outcome of the Maji Maji Rebellion made it easier to declare depopulated areas 'uncultivated wilderness' and 'terra nullius'. This was exacerbated by repeated 'punitive expeditions' that helped create 'the empty landscape of the reserve' by driving away native farmers.[53] Indigenous hunting was to be limited in order to coerce African people onto the labour market.[54]

---

[50]Gissibl, *The Nature of German Imperialism*, pp. 141, 161; on its failure, see pp. 191–3. On later, more media-driven modes of conservation, see Thomas M. Lekan, *Our Gigantic Zoo. A German Quest to Save the Serengeti* (New York: Oxford University Press, 2020).
[51]Gissibl, *The Nature of German Imperialism*, p. 185.
[52]Gissibl, *The Nature of German Imperialism*, p. 202.
[53]Gissibl, *The Nature of German Imperialism*, p. 206.
[54]Gissibl, *The Nature of German Imperialism*, p. 208.

Gissibl continues to highlight the scope of 'transimperial cooperation and mutual exchange in the early stages of African conservation'. This is especially important, he writes, since the story of conservation was hitherto largely told from a British perspective, as with the example of Kenya in Steinhart's work above: 'wildlife policies in the East African colonies were no self-contained phenomena, but interacted'.[55] This encompassed the already mentioned fields of game legislation, the organization of safari tourism, but also competition in the ivory trade. Furthermore, scientists like the German physician and microbiologist Robert Koch (1843–1910) participated in an exchange of knowledge across imperial boundaries on questions of epidemiology and other issues. 'Imperialism was tied to internationalism in complex ways,' Gissibl quips before he delves into some of the intricacies of the International Conference on the Preservation of Wild Animals, Birds, and Fish in Africa of 1900 that spawned the above-mentioned London Convention of the same descriptive title. In its scope, it was misleading, however, as it focused largely on the hunting of charismatic megafauna like the elephant. A diplomatic event that connected functionaries, hunters and naturalists, it was met with mixed interest by the European powers. Its overall limited effect notwithstanding, Gissibl recognizes the convention as 'a milestone in international environmentalism' because it 'established as an international norm that wildlife was, in principle, to be preserved and the extinction of certain animals averted'.[56] Governments could potentially be held accountable now based on the jointly formulated – if not ratified – papers on wildlife conservation. This momentum fed into more globalized discussions that continued to inform policies on colonial ground.

The First World War resulted in the international isolation of Germany that neither took part in the conferences on nature conservation in Paris (1923, 1931) nor in London (1933). The years under Nazi leadership were marred by what Gissibl broadly labels 'impressive exercises at imaginary conservation' as it lacked the necessary international respect and influence. It was only during the 1950s that German protagonists returned to the scene as 'honest brokers' through the activities of organizations like the International Union for Conservation of Nature (IUCN), the United Nations Educational, Scientific and Cultural Organization (UNESCO) and, since the 1960s, the World Wildlife Fund (WWF, now called the World Wide Fund for Nature) which 'increasingly took over stewardship for East African wildlife (...) seemingly untainted by colonial baggage or other obvious stakes in East African conservation'.[57] The

---

[55]Gissibl, *The Nature of German Imperialism*, p. 234.
[56]Gissibl, *The Nature of German Imperialism*, p. 253.
[57]Gissibl, *The Nature of German Imperialism*, p. 304.

persistence of hegemonic structures has been a strong point of contention ever since.

Gissibl's study leaves us with a fragmented picture. The label of animal history is misleading, as animal agency itself hardly plays a role in the legalist discussion throughout his book that rather deals with racist asymmetries in colonial politics vis-à-vis the Indigenous population. Nonetheless, it presents its readers with important details on wildlife governance based on strong empirical work in a range of archives. More to the point is an article he published in a German journal that is focused on ongoing practical aspects of historical research titled *The colonized animal. On the ecology of the contact zones of German colonialism*: 'If one takes the claim of the colonial rulers seriously, then the animal and plant world inevitably belonged to the total formation of colonial rule.'[58] Consequently, he speaks of 'multiple agencies' that can be ascribed to humans and non-humans:

> The colonial claim to power was also realized through the bodies of animals; animal action challenged human action and was involved in the creation of social and cultural realities that were constitutive for colonialism as a system of domination. The self-determined and externally determined activities of animals must be the subject of historiography simply because they stood in relation to human action and were thus socially relevant.[59]

While this argument, circular as it may seem, would surely not be doubted by contemporary ecologically minded scholars, it is not easy to be put into practice, as the hitherto discussed works on colonial history have shown. Often, documentation is one-sided and lacking a non-Western perspective, which extends to the epistemic background of the researchers: grasping Sub-Saharan Africa in its ethnocultural and linguistic diversity is a daunting task, to say the least. In his article, Gissibl suggests to use discourses and practices of domestication as an analytical avenue. Faced with the 'unsuitability of European domestic and farm animals for the tropics', he writes, 'the taming of native animal species, their cross-breeding with related European species and the import of already domesticated species from other tropical regions were among the measures intended to "improve" the biological make-up of colonized areas'. This takes us back to the image of the mounted zebra on his book cover, as he stresses that 'attempts to tame and breed African large mammals were unsuccessful, but not insignificant' in the way they

---

[58]Bernhard Gissibl, 'Das kolonisierte Tier: Zur Ökologie der Kontaktzonen des deutschen Kolonialismus' *WerktstattGeschichte* 56 (2010), pp. 7–28, here p. 8.
[59]Gissibl, 'Das kolonisierte Tier', p. 9.

demonstrate colonial aspirations. These, Gissibl continues, extended to a 'claim to the domestication of the entire continent and its inhabitants' in all its perceived wilderness.[60]

He also underlines the 'hegemonic masculinity' of white colonizers reflected in their hunting practices through participation, privilege and identification: 'Only the killing of the wild animal and the appropriation of the animal in the hunting trophy restored the humanity and imperial masculinity of the white hunter and his claim to power over the African wilderness.' Big game hunting was even presented 'as an instance of education towards a supposedly more natural, vital and violent masculinity' with regard to the domestic reading public that was to be delineated from Indigenous practices. Hunting women remained marginal.[61]

> Big game hunting thus constituted a masculinity of civilized naturalness that incorporated the animalistic as natural and authentic, contained a critique of civilization and self-civilization in equal measure, and thus responded to the much-discussed crisis of masculinity in Western modernity.[62]

Ultimately, according to Gissibl, colonial tendencies to conserve nature created the basis for an African modernity with wild animals as an integral part of the environment that stood in contrast to European models of rationalization (see also Chapter 7). Thus, 'Western capital and knowledge, Western concepts of nature and conservation interests, a strong central state and a largely marginalized local population characterize the governance structures for the protection of African big game to the present day.'[63] This shows that much remains to be done in this field to better understand the inherent ambivalences of hunting, conservation and colonial rule that show in traditions, laws and everyday acts of violence.[64]

---

[60]Gissibl, 'Das kolonisierte Tier', pp. 12, 14, 15.
[61]Gissibl, 'Das kolonisierte Tier', pp. 20–1. See also Callum Mckenzie, '"Sadly Neglected" – Hunting and Gendered Identities: A Study in Gender Construction' The International Journal of the History of Sport 22(4) (2005), pp. 545–62 who speaks of 'stoicism, peseverence [sic] and robustness' as aspired qualities – p. 547.
[62]Gissibl, 'Das kolonisierte Tier', p. 22.
[63]Gissibl, 'Das kolonisierte Tier', p. 28.
[64]For a more integrated historiographic approach that explicitly tries to capture the voices and actions of animals, see Sandra Swart, The Lion's Historian. Africa's Animal Past (Johannesburg: Jacana Press, 2023).

6

Commodifying animals: Whaling and the exploitation of the oceans

There is, one knows not what sweet mystery about this sea, whose gently awful stirrings seem to speak of some hidden soul beneath; like those fabled undulations of the Ephesian sod over the buried Evangelist St. John. And meet it is, that over these sea-pastures, wide-rolling watery prairies and Potters' Fields of all four continents, the waves should rise and fall, and ebb and flow unceasingly; for here, millions of mixed shades and shadows, drowned dreams, somnambulisms, reveries; all that we call lives and souls, lie dreaming, dreaming, still; tossing like slumberers in their beds; the ever-rolling waves but made so by their restlessness.

– HERMAN MELVILLE, *MOBY-DICK; OR, THE WHALE* (1851), CHAPTER CXI: THE PACIFIC

Death and glory were closely knit on the world's oceans. As Herman Melville describes in impressive detail throughout his classic work of literature, the fate of seafarers was subjected to the forces of nature. At the same time, it is a highly philosophical metaphor on the meaning of life that ultimately remains unfathomable, beyond comprehension. Humanity's struggle to control – or at least exploit – the environment may well lead to its downfall, as in the figure of Captain Ahab who is drawn into the depths bound to the mighty white whale he was chasing. It thus seems only fitting to begin a study about the Northern Pacific with the disappearance of one of its fabled species before later returning to cetaceans and their plight: Steller's sea cow. Hunted for its meat by Russian fur traders who made their way across the Bering Strait into North America, it serves as an example of anthropogenic destruction and what Ryan Tucker Jones in *Empire of Extinction* labels 'the haunting sense of loss that extinction has left on colonial landscapes and seascapes'.[1] He thereby asks the question how indicative this irrecoverable loss of animal life since the eighteenth century is for imperial rule. Land, water and animals are assigned the status of 'leading characters' in his book, 'alongside Russians, Aleuts, Germans, and other members of the human species'.[2]

According to Jones, the possibility of extinction – let alone unsustainability – transcended the contemporary imagination. Nature's resources were there for the taking, and the integration of representatives of natural history into imperial expansion was 'commonplace'.[3] The Second Kamchatka Expedition (around 1733 to 1743, also called 'The Great Northern Expedition') under the command of the Danish captain Vitus Bering (1681–1741) is a fitting example. In search of navigable routes and riches along the east Siberian coast, natural scientists were employed to mark discoveries considered of benefit to the Russian Empire.[4] This followed an expansive drive that had begun in the late sixteenth century with the decline of the Khanate of Sibir as a successor to the mighty Mongol Empire that once stretched across Eurasia.

For Russia, this came at a time when academic culture was still in a fledgling state. Reports by Cossack colonizers about lavish fauna, of a 'great many whales, seals and sea otters in the sea' made their way from Kamchatka to the imperial centre of Moscow that 'did not promote the economic development of the peninsula, but rather its plunder' through a system of tribute collection (commonly referred to as *yasak*) known since the rule of the khans.[5]

The abundance of animals in and around Kamchatka supplied the environmental conditions necessary to support a dense human population. Huge seasonal salmon runs provided Kamchatka's humans easy access to food. In the south of the peninsula, the Kamchadals (also known as Itelmen) had inhabited the land for nearly thirty thousand years by the time

---

[1] Ryan Tucker Jones, *Empire of Extinction. Russians and the North Pacific's Strange Beasts of the Sea, 1741–1867* (Oxford and New York: Oxford University Press, 2014; online edition: Oxford Academic), p. 3.
[2] Jones, *Empire of Extinction*, p. 9.
[3] Jones, *Empire of Extinction*, p. 15.
[4] See also Andreas Renner, *Nordostpassage. Geschichte eines Seewegs* (Hamburg: mareverlag, 2024).
[5] Jones, *Empire of Extinction*, pp. 28–9. He later writes: 'The military officers and political exiles who received governorships in the towns and regions of Siberia supplemented their small or nonexistent salary with massive extortion and control of the government monopolies on furs and liquors' – p. 38.

of Russian contact. They harvested river-running salmon in the summer and fall, drying and storing them by the thousands for winter provisions to feed themselves and the dogs that pull their sleds (...) Kamchadals a so harvested the abundance of the sea, killing fur seals, sea lions, sea otters, and – more rarely – whales. On occasion they would also kill the peninsula's giant brown bears, impaling them to death with wooden poles.[6]

As with the conquest of the Americas (discussed in Chapter 4), such natural wealth attracted an array of fortune seekers and adventurers, prime among them the so-called *promyshlenniki*, industrious trappers and fur-traders.[7] The German physician and naturalist Georg Wilhelm Steller (1709–46), who first described his namesake sirenian mentioned at the beginning of this chapter, deplored 'the poor sea otters, which were needlessly and thoughtlessly killed merely for their pelts, the meat being thrown away'.[8] Simultaneously, the advancement of tsarist Russia and its tax collectors across Siberia caused resistance among old and new local dwellers: 'Extortionate *yasak* demands and a failure to carry out the state's benevolent policy toward the Kamchadals constituted the Russians' chief sins in Kamchatka', Jones asserts, and people like Steller were to play 'a key role in producing the knowledge that would lead to a more complete exploitation of nature'.[9]

Considering the profitability of trading furs, it is no surprise that many government servitors who represented the 'loose bureaucracy' of Kamchatka and other provinces of the Far East soon counted themselves among the promyshlenniki. They were followed by more affluent merchants from Moscow and Irkutsk that aimed to expand their business east and eventua lly came to dominate the maritime fur exchange.[10] As in the case of European colonialism in Africa (see Chapter 5), Indigenous populations were relied on

---

[6]Jones, *Empire of Extinction*, pp. 30–1.
[7]See also John F. Richards, *The World Hunt: An Environmental History of the Commodification of Animals* (Berkeley: University of California Press, 2014), pp. 55–84 for a helpful overview on 'The Hunt for Furs in Siberia' from the 1500s to the eighteenth century based on more classical works. It was posthumously extracted from the author's *The Unending Frontier: An Environmental History of the Early Modern World* (2003). John M. MacKenzie, *The Empire of Nature. Hunting, Conservation and British Imperialism* (Manchester: Manchester University Press, 1988), p. 296 highlights this parallelism as well.
[8]Jones, *Empire of Extinction*, p. 48. See also Martina Winkler, *Das Imperium und die Seeotter. Die Expansion Russlands in den nordpazifischen Raum, 1700–1867* (Göttingen: Vandenhoeck & Ruprecht, 2016). Though sea otters figure less than expected as agents, the book is an important work of cultural history deeply influenced by the spatial turn. It surveys the North Pacific region as an imperial arena which was considered an integral part of the Russian Empire by the eighteenth century as it is mirrored in the documents of scientists and voyagers.
[9]Jones, *Empire of Extinction*, pp. 51, 44, respectively.
[10]Jones, *Empire of Extinction*, p. 66.

to hunt and to provide traders. This was spurred by threats of violence and hostage-taking.[11] Russian naturalists, who were pondering alternatives to the slaughter of marine mammals in the form of European-styled agriculture and livestock farming, soon realized that the number of animals was in decline. This corresponded to reports by promyshlenniki that were in close contact with Indigenous hunters, though they were paid little respect in the recently established imperial centre of St Petersburg until the end of the eighteenth century.[12]

As in other colonial contexts, native populations were often held responsible for declining numbers of animals due to their supposedly uncultivated practices and unrestrained nature. 'Part of the critique's effectiveness can be explained by the fact that it had caught up with the broader sentiments of colonial Europeans, who tended to blame their indigenous trading partners or colonized subjects for their own environmental troubles', Jones observes.[13] In a cynical manner, they thus prepared the ground for conservation measures that further limited native freedoms – not least by suggesting to close hunting grounds for years on end. Quotas were allocated to specific districts by the Russian-American Company (RAC) which until the 1860s held a trading monopoly as well as administrative competencies for the parts of North America under tsarist control before the Alaska Purchase by the United States in 1867:

> If the Aleuts killed too many sea otters in one year, they would have a smaller quota the next. The method of hunting also came under control, with extra precautions taken not to frighten the sea otters reserved for hunting in future years. No firearms were to be used, and fires had to be lit far away from the sea otter herds, smoke being considered one of the chief culprits in driving away the animals. Females, too, were spared, as far as this was possible considering that the animals were killed at sea. Young Aleuts were taught to distinguish the sexes by noticing the 'color and shape of its head and neck.' Whether this was longstanding Aleut practice or a Company innovation is not clear.[14]

The company's conservation policies – which were not motivated by compassion for the hunted animals but rather aimed at securing its core economic interests – remained 'strictly reactive', Jones observes, as 'an attempt to breathe some flicker of life back into badly depleted areas'.[15] It was

---

[11]Jones, *Empire of Extinction*, p. 84.
[12]See Jones, *Empire of Extinction*, pp. 102–37 (Chapter 3: Naturalists Plan a North Pacific Empire).
[13]Jones, *Empire of Extinction*, p. 204; see also pp. 223–4.
[14]Jones, *Empire of Extinction*, p. 210.
[15]Jones, *Empire of Extinction*, p. 220.

not until the North Pacific Fur Seal Convention of 1911, as some authors have argued, that the conservation of endangered species and biodiversity became a non-utilitarian focus with this precursor to contemporary environmental legislation.[16] As Robert Kindler highlights, this change in perspective has to be seen in the context of power shifts in international diplomacy after Russia's defeat in the Russo-Japanese War of 1904–5: the weakened stance of the tsarist empire on the international arena 'contributed significantly to the conservation of fur seals' as it could hardly defend its immediate economic interests and searched to gain prestige by demonstrating agency through participation in such highly publicized diplomatic events.[17]

The eastward drive

The history of extinction in Russia's Far East is closely tied to the empire's expansion. Here, hunters and merchants pursued wild animals in what became a *commodity frontier* of the fur-trade, as Robert Kindler has shown in his book on the *Realm of the Seals*. Russia's authority over people and animals remained fragmented, however, and the interaction of humans with non-human protagonists constantly 'changed, influenced' and thus 'created the North Pacific region'.[18] Both groups of actors contoured this transnational space of communication and conflict where animals as a natural resource were 'inextricably linked' to efforts of state-building and assertions of power.[19] In one subchapter, Kindler highlights the brute force and unbearable violence of seal hunting as these animals were clubbed to death and often-times skinned alive – much to the dismay of less experienced onlookers who believed to see tears running down the animals' helpless faces. The anthropomorphism of those who criticized such barbarity, in turn, proved fatal for the Indigenous people, Kindler argues:

> Because if observers felt sympathy for the 'mourning' seals, this inevitably must have had a negative effect on the perception of those who slew the

---

[16]For a short overview, see Robert Kindler, *Robbenreich. Russland und die Grenzen der Macht am Nordpazifik* (Hamburg: Hamburger Edition, 2022), pp. 27–30; for a characterization of the immediate events after the Alaska purchase as 'lawless as any goldrush in its early days', pp. 68–72; on the diplomatic dimension, see pp. 289–98.

[17]Kindler, *Robbenreich*, p. 268 (quote), pp. 305–6.

[18]Kindler, *Robbenreich*, p. 10 (*commodity frontier*), p. 15 (*fragmented authority*), quote p. 19. Kindler refers to recent discussions as presented in Sven Beckert, Ulbe Bosma, Mindi Schneider, and Eric Vanhaute, 'Commodity Frontiers and the Transformation of the Global Countryside: A Research Agenda' *Journal of Global History* 16(3) (2021), pp. 435–50.

[19]Kindler, *Robbenreich*, p. 11.

seals. And indeed, some texts dealing with the relationship between the Aleuts and fur seals revealed a certain sympathy for the graceful and agile animals, which often stood in sharp contrast to a barely concealed dislike of the Aleuts (...) The ambivalent positioning of the islanders – on the one hand they were considered indispensable experts, on the other hand they were regarded as cruel butchers and people of low rank – contributed significantly to the fact that they had to lead a life on the sidelines.[20]

Following the animals through the North Pacific, hunters soon found themselves on the high seas. With prices rising for sealskins in the trading hubs of Europe – especially London – this business became increasingly lucrative. The indiscriminate killing of fertile females put ever more strain on herd populations, whose numbers were visibly dwindling towards the end of the nineteenth century. The push onto the oceans was exacerbated by the decline of the American whaling industry that sought less risky alternatives, thus many whalers became sealers.[21] It reached its pinnacle between 1870 and 1910, before the ratification of the above-mentioned Fur Seal Convention deemed it illegal. During these decades, about 1.3 million sealskins were traded, which accounted only for a portion of the overall animals killed, as it was estimated that between half and two-thirds of them could not be retrieved in time before sinking to the bottom.[22] When the Fur Seal Convention of 1911 came into effect, the damage of decades of exploitation was done: 'Local populations were impoverished and, in some cases, had to fear for their existence, fur seal populations were scarred by the devastation of the past and entire ecosystems underwent irreversible long-term changes', Kindler observes.[23]

The killing of seals was just one aspect of the 'great hunt' on the world's oceans, however, and pelagic extinction continued in Soviet times with rigid economic planning, extensive resource use, fragile infrastructures, lacking investments and the destruction of habitats that remains unresolved until today.[24] In his second book, *Red Leviathan*, Ryan Tucker Jones promises to tell 'The Secret History of Soviet Whaling' that retraces the expansion of the industry. With regard to commercial whaling, Russia had arrived somewhat late on the international scene: while in the 'Great Year' of 1697 mainly

---

[20]Kindler, *Robbenreich*, pp. 141–50, quote p. 150. See also Robert Kindler, 'Robben töten. Jagdpraktiken, Anthropomorphismus und Sozialdisziplinierung im Nordpazifik', in Iris Därmann and Stephan Zandt (eds), *Andere Ökologien. Transformationen von Mensch und Tier* (München: Wilhelm Fink, 2017), pp. 101–20.

[21]Kindler, *Robbenreich*, pp. 162–4.

[22]Kindler, *Robbenreich*, p. 172; the argument is repeated on pp. 212–13.

[23]Kindler, *Robbenreich*, p. 398.

[24]Kindler, *Robbenreich*, pp. 368, 405–6.

British, Dutch and German ships were engaged near Spitsbergen where catches reached a record high of 2,000 Atlantic right whales, it was not until the eighteenth century that the tsarist empire 'became directly invo ved in promoting, financing, and controlling whaling' thanks to the westward orientation and maritime interests of Peter the Great (1672–1725).[25] Even though Jones at times fails to discern what he actually understands as 'Russian' in his story – one should be reminded that the empire encompassed a plethora of ethnicities and employed a number of foreign experts – he rightly highlights the important influence of Indigenous hunters in the making of the industry, which were broadly identified as 'Aleuts' or 'Chukchi' by their non-native contemporaries.[26] The Russian state's claim to power even went so far as to trigger a paternalistic instinct to protect 'the interests' of these peoples against 'foreign incursions' by American whalers in the North Pacific.[27]

Onto the seas

The history of whaling with its complex international entanglements is difficult to present in a linear fashion. Until early modern times, it was generally a littoral affair. Hunters focused on their shorelines and only slowly made their way further onto the ocean. While the Basques are usually credited with starting commercial whaling in the 1500s using specially equipped ships that sailed the North Atlantic,[28] it must be noted that a modern processing industry was only created in the nineteenth century. According to John F. Richards, it was the walrus with 'its extended ivory tusks, tough, thick hide, and copious fat' that eventually attracted hunters to the Arctic Ocean. Soon, they also focused on bowhead and right whales, which had the great advantage that most of them did not sink to the ground right away but could be processed at sea or towed to the shore.[29] Not only was whaling considered to be more 'cost-effective', by 1850 walruses had become extinct in the marine ecosystems around Spitsbergen.[30]

---

[25]Ryan Tucker Jones, *Red Leviathan. The Secret History of Soviet Whaling* (Chicago and London: The University of Chicago Press, 2022), p. 4. For a critical evaluation, see Timm Schönfelder, 'Review of Ryan Tucker Jones: Red Leviathan. The Secret History of Soviet Whaling' *Jahrbücher für Geschichte Osteuropas* 72(3) (2024), pp. 511–13.

[26]On the problem of exonyms in non-native sources, see Kindler, *Robbenreich*, pp. 34–5.

[27]Jones, *Red Leviathan*, p. 15.

[28]Richards, *The World Hunt*, p. 123.

[29]Richards, *The World Hunt*, pp. 113–14.

[30]Richards, *The World Hunt*, pp. 146–7. For more detail on the local industry, see Louwrens Hacquebord, 'Three Centuries of Whaling and Walrus Hunting in Svalbard and its Impact on the Arctic Ecosystem' *Environment and History* 7(2) (2001), pp. 169–85.

Whales were killed to produce a range of goods: apart from their edible meat, blubber was rendered into oil for lamps, used as a lubricant for machines or as a basis for cosmetics and soaps (and, in the case of Japan, as an insect repellent in rice production); baleen bones were fashioned into umbrellas, corsets or whips, and larger ones could be used for construction, notably by Indigenous communities.[31] 'Arctic whaling displayed the characteristic pattern of commercially driven resource extraction. No allowance was made for any sort of conservation or sustainable use of these stocks', Richards laments. Entire herds were killed 'without any discernible restraint on the part of the users' while, as a result, 'the whalers shifted to more and more distant, difficult, and dangerous regions'.[32] Whaling spread across the world's oceans through technological advances, expanding trade networks and growing demand for whale products. The industry saw its share of ups and downs against the backdrop of world politics, with companies being dissolved or merged. It expanded into the North Atlantic, the Pacific and Southern Oceans, and ultimately affected whale populations in nearly every oceanic region. As such, New England whalers reached Hawai'i in the early nineteenth century.

'Being a whaling nation made the United States an imperial one, in the Pacific – an empire that saw civilization as having commercial potential, and commerce as having the potential to civilize', Bathsheba Demuth observes.[33] Similar to the tsarist case, Jakobina K. Arch wrote that 'foreign incursions' of Russian, British, French and American vessels drew Japan 'into the Pacific World' towards the end of the Tokugawa/Edo period in the nineteenth century (cf. Chapter 2).[34] Local whalers soon adopted new technologies that included steam-engines, iron hulls and harpoon guns which were mounted to the bow. This modernization, Arch observes, 'brought Japanese techniques and targets in line with other global whaling efforts'. As a result of the depletion of cetacean populations near the shores, such endeavours 'were generally conducted far from the home ports of the whaling ships', and they focused on a number of new species like grey and humpback whales. In the wake of the above-mentioned Russo-Japanese War of 1904–5, Japan even acquired Russian factory ships. Ultimately, Arch warns, this industrializing drive 'removes the personal experiences' and fosters 'a modern urban forgetfulness about the

---

[31]For an overview, see Bathsheba Demuth, *Floating Coast. An Environmental History of the Bering Strait* (New York: W. W. Norton & Company, 2019), pp. 26–7.

[32]Richards, *The World Hunt*, p. 148.

[33]Demuth, *Floating Coast*, p. 29.

[34]Jakobina K. Arch, *Bringing Whales Ashore. Oceans and the Environment of Early Modern Japan* (Seattle: University of Washington Press, 2018), pp. 183–4. For a strong focus on Indigenous communities, see the rich contributions in Ryan Tucker Jones and Angela Wanhalla (eds), *Across Species and Cultures. Whales, Humans, and Pacific Worlds* (Honolulu: University of Hawai'i Press, 2022).

physical realities and importance of the oceans' (this form of alienation, of course, is a common phenomenon that will also be discussed in the following chapter on farm animals in food production).[35]

In her environmental history of the Bering Strait *Floating Coast*, Bathsheba Demuth follows these changes as she traces the transformation of matter into energy from plankton to whales to human use. Here, the industrious whaler who was mainly interested in profit clashed with the habits of Chuckchi and Yupik that appeared not to 'labor beyond their present necessities'. There were strong rifts in perception of nature and the environment: 'That whales and their hunting contained history – a history of wars and ceremonies and trade alliances – did not pass the lines of cultures', Demuth notes.[36] This pitted ships with their 'Babel of languages and colors' and their crews as 'commerce personified, willing to sell anything, hunt anytime' against localized Indigenous communities. Soon, however, these were hired as inexpensive labourers 'desperate to make a living amid hunger and epidemics'.[37] Demuth's account is close to the voices on the ground, following whalers on their journeys through the diaries and reports they left behind, and collecting a wide range of ethnographic impressions on native life. She also focuses on animals and their diverging temporalities with something she calls 'whale time' at one point

> Commercial whaling was just one sort of production bound to whales, but one particularly unsuited to animals that give birth only a few times a decade. Despite the statements of faith regarding more whales just beyond the ice, bowhead time is slow. It takes years to strain the light fixed by plankton into tons of flesh. As a result, whaling could not obey the simple economic formula of innovation creating efficiency and efficiency leading to more production. With every technological adaptation increasing the speed, lethality, or range of the whaling kit, more whales died. More dead whales meant fewer future whales, which made future whale profits less certain. Efficiency could consume more, but not produce more. By the end of the 1890s, a good year for the industry [in Beringia's seas] was one in which fifty whales died. The remaining population was likely fewer than five thousand animals.[38]

Demuth's narration follows a circular motion from the sea to the shore, to land, underground and back to the ocean. Whales are succeeded by walruses, arctic foxes, reindeer, wolves and minerals before moving into focus again.

---

35 Arch, *Bringing Whales Ashore*, pp. 186–8.
36 Demuth, *Floating Coast*, p. 42.
37 Demuth, *Floating Coast*, pp. 65, 60.
38 Demuth, *Floating Coast*, p. 68.

This concept harks back to native worldviews where, as one scholar wrote, 'everything transforms into everything else'. In such animist concepts that did not delineate culture from nature (*cf.* Chapter 2), animals like the walrus 'existed in a state of change: between human and not, between rage and sacrifice'.[39] This transformation went so far that, thanks to the resourcefulness of chemists, whale blubber lost its signatory taste in the early twentieth century through a process called 'hydrogenation' and could be spread on toast as margarine that provided much-needed calories to crisis-ridden Europeans.[40]

A cetacean genocide?

Central to Ryan Tucker Jones' work on Soviet whaling is the notion of a lasting 'war between humans and whales'.[41] This conflict reached new heights with the Norwegian invention of the stern slipway in 1922, when the Soviet Union was created after years of revolutionary unrest. It 'allowed whales to be hauled directly on to the ship's deck and processed there'. It was accompanied by a 'clanking, grinding, seething apparatus of saws, boilers, and canners [that] appeared on board. Production speed and volume increased dramatically. Distant seas such as the Antarctic, which held untold thousands of whales, beckoned'. By then, Norwegian ships had replaced Dutch and American vessels 'as indisputable masters of the trade'.[42] The first Five-Year Plan, implemented in 1928, laid the groundwork for a modern Soviet whaling fleet. Soon, it practised 'industrialized warfare against an enemy equipped only with fat, muscle, and the assistance of companions, who lacked the hands that might have helped'.[43] Treaties like the 1931 Geneva Convention for the Regulation of Whaling – an important precursor to the creation of the International Whaling Commission (IWC) in 1946 – that restricted hunting to avoid overexploitation had been adopted without the Soviet Union's participation, which was still a diplomatic outcast in the early 1930s. Thus, 'the Soviets' continued unchecked, 'killing both nursing mothers and their young'.[44]

The USSR's share in global whaling remained small until the end of the Second World War. The spoils of victory, however, allowed them to significantly expand their fleet with catcher ships donated by the United States, who had

---

[39]Demuth, *Floating Coast*, p. 77.
[40]Demuth, *Floating Coast*, p. 262. See also Jones, *Red Leviathan*, p. 58 on whale oil as 'the cheapest source' of edible fat, and p. 163 on the production of margarine.
[41]Jones, *Red Leviathan*, p. 18.
[42]Jones, *Red Leviathan*, p. 28.
[43]Jones, *Red Leviathan*, p. 44. See also Demuth, *Floating Coast*, pp. 257–72.
[44]Jones, *Red Leviathan*, p. 48; Demuth, *Floating Coast*, pp. 276–8, 292–3.

given up pelagic whaling for good, and German-built floating factories.[45] Even though the Soviet Union ultimately signed the International Convention for the Regulation of Whaling in 1946 and, according to Jones, 'emerged as one of the most outspoken advocates of conservation',[46] it did not stop to hunt down protected species, usualy also out of season, as it was lamented in Western media in the mid-1950s.[47] While Great Britain and Norway reduced their whaling fleets, the Soviet Union aspired to become 'the world's largest whaling power', a goal that was achieved in the early 1960s.[48] For this, it invested heavily in new ships that employed scientists on highly dubious research missions into whale behaviour. As the marine biologist Iurii Mikhalev (born 1938) observed, 'Soviet whaling brought whale populations to near-extinction, was unprofitable, amoral and politically damaging for the country.'[49] This went hand in hand with clandestine practices: within four years around the turn of the 1960s, 'the Sovet Union had killed nearly 30,000 humpbacks while reporting less than a thousand' in Antarctic waters, Jones writes. In 1964, the industrialized slaughter reached its pinnacle 'with the Soviets contributing around 40 per cent of the 91,783 animals killed that year'.[50] Overall, it is estimated that at least 541,766 cetaceans had died at their hands between 1932 and 1987, when the Soviet delegation to the International Whaling Commission declared 'a temporary stop in the Antarctic commercial whaling (...) due to technical reasons'.[51]

Soviets had taken roughly one of every six whales killed in the twentieth century (...) After World War II, when 99 percent of their own kills took place, the Soviets had been the world's most prolific whalers, and the only whaling nation to kill every species of whale they came across, regardless of whether the animal they targeted was one of the last scattered members of its tribe.[52]

---

[45]Jones, *Red Leviathan*, p. 60.
[46]Jones, *Red Leviathan*, p. 69. For a detailed assessment of the International Convention for the Regulation of Whaling and the subsequent creation of the International Whaling Commission, see Malgosia Fitzmaurice, *Whaling and International Law* (Cambridge: Cambridge University Press, 2015), pp. 29–56 and 57–122.
[47]Jones, *Red Leviathan*, p. 81.
[48]Jones, *Red Leviathan*, p. 92.
[49]Jones, *Red Leviathan*, p. xiii.
[50]Jones, *Red Leviathan*, p. 95. Demutn, *Floating Coast*, p. 286 mentions the practice of labelling catches by certain Soviet ships as 'indigenous exemption' in questionable accordance with IWC guidelines.
[51]Jones, *Red Leviathan*, p. 209.
[52]Jones, *Red Leviathan*, p. 210.

These statistics culminate in the accusation of a 'cetacean genocide' that according to Jones was committed by the Soviet Union and hunters of other nations during the twentieth century:

> Blue whales, fin whales, humpback whales, sperm whales, seis, and minkes everywhere experienced a twentieth century that looked, sounded, and felt so different from the one humans experienced. While humans lived longer and in far greater numbers than ever before, whales went through an unprecedented horror. Nearly every single year from the 1910s through the 1970s they saw and heard hundreds and sometimes thousands of their companions writhing and groaning in pain before dying and disappearing. For a period in the early 1960s, just as human economic growth peaked, the killing came nearly without pause or refuge. The oceans turned red, and, in a transformation that must have been just as strange for the whales, they grew silent.[53]

Weighing the plight of these creatures against human suffering and suggesting that the latter were better off during the twentieth century that saw the Shoa, two world wars and many other atrocities, is highly questionable, to say the least. The notion of a 'cetacean genocide' invites the same criticism that one encounters with animal rights organizations like PETA which have accused the meat industry of committing an 'animal holocaust'.[54] As the political scientist David B. MacDonald wrote, 'Morality is on the side of those who seek to retain the cautionary lessons of the Holocaust, while ensuring that its images and symbolism are not abused and trivialized.'[55] Although the Soviets were known to cook their books to hide the thousands of whales that were illegally killed to fulfil the demanding plan targets,[56] the claim that their practices represent anything comparable to genocide misses the mark. At the core of the discussion, as Bathsheba Demuth so eloquently shows, was the relationship of hunter and prey: were whales merely 'part of a larger equilibrium that included human predation' or were they 'bearing selves – souls, even – granting each individual rights'?[57] While the International Whaling Commission ultimately sided with the latter view at a time of increased ecological sensitivity, ongoing

---

[53]Jones, *Red Leviathan*, p. 217.
[54]Schönfelder, 'Review of Ryan Tucker Jones: Red Leviathan', p. 512.
[55]David B. MacDonald, 'Pushing the Limits of Humanity? Reinterpreting Animal Rights and "Personhood" Through the Prism of the Holocaust' *Journal of Human Rights* 5(4) (2006), pp. 417–37, here p. 433.
[56]Demuth, *Floating Coast*, p. 293.
[57]Demuth, *Floating Coast*, p. 303.

disputes about Indigenous hunting rights or even 'whaling in the name of science', as some flimsily claim to do,[58] complicate the picture.

Facing extinction

Fishing, much like whaling, is representative of close interconnections between humans and their environment.[59] As anthropological studies have highlighted, fish 'mediate relationships between actors' who must possess 'specific knowledge' that stems from being a part of both the environment and a community. In an attempt to avoid 'extinction' of cultural practices, Indigenous communities combine traditional and contemporary forms of knowledge into a new hybrid in a process that aims to grasp 'differing understandings and conceptualizations of fish, which were sometimes complementary and sometimes contradictory'. Understood as a highly situational approach to human–fish relationships, it encompasses the vast range of 'catching, preparation, storage, consumption, storytelling, philosophizing, sharing, theorizing, songs, ways of respecting, and linguistic definitions of, about, for, or with fish and fishy beings within the community'.[60] Joshua Schuster's account that aims to answer the question *What Is Extinction?* starts with the destruction of such habitats. While 'extinction is a fact of biological regularity apparent in the deep-time scale of species history', he acknowledges that 'the increasing rate of the depletion of life is also a marker of modernity and of the present'.[61] In what is often termed the 'sixth wave' of such mass events, he notes:

> Extinction rates are rising largely due to human causes, including hunting and fishing; habitat destruction; deforestation; global heating; ocean acidification; pollution; pesticides; the harvesting of rare animals as pets or for food and medicines; and the introduction of new predators to new habitats.[62]

---

[58]Cf. Virginia Morell, 'Court Slams Japan's Scientific Whaling' *Science* 344(6179) (2014), p. 22.

[59]For an overview on the evolution of fishing (and whaling) from prehistoric times to the late twentieth century, see Dietrich Sahrhage and Johannes Lundbeck, *A History of Fishing* (Berlin and Heidelberg: Springer, 1992).

[60]Zoe Todd, 'Fish pluralities: Human-animal relations and sites of engagement in Paulatuuq, Arctic Canada' *Études/Inuit/Studies* 38(1/2) (2014), pp. 217–38, here pp. 222, 229, 219, 222, respectively.

[61]Joshua Schuster, *What Is Extinction? A Natural and Cultural History of Last Animals* (New York: Fordham University Press, 2023), p. 3.

[62]Schuster, *What Is Extinction?*, p. 4.

This also touches upon the so-called genocide–ecocide nexus as we have experienced it in the case of the *Columbian Exchange* of species that went hand-in-hand with the eradication of the native population (*cf.* Chapter 4). As it was seen above with the disappearance of Steller's sea cow, the witnessed extinction of species marked a change in perception during the eighteenth century. Contemporaries like the French naturalist Georges-Louis Leclerc, Comte de Buffon (1707–88) concluded from the impressive skeletal remains of what was later called the mastodon found in North America at the beginning of the century that it was the simpler explanation to presume there were no living specimens left than to expect to find them in more remote parts of this continent. From this, de Buffon deduced: 'since it has disappeared, how many others – smaller, weaker, and less noticeable – must have perished without having left us either evidence or information about their past existence?'[63] These ideas were further refined in the decades that followed and soon blended with theories on catastrophe, evolution and adaptive change in species. 'Extinction is central to evolutionary processes', Schuster resumes referring to Charles Darwin, 'but also the radical end and undoing of these processes of speciation'.[64] Thanks to its photographic documentation, the disappearance of the bison in North America 'was witnessed and debated in real time'.[65] So-called extinction shots and images of last animals showed the accelerating violence of industrialization.

Arguably, this process culminated in the eradication policies of Nazi Germany. Notions like 'state biology' (*Staatsbiologie*), as used by one of the pioneers of modern ecology Jakob Johann von Uexküll (1864–1944), underlined a 'fusion of politics and biology' that directly spoke to the interest of fascist ideologues and politicians: 'the Nazis were obsessed with ideas of extinction', Schuster writes, 'viewing the decline and decimation of races and species as having an ultimate causal power and casting definitive judgment across all life'.[66] They both feared that 'their people' would be wiped off the earth and understood that this could be used as an effective tool for domination. As Schuster continues to highlight, the basis for this view can be found in a selective reading of scientific and pseudo-scientific concepts of the time 'drawn from biology, racial eugenics, medicine, ecology, and perceptions of animals'.[67]

National Socialists proclaimed that racially pure Germans, as well as regional animals and the landscape itself, formed a biotic unity, an '*organische*

---

[63]Schuster, *What Is Extinction?*, p. 15.
[64]Schuster, *What Is Extinction?*, p. 28.
[65]Schuster, *What Is Extinction?*, p. 51.
[66]Schuster, *What Is Extinction?*, p. 134.
[67]Schuster, *What Is Extinction?*, p. 135.

Lebensgemeinschaft' (organic life-community). The dictum of 'blood and soil' asserted Germanic racial family lineage and historically Germanic lands as the essential standard of value in the world and the basis for assessing and hierarchizing all life and land across the planet. The Nazis hierarchized animals according to similar principles, where purity of breed, nativity to Germanic-associated lands, perceived historical importance and nobility, and robustness of stock would rank as best.[68]

While this, at first glance, appears to be a far cry from the topic of this chapter – whaling and the exploitation of the oceans – it seems nonetheless important to delve into the framework of these policies. This should provide more context to the idea presented by Ryan Tucker Jones and others in the animal right's community that accepting the possibility of extinction (as it was the case in Soviet whaling) can be paralleled with a premeditated and targeted annihilation of people. The quote above already shows that whaling was not about biological selection. Whalers did not pursue the goal of 'weeding out the weak' to strengthen their own or any other species. They took what they needed to make a quick profit, knowing full well at least with the creation of the International Whaling Commission (IWC) in 1946 that their days may be numbered. This corresponded to the experience of extinction as highlighted throughout this chapter – be it Steller's sea cow, North America's bison or the walrus around Spitzbergen. Naturally, the goal of commodifying animals into food, fuel, fertilizer, lubricants or clothing did not result in a 'fight for survival' with these species. Cynically enough, it resulted in the disappearance of Indigenous communities that along with these animals were deprived of their means to survive. If we focus our attention on actual Nazi politics, we notice a strong romanticization of the supposedly untainted primeval through politics of 'racial hygiene':

The Nazis conflated biology and myth, natural history and conspiracy, in their insistence that the immediate situation in Germany could result in only one of the two outcomes: biological downfall or biological utopia (...) The Nazis believed they could regenerate themselves through the extinction of others.[69]

This was driven to the extreme of *genocide*, a term that was coined only in 1944 by the lawyer Raphael Lemkin (1900–1959) to describe Nazi atrocities. The concept gained prominence during the Nuremberg trials and motivated the approval of the Convention on the Prevention and Punishment of Genocide

---

[68]Schuster, *What Is Extinction?*, p. 137.
[69]Schuster, *What Is Extinction?*, p. 143.

by the United Nations in 1948.[70] Ryan Tucker Jones rightly points to an inhumane playfulness when crewmembers were photographed happily riding a dead 'near-term fetus' on board a Soviet whaling ship or seen drinking the milk 'from slain lactating mothers' as evidence that some whalers celebrated the destruction of 'families in creation' through the desecration of whale carcasses.[71] The implications of genocide, as summed up by Schuster, greatly transcended such slaughter of marine mammals, however:

> Genocide included eradication with humiliation, forcing the victims to participate in their own annihilation, blaming the victim, and seeking the victim's erasure physically and metaphysically, destroying the physical body as well as the very idea of a group of people. The Nazis sought to use politically-motivated extinction to go beyond and render incoherent the natural history of extinction, practicing what Saul Friedländer calls an 'amorality beyond all categories of evil'.[72]

Seeing societal corruption in such practices like whaling is problematic as well, though surely more telling than the introduction of a victim–perpetrator binarism of humans and cetaceans. In Nazi Germany, Schuster observes, 'the loss in wildlife and the rise in domestic animals pertains to the relevance of the romanticization of Germanic animals and extinction'.[73] The reanimation of lost species like the aurochs became a central ideological interest with a niche economic impact (as will be touched upon in the following chapters). Ultimately, 'there must be the utmost vigilance over the terms, concepts, and rhetoric of extinction and genocide'.[74] Only this way, Schuster reminds us, can we avoid that they become 'meaningless referents'.

Do whales have a history?

In his musings on the 'cetacean genocide', Ryan Tucker Jones implies the idea that animals, especially whales in this case, have a common culture and, resulting from this, a history. As he and his co-author Angela Wanhalla mention

---

[70]Cf. the introduction to a special issue by Donna-Lee Frieze, 'New Approaches to Raphael Lemkin' *Journal of Genocide Research* 15(3) (2013), pp. 247–52.
[71]Jones, *Red Leviathan*, p. 128.
[72]Schuster, *What Is Extinction?*, p. 144.
[73]Schuster, *What Is Extinction?*, p. 144. See J. W. Mohnhaupt and John R. J. Eyck, *Animals under the Swastika* (Madison: University of Wisconsin Press, 2022) for a popular overview, and Boria Sax, *Animals in the Third Reich. Pets, Scapegoats, and the Holocaust* (New York and London: Continuum, 2000) for an essayistic account.
[74]Schuster, *What Is Extinction?*, p. 163.

in their introduction to an edited volume on the history of whaling in the Pacific, a collaborative publication by two marine biologists – Hal Whitehead, a whale expert, and Luke Rendell, who specializes in the evolution of social learning – was an important inspiration.[75] In *The Cultural Lives of Whales and Dolphins*, Whitehead and Rendell base their argument on the broad definition that 'culture is a flow of information moving from animal to animal'.[76] Such an exchange of information includes humpback songs as a means of communication that these whales learn from one another and pass on to the younger generations. 'Some liken it to human music, others to the songs of birds; it has elements of both', the authors state.[77] As the biologists continue to highlight, a central interest of theirs is the development of behaviour among animals that transcends the popular understanding of deterministic genetic coding. In other words: whales and dolphins learn to behave through a range of social inputs. Here, Whitehead and Rendell draw a strong comparison to us hominids:

> Human language is another example of these complex interactions. While still arguing about the details, most who have studied its evolution conclude that we are born with a genetic template that allows us to learn *a* language effortlessly between the ages of one and four, but *the* language we learn is completely determined by social input during this period – we learn it from others. It is part of our culture.[78]

Following this line of thought, cetacean communities share a culture which is passed on through imitation and emulation. Their interaction may set them apart from other groups of individuals, yet clear boundaries are difficult to draw: 'We do not expect sharp cultural divisions within the population', the authors continue, 'but much of their behaviour may be cultural. There may be clines, with more of this behaviour over here and more of that over there'.[79] Human activities interfered violently with these communities, and the mass killing of whales might have left its mark on migration patterns, as Jones points out at the end of his already-mentioned chapter on the 'cetacean genocide':

---

[75]Ryan Tucker Jones and Angela Wanhalla 'Introduction: The Pacific Worlds of Whales and Humans' in Ryan Tucker Jones and Angela Wanhalla (eds), *Across Species and Cultures. Whales, Humans, and Pacific Worlds* (Honolulu: University of Hawai'i Press, 2022), pp. 1–6, here p. 4.
[76]Hal Whitehead and Luke Rendell, *The Cultural Lives of Whales and Dolphins* (Chicago and London: The University of Chicago Press, 2015), p. 3.
[77]Whitehead and Rendell, *The Cultural Lives of Whales and Dolphins*, p. 2. This argument is further elaborated in Chapter 4 *Song of the Whale*, pp. 67–97.
[78]Whitehead and Rendell, *The Cultural Lives of Whales and Dolphins*, p. 4.
[79]Whitehead and Rendell, *The Cultural Lives of Whales and Dolphins*, p. 18.

We can at least guess that they did realize it in some way: records over subsequent decades suggest that humpback whales abandoned some breeding grounds – Fiji, for example – in favor of other places where more of their own kind could be found, such as Eastern Australia. Alone in a lagoon, having seen and heard the last moments of their families and companions, those still left ventured out into the unknown, across empty ocean, until they heard again the familiar songs, low and mournful, drawing them toward new lives and the survival of their kind.[80]

Thus, one may argue that the trajectory of their cultural evolution which determines certain group dynamics is their history. The question then, of course, would be how they keep and convey this history, given that 'there is simply no evidence that any nonhuman possesses the kind of open-ended and recursive communication system we recognize as language', as Whitehead and Rendell remind us.[81] Jones argues that the stressful experiences of surviving whales can be traced through hormones like cortisol which are found in their earwax that accumulates like tree rings:

> As the earplugs measure the stress of animals that survived years of hunting before finally being killed, they likely indicate that a whale's anguish resulted as much from the death of its companions as from being chased itself. Indeed, those whales that were chased were very unlikely to have survived long enough to accumulate earplugs with any time depth.[82]

Ultimately, the question whether cetaceans have something like a history remains a matter of definition. Recent studies prefer to speak of 'animal histories' in the plural, underlining the manifold experiences of non-human protagonists and their dynamic adaptations to changing environments that produce 'lively worlds' with other species 'that overlap, at times, and exist apart, at others'.[83] Or in the words of Whitehead and Rendell: 'Without the information they learn from each other, their behavior would be very different.'[84] They continue to state:

---

[80]Jones, *Red Leviathan*, p. 133. On the possibility of 'cultural transmission of migration routes from mother to calf', see Whitehead and Rendell, *The Cultural Lives of Whales and Dolphins*, p. 196.

[81]Whitehead and Rendell, *The Cultural Lives of Whales and Dolphins*, p. 38.

[82]Jones, *Red Leviathan*, p. 133.

[83]Dan Vandersommers, Thomas Aiello and Susan Nance, 'Animal History: A Brief Introduction to Its Past and Future' *Animal History* 1(1) (2025), pp. 5–12, here p. 9.

[84]Whitehead and Rendell, *The Cultural Lives of Whales and Dolphins*, p. 44.

[T]he ocean is [a] habitat where culture is potentially extremely useful. The resources of the ocean vary hugely over scales of space and time so large that it is hard for one animal to make sense of. The accumulated knowledge of others is potentially a wonderful resource. But to make good use of this knowledge pool, an animal needs several attributes: a social structure with important bonds, a longish life, and an effective decision-making system.[85]

Potentially, cetaceans fulfil these broad requirements – as do elephants and great apes. Their 'history', according to the authors, is mirrored in the evolution of behavioural traits that are passed on genetically and through social learning. Meanwhile, a range of ethical implications stem from the pioneering work done by Whitehead and Rendel that may inspire a stronger sense of humility among humans: are animals that have 'culture' especially worth saving?[86] And does this imply a hierarchy over or an opposition to those that appear to be organized in less complex societies? Future studies may take this as a starting point to draw a more diverse and elaborated picture of marine (and terrestrial) animal agency.

---

[85]Whitehead and Rendell, *The Cultural Lives of Whales and Dolphins*, p. 65.
[86]Cf. Jacob Brandler, 'Do "Animals" Have Histor(ies)? Can/Should Humans Know Them? A Heuristic Reframing of Animal-Human Relationships' *Journal of Animal Ethics* 12(2) (2022), pp. 148–57

7

From farm to table: Industrialized animals and food production

According to Richard W. Bulliet in *Hunters, Herders, and Hamburgers*, most people in the so-called developed world (or the 'Global North' – both with their own share of problematic implications) live in 'postdomestic' societies that are marked by two key characteristics: First, 'postdomestic people live far away, both physically and psychologically, from the animals that produce the food, fiber, and hides they depend on, and they never witness the births, sexual congress, and slaughter of these animals'. Yet at the same time, they feel very close to certain companion species that they interact with daily (as seen in Chapter 3). The second defining attribute, according to Bulliet, is that members of such a society – while consuming animal products in abundance – 'experience feelings of guilt, shame, and disgust when they think (as seldom as possible) about the industrial processes by which domestic animals are rendered into products and about how those products come to market'.[1] The contradictions of these observations are palpable in the longing for emotional connections to some animals while the suffering of others is skilfully ignored. Such *cognitive dissonance* – a tension one may experience when notions, beliefs or ideas do not align in everyday practice – is arguably at the heart of industrialized production. 'Domestic societies', in contrast, 'take for granted the killing of animals and experience few moral qualms in consuming animal products'.[2]

---

[1]Richard W. Bulliet, *Hunters, Herders, and Hamburgers. The Past and Future of Human-Animal Relationships* (New York: Columbia University Press, 2005), p. 3.
[2]Bulliet, *Hunters, Herders, and Hamburgers*, p. 3.

This chapter explores the rise of industrialized agriculture in capitalist and totalitarian states through competing regimes of meat production. Naturally, eating animals involves the trifecta of killing, butchering and cooking.[3] In her classical treatise *Animal to Edible* anthropologist Noëlie Vialles has looked at the operation that turns living beings into meat by focusing on the abattoirs of the Adour region of southwest France. Not only does she offer insights into the string-like organization of slaughterhouses, but she also underlines the increased anonymity of the process in modern times: 'The urban consumer is never, in terms of his daily alimentary experience, brought face to face with the animal (...) the origin of that meat is entirely hidden from view.'[4] As Dorothee Brantz has continued to argue, this banning of the animalistic from what was perceived as civilized life answered to bourgeois sensibilities.[5] Population growth spurred the demand for protein, and urban agglomerations had to find new ways of satisfying these needs. According to Harriet Ritvo, 'the weight of ordinary English cattle and sheep at slaughter nearly doubled in the course of the eighteenth century'.[6] Indeed, meat consumption rose notably during the nineteenth century in the wake of industrialization.[7] While ranching of imported cattle, pigs, sheep and chicken created what Bulliet calls a 'meat-centred industry' in Argentina, the United States and Australia, Victorian England had not only taken the lead in livestock breeding, but also in 'separating city dwellers from domestic animals used for production'.[8] This separation is mirrored by an increasingly automated process of 'de-animalization' in slaughterhouses where every step is planned in minute technical detail.[9] It follows the process of killing the animal per se ('de-animation') that is accompanied by bloodletting: 'The carcass obtained in this way no longer has anything to do with the animal from which it has in a sense been extracted. It is a foodstuff, a *substance*; all the links that attached it to a once living body have been severed,' Vialles writes.[10] Being considered 'service structures' that – as noted above – better remained unseen by the

---

[3]Bulliet, *Hunters, Herders, and Hamburgers*, p. 56.

[4]Noëlie Vialles, *Animal to Edible* (Cambridge: Cambridge University Press, 1994; first published in French as *Le sang et la chair. Les abattoirs du pays de l'Adour* in 1987), p. 28.

[5]Dorothee Brantz, 'Recollecting the Slaughterhouse' *Cabinet* (4) (Fall 2001), pp. 118–23.

[6]Harriet Ritvo, *The Animal Estate. The English and Other Creatures in the Victorian Age* (Cambridge: Harvard University Press, 1987), p. 69.

[7]See Roger Horowitz, *Putting Meat on the American Table. Taste, Technology, Transformation* (Baltimore: The Johns Hopkins University Press, 2006) for an overview on changing tastes since colonial times.

[8]Bulliet, *Hunters, Herders, and Hamburgers*, p. 185. See also Ritvo, *The Animal Estate*, pp. 45–81. For a tentative treatment of swine, see Robert Malcolmson and Stephanos Mastoris, *The English Pig. A History* (Rio Grande, Ohio and London: Hambledon, 1998).

[9]Cf. Vialles, *Animal to Edible*, p. 65.

[10]Vialles, *Animal to Edible*, p. 127.

public eye, 'the slaughterhouse system inaugurated a radical shift in human-animal relations, as it institutionalized the industrial compartmentalization of a particular segment of the animal kingdom', Paula Young Lee argues.[11]

As Wilson J. Warren highlights in *Meat Makes People Powerful*, global animal slaughtering observed the European example in taste and technology. In this, France became a model for the construction of public abattoirs ('public' referring to the state and its welfare policies) during the first reign of Napoleon (1804–14) that was emulated across continental Europe, including Brussels (1840), Vienna (1851), Lyon (1858), Milan (1863), Munich (1865), Zurich (1868) and Berlin (1881).[12] Among them, La Villette – which was opened in 1867 as a result of Haussmann's renovation of Paris under Napoleon III (1852–70) that remade the city into a modern metropolis – was referred to as 'the greatest market and slaughterhouse complex'; soon, La Villette received the questionable moniker *La Cité du Sang* ('The City of Blood').[13] Consequently, production increased notably, and Paris as well as London evolved into the European capitals of meat consumption.[14] This reached a new dimension with the opening of 'slaughter-factories', as some contemporaries called them, that 'implacably dismember[ed] animals as if they were raw materials no different from hay or cut trees'.[15] As such, Chicago became the United States' 'earliest and most important terminal and transfer market for meat products' since the mid-1860s thanks to the expansion of the railroad and soon-to-follow mechanical refrigeration that allowed long-distance transport of dressed meat.[16] Under the aegis of the newly founded Union Stock Yard & Transit Company, Chicago's stockyards were the epitome of industrialized killing. Named 'the slaughterhouse of the world', it became a spectacle for visitors and even a tourist attraction. According to a local saying, 'the packers used everything (...) but the squeal of the vanquished hog'.[17] This created a

---

[11]Paula Young Lee, 'Introduction: Housing Slaughter', in Paula Young Lee (ed.), *Meat, Modernity, and the Rise of the Slaughterhouse* (Durham: University of New Hampshire Press, 2008), pp. 1–9, here p. 2.

[12]Wilson J. Warren, *Meat Makes People Powerful. A Global History of the Modern Era* (Iowa City: University of Iowa Press, 2018), pp. 1–27. On the meaning of 'public', see Brantz, 'Recollecting the Slaughterhouse'.

[13]Kyri Claflin, 'La Villette: City of Blood (1867–1914)', in Paula Young Lee (ed.), *Meat, Modernity, and the Rise of the Slaughterhouse* (Durham: University of New Hampshire Press, 2008), pp. 27–45, quote p. 27.

[14]Warren, *Meat Makes People Powerful*, p. 16.

[15]Lee, 'Introduction', p. 7.

[16]Warren, *Meat Makes People Powerful*, p. 17.

[17]Dominic A. Pacyga, *Slaughterhouse. Chicago's Union Stock Yard and the World It Made* (Chicago and London: The University of Chicago Press, 2015), p. xi. See also the classical study by William Cronon, *Nature's Metropolis. Chicago and the Great West* (New York and London: W. W. Norton and Company, 1991), pp. 207–59 that explores the nexus of nature and capital.

vast range of by-products that subsidized low meat prices. After the Second World War, local industry was in decline, however, and the yards were closed for good in 1971.

The rise of industrialized slaughter went hand in hand with the industrialization of agriculture that reached a first climax in the United States during the 1920s before the time of the Great Depression.[18] Draft animals were replaced by machines like tractors, and the production of grain to feed livestock was encouraged to satisfy the growing demand for animal protein.[19] This slowly replaced the huge herds of grass-fed cattle that were held on the prairies before they were moved to the holding pens of the slaughterhouses, which had in turn contributed to the extinction of the American bison (as discussed in Chapter 4). The innovations of the US-American industry and the scale of its output soon became the envy of European abattoirs. Under the guise of promoting hygiene and, to a lesser degree, better working conditions and animal ethics, they scrambled to modernize. This drive mixed with highly politicized goals to ostracize or outright ban non-gentile practices which was mirrored in the prolonged debates about the prerequisite to stun animals before slaughtering. While this was considered to ensure humane treatment by animal protectionists, Jewish communities saw it as an affront to their dietary laws and traditions.[20]

Totalitarian swine

As Tiago Saraiva underlines in the conclusion to his *Fascist Pigs*, anti-Semitism was deep-seated in German philosophy. In Saraiva's reading, Martin Heidegger notoriously classified Jews as 'a calculative nomadic race' that was not 'rooted in the soil, for they didn't know how to dwell, they were all about machination and breeding'. Yet Heidegger was, Saraiva continues, also sceptical of the Nazis' grandiose technological projects which found their expression in industrialized agriculture.[21] At the core of these seemingly contradictory views was a deep criticism of 'Western progress', as others have highlighted, that allegedly neglects authenticity in favour of rationalization.[22] Although Heidegger did

---

[18]Deborah Fitzgerald, *Every Farm a Factory. The Industrial Ideal in American Agriculture* (New Haven and London: Yale University Press, 2003), p. 184.

[19]Warren, *Meat Makes People Powerful*, p. 44. Fitzgerald, *Every Farm a Factory*.

[20]Dorothee Brantz, 'Stunning Bodies: Animal Slaughter, Judaism, and the Meaning of Humanity in Imperial Germany' *Central European History* 35(2) (2002), pp. 167–94, here pp. 177–8.

[21]Tiago Saraiva, *Fascist Pigs. Technoscientific Organisms and the History of Fascism* (Cambridge and London: The MIT Press, 2016), pp. 239–40.

[22]Cf. Donatella Di Cesare, *Heidegger and the Jews. The* Black Notebooks (Cambridge: Polity Press, 2018; first published in Italian in 2014, translated by Murtha Baca).

not directly engage with the concept, his thoughts address a phenomenon commonly referred to as 'high modernism'. The idea behind it suggests that industrialized states have a penchant for centralized control that is based on a strong trust in science and technology. This is often accompanied by state superstructures and a rule of experts. It aims at making people – and arguably also animals – 'legible'. *Legibility* means that their actions can be influenced or subverted in accordance with state policies and expectations.[23]

As Ulrich Herbert has underlined, modernization does not necessarily rely on democratic structures: 'in most societies, the transition, especially from an early to an advanced industrial society, tends to be best implemented with authoritarian and even dictatorial methods'.[24] Yet Nazism's relationship to high modernism is not straightforward: a mystical belief in 'Aryan' racial-genetic superiority along with blood-and-soil ideology and a sense of national pride are used in propaganda to mobilize the masses – all a far-cry from modern scientific achievement. 'The escape into backward-looking utopias of an agrarian state', Herbert writes, 'the escapist modes of esotericism, the search for protection in the bosom of the nation or "Volk", or in the solidarity halls of the workers' movement – they were all part of this quest for reinsurance in the maelstrom of high modernity'. In this reading, fascist ideology is an answer to a rapidly changing world: 'Modernity had now emerged in its multiple effects as such a destructive force that it seemed it could only be countered and tamed by totalitarian means.'[25]

Tiago Saraiva addresses the interpretative conflict surrounding the old question what fascism actually entails and to what degree variations can be discerned through a focus on *biopolitics*, a loosely defined concept that underlines state intervention in biological and social life. At the outset of *Fascist Pigs*, he therefore posits to investigate 'the making and growing of animals and plants embodying fascism' and to describe 'how technoscientific organisms designed to feed the national community (...) became important elements in the institutionalization and expansion of the regimes of Mussolini, Salazar, and Hitler'.[26] Through case studies on Italy, Portugal and Germany along with their colonial aspirations in Africa and Eastern Europe, Saraiva looks at fascism as 'an all-encompassing modernist social experiment with the purpose of inventing a new national community'.[27] Food production

---

[23]For more details on the concept, see James C. Scott, *Seeing Like a State. How Certain Schemes to Improve the Human Condition Have Failed* (New Haven and London: Yale University Press, 1998).
[24]Ulrich Herbert, 'Europe in High Modernity. Reflections on a Theory of the 20th Century' *Journal of Modern European History* 5(1) (2007), pp. 5–21, here p. 9.
[25]Herbert, 'Europe in High Modernity', pp. 12–13. For a different view, *cf.* Roger Griffin, 'Fascism's Modernist Revolution: A New Paradigm for the Study of Right-wing Dictatorships' *Fascism* 5(2) (2016), pp. 105–29.
[26]Saraiva, *Fascist Pigs*, p. 2.
[27]Saraiva, *Fascist Pigs*, p. 5.

appears as a uniting challenge for these societies, especially after the end of the First World War. This places agriculture at the centre of interest. Especially for Nazi Germany, Saraiva sees an important concept in the term 'Bodenständigkeit' that – akin to Heidegger's crude ideas above – conveys a rootedness in the soil.[28] Consequently, he starts out with authoritarian policies of wheat cultivation in Italy and Portugal since the 1920s. Both states, and later Germany, followed the idea to attain a higher degree of independence from globalized grain markets by introducing new types of seeds and enforcing land reclamation on a large scale that was accompanied by targeted fertilization. While new hybrid strains of wheat were better adapted to local conditions, the planting of monocultures soon took its toll through soil erosion. In the cases of Italy and Portugal, large landowners profited from these reforms.[29]

Meanwhile, and with an even stronger focus since the 1930s, Germans – who are jokingly referred to as 'children of the potato' here – consumed these 'apples of the earth' (Erdäpfel) as a convenient staple food that also served to nourish pigs (these devoured more than half of the potatoes grown in the Reich). The logic of favouring this crop was similar to the one already employed in the authoritarian states of Italy and Portugal, namely to decidedly reduce dependence on international markets and to further the national economy:

A significant increase in productivity in potato cultivation also meant diminishing imports of animal feed, the main source of concern for those aiming at sustaining Germans on produce from the national soil. To win the Battle for Production ['Erzeugungsschlacht', in Nazi speak], the nutritional basis of both pig farming and dairy farming had to be radically changed toward domestically produced feeds, thus placing higher demands on Germany's potato crop.[30]

In fascist propaganda, the pig was imagined as a 'leading animal of the Germanic people', not least since it served to differentiate the 'northern peoples' from the 'Semites'. This anti-Semitic stance had been elaborated with regard to agriculture and food production by Richard Walther Darré (1895–1953), one of the main ideologues behind the motto of 'blood and soil' (Blut und Boden) who became Reich minister for food and agriculture in 1933, shortly after the Nazis' 'seizure of power':

---

[28]Saraiva, Fascist Pigs, p. 15.
[29]Saraiva, Fascist Pigs, pp. 21–69.
[30]Saraiva, Fascist Pigs, pp. 71–2. On the menace of the potato beetle to these endeavours, see pp. 87–90.

Not only did Darré argue that the sacrificial pig was a favorite among the gods of ancient Aryans; he argued that the pig's physiological properties justified such distinguished treatment. Pigs, he noted, were not easily transported over long distances and thus were not suitable livestock for the nomadic Semites. The northern forests, home of the true Germans, provided acorns for pigs, whose high fat content helped local people to survive harsh winters. Pigs performed the distinction between agrarians and nomads – or in Nazi terms, between rooted Germans and uprooted Jews.[31]

Here, a supposedly determining connection of 'living space' (*Lebensraum*) and physiology is presented that furthermore suggests parallels to evaluating the 'racial purity' of humans in line with national socialist worldviews. Raising pigs, Darré reckoned, was 'a constitutive element of being German'.[32] In order to feed the population, these were to thrive on local foodstuff. As Saraiva stresses, this motivated an intensified search for highly adapted and reliable breeds that fattened nicely. One must be careful, however, not to see explicit Nazi politics at play in all of these programmes as the author tends to do: not only did most of the notable research stations involved in this exist independently of fascist structures before the 1930s, but they also followed breeding practices and traditions that had evolved during the nineteenth century, as it was shortly highlighted at the beginning of this chapter; their efforts had received a jolt during the interwar years in line with the task to provide animal protein.[33] It has been widely documented that Nazi propagandists gladly sold successful breakthroughs in science and technology as their own merit, with the Autobahn only being one example among many.[34]

Nonetheless, the institution of the *Reichsnährstand* ('State Food Society') enforced breeding initiatives and generalized performance evaluations, as Saraiva relates: 'increasing pigs' fat content was to root Germans in the national soil by increasing their domestic fat intake'. Pork meanwhile covered about two-thirds of meat consumption.[35] Soon, the goal to close the 'fats gap' in the German diet was confronted with demands to prepare the economy for war under the aegis of 'Plenipotentiary' Hermann Göring (1893–1946), which were voiced in Hitler's 1936 Four-Year-Plan memorandum. 'Although the

---

[31]Saraiva, *Fascist Pigs*, p. 101.

[32]Saraiva, *Fascist Pigs*, p. 105.

[33]Cf. Saraiva, *Fascist Pigs*, p. 107. Stating that German hogs 'were fatter' and 'bred to thrive on a potato-based diet' as clearly distinctive marks from British and American swine is not entirely convincing (p. 135).

[34]For an associative introduction to the thematic complex, one may refer to Paul R. Josephson, *Totalitarian Science and Technology* (Amherst: Humanity Books, [2]2005).

[35]Saraiva, *Fascist Pigs*, p. 123.

issues of self-sufficiency in raw materials, energy, and food had been present since the beginning of the Nazi regime, they now assumed unprecedented urgency', Saraiva underlines.[36] While the economic rationale is understood, the author overextends the interpretative force of his argument – which is largely based on published sources like journals – when he stresses that pigs were made to contribute 'to the Nazi regime through militarism, nationalism, transcendentalism, and statism' by ensuring they 'were fat and rooted in the soil (bodenständig)'. Deriving from these 'four dimensions' which 'condense much of the phenomenon of fascism' that 'it is thus reasonable to assert that performance tests selected those pigs performing fascism. In other words, performance tests were designed to produce fascist pigs' is a long shot.[37] Trite as it may sound, it was not the animals themselves that were fascists, but the people coordinating the breeding programmes and the regime's propagandist mouthpieces that Saraiva bases his arguments on. Surely one would have gained more from focusing on the enforced dietary customs that set apart the supposedly 'Aryan' population from their Jewish neighbours, and the slaughtering practices this entailed.[38] Another important aspect within biopolitics – which, unfortunately, remains only implicated as a guiding concept throughout Saraiva's work – is the relationship of Nazi policies of conservation, sustainability and 'völkisch' ideology as it was discussed by Frank Uekötter.[39] The underlying reactionary modernism is famously mirrored in the rewilding experiments with Heck cattle during the 1930s, brought to life by German zoologists in an attempt to recreate the long extinct aurochs as a supposedly 'racially pure breed'.[40]

Comrades in barns

While we do not hear from Tiago Saraiva how the story of his allegedly 'fascist pigs' ends in the fiery destruction of the Second World War, Thomas

---

[36]Saraiva, *Fascist Pigs*, p. 122.

[37]Saraiva, *Fascist Pigs*, pp. 133–4. Such issues of over-interpretation extend throughout the book and are accompanied by stressed etymologies and the erroneous spelling of German designations, names and titles – a problem that Thomas Fleischman (see below) obviously also struggles with.

[38]As above, Brantz, 'Stunning Bodies' and Dorothee Brantz, 'Animal Bodies, Human Health, and the Reform of Slaughterhouses in Nineteenth-Century Berlin' *Food and History* 3(2) (January 2005), pp. 193–215.

[39]Frank Uekötter, *The Greenest Nation? A New History of German Environmentalism* (Cambridge and London: The MIT Press, 2014) and Frank Uekötter, 'Green Nazis? Reassessing the Environmental History of Nazi Germany' *German Studies Review* 30(2) (2007), pp. 267–87.

[40]Cf. Jamie Lorimer and Clemens Driessen, 'From "Nazi Cows" to Cosmopolitan "Ecological Engineers": Specifying Rewilding Through a History of Heck Cattle' *Annals of the American Association of Geographers* 106(3) (2016), pp. 631–52.

Fleischman picks up the pieces. In his *Communist Pigs*, he relates the evolution of East German animal rearing and, as he states, its convergence with capitalist modes of production.[41] Presenting the socio-economic history of the German Democratic Republic in broad strokes, Fleischman nicely ties in the wild boar, the garden pig and the industrial pig – all three depicted on the cover of his book. He thereby underlines that the GDR combined a capitalist with a fascist tradition of production, despite all the propagandist vows that suggested otherwise. In this, he addresses the issue raised with Saraiva above about the relationship of ideology and animals:

> For example, while fascism or communism can bring a pig into existence, give it shape, and place it within a particular economic system, does that pig continue to 'perform' those ideologies when the system that created it no longer exists? Or if a pig bred for one system is deployed in another, as was the case with capitalist pigs traded to communist countries, does the pig cease its capitalist behaviors once it enters a non-capitalist society? As East Germany's pigs show, ideological distinctions are not so neat. Just as pigs reveal ideology in their bodies, behaviors, and diets, they also transform ideology – its meaning and performance – along the way. When enacted through living creatures, ideology becomes much more pliable, messy, and, as was the case for East German communism, quite brittle.[42]

Fleischman begins his story with the import of more than nine thousand breeding hogs from Yugoslavia to the GDR via airplanes from November 1969 to March 1970. These were to jumpstart East Germany's own industrial pig sector, following the model of the factory farm which preferred large-scale state-owned agricultural complexes. The village of Eberswalde, situated northeast of Berlin about twenty kilometres from the Polish border, was to become the largest industrial pig farm and slaughter complex in the world with up to 400,000 animals raised and killed per year: 'Eberswalde's leaders pioneered a troika of industrial facilities that disaggregated the entire life cycle of the hog into three branches of inputs and out-puts: grain, breeding, and meat.'[43] The aim was to unite and coordinate every step of commodification. After the First World War, the 'American model' that turned farms into factories had been the envy of Germans and Soviets alike. In the 1920s, standardization, mecharization and Fordist mass production became

---

[41]Thomas Fleischman, *Communist Pigs. An Animal History of East Germany's Rise and Fall* (Seattle: University of Washington Press, 2020), p. 4.
[42]Fleischman, *Communist Pigs*, p. 13.
[43]Fleischman, *Communist Pigs*, pp. 18–21, quote p. 20.

the keywords for industrialization.[44] As Fleischman highlights, this not only inspired the violent collectivization of agriculture under Stalin in the 1930s, but also the already-mentioned *Reichsnährstand* as 'the largest single economic unit in the world' that 'controlled all agricultural production within Germany. It determined prices and production levels in every village, town, and regional city, coordinating food production between farmers and processors'.[45] Repeated efforts at collectivization in post-war East Germany were met with strong resistance by farmers who killed or maimed their livestock in protest: 'In 1959 and 1960, neglect, injury, and premature slaughtering of privately owned livestock resulted in the death of 1.25 million pigs, 200,000 cattle, and 115,000 sheep.'[46] Cynically enough, this only mirrored the Soviet experience.[47] Adding to this was the loss of skilled labourers who either took well-paying industrial jobs or left the country altogether. There were also strong parallels to the American ideal of *agribusiness*, which was coined in the mid-1950s and soon promoted by the United States Department of Agriculture (USDA). As could be witnessed in Iowa, it drove small landholders away in a process of vertical integration with large producers that according to Fleischman resembled 'a market-based collectivization drive'.[48]

A deciding link for these regimes that stood in Cold War competition was the non-aligned state of Yugoslavia. It benefited from US attempts to undermine Soviet influence and had access to modern Western agricultural technology, including from West Germany and Italy. In the mid-1960s, its factory farms (*agro-combines*) drew the attention of East German leaders who 'marveled at the advanced automation that controlled everything from feeding to heating and lighting'. First Secretary of the Central Committee of the Socialist Unity Party of Germany (SED) Walter Ulbricht (1893–1973, in power 1950–71) recognized this as the future of production, and Yugoslav experts were invited to the GDR – first to build chicken and cattle farms, later to design the facilities of Eberswalde. This then laid the groundwork for the import of breeding hogs as told at the beginning of Fleischman's book that were known to be compatible with such unforgiving methods of production.[49]

Eberswalde soon spawned its own breeds like the newly created hybrid hog *Leicoma* in 1976, a portmanteau that represented the collaborative effort of

---

[44]Fleischman, *Communist Pigs*, p. 24. Yet he rightly notes that it was the state of Saxony that had created one of the first agricultural experiment stations near Leipzig in 1850 – p. 25. See also Alex Blanchette, *Porkopolis. American Animality, Standardized Life, and the Factory Farm* (New York: Duke University Press, 2020).
[45]Fleischman, *Communist Pigs*, p. 29.
[46]Fleischman, *Communist Pigs*, p. 33.
[47]See Lynne Viola, *Peasant Rebels under Stalin. Collectivization and the Culture of Peasant Resistance* (New York and Oxford: Oxford University Press, 1996).
[48]Fleischman, *Communist Pigs*, p. 35.
[49]Fleischman, *Communist Pigs*, pp. 38–42, quote p. 40.

facilities in the districts of Leipzig, Cottbus and Magdeburg. Notwithstanding its designation, this pig was 'a truly transnational animal', as it combined pedigree from Yugoslavia, West Germany and the United States.[50] As Fleischman impressively shows, it was also the GDR's experience of a changing global economic system paired with protests in Poland against rising food prices during the 1970s that motivated the new First Party Secretary Erich Honecker (1912–94, in power 1971–89) to avoid shortages of sustenance and spikes in living costs. In the years that followed, the GDR became an important player in the so-called meatification of diets that increasingly used grains for fodder to yield animal protein instead of cereals.[51] This was accompanied by agrarian reforms that further specialized and intensified production. They encouraged a focus on monocultures which led to the loss of habitats and biodiversity. Animals became sick as a result of poor fodder quality and an overuse of fertilizers that caused nitrate poisonings. Swaths of land were polluted with the heaps of manure coming from the factory farms. It reached the digestive tracts of the population through drinking water.[52]

One response to the issues with large-scale farms was the keeping of private 'garden pigs'. As Fleischman relates, it became an acceptable option when this form of subsistence seemed to have lost its bourgeois taint by the mid-1970s. Thus, at the Ninth Party Congress in 1976 'the regime abandoned the view of gardening as a threat to socialist production' and 'formally endorsed the practice as a worthy socialist recreational activity'. Eventually, about a third of the GDR's population became involved, cultivating more than a tenth of the arable land which awarded it the title of a 'small-garden paradise' (*Kleingartenparadies*). The animals they kept could either be consumed privately or sold to state-owned slaughterhouses.[53] However, one must be careful not to confuse the varied private forms of production, as the collective farms did also allow for private plots where large animals (namely the 'garden pig' and cattle) could be raised by the workers. In the case of the Soviet Union – which served as a role-model in this – the private garden plots were much more productive than the communal land, not least since they provided a direct incentive due to the personal use of the produce that could be eaten, sold or traded and thus formed an important part of the black-market second economy.[54]

During the 1980s, Fleischman underlines, this strain resulted in a 'growing sense of division' between an industrial system for food production 'which privileged Western markets, Berlin, and other large cities' and a traditional,

---

[50]Fleischman, *Communist Pigs*, pp. 45–6.
[51]Fleischman, *Communist Pigs*, pp. 64, 66.
[52]Fleischman, *Communist Pigs*, pp. 81, 87–9; on 'the manure crisis' of the 1980s, see pp. 92–117.
[53]Fleischman, *Communist Pigs*, p. 120.
[54]See Zhores A. Medvedev, *Soviet Agriculture* (New York and London: W. W. Norton & Company, 1987) for a classical yet well-informed study.

decentralized one 'which was largely oriented toward rural communities'. Yet these two systems, he continues, were closely intertwined – they 'produced each other' and could not function independently.[55] State-mandated increases in prices of livestock and fodder made the second option even more attractive as pigs could be fattened relatively cheaply due to the ready availability of highly subsidized basic foodstuffs like bread and butter. As a result, the share of individual production doubled between 1983 and 1984, reaching almost 20 per cent.[56] A notable side-effect of large-scale agricultural development was the rise in wild boar populations that only too gladly rummaged through the vast grain fields. Since access to weapons was strictly regulated, controlling these animals proved difficult. What is more, the nomenklatura enjoyed hunting outings in their exclusive preserves while wild animals made their way into cities and settlements.[57]

The state farms, meanwhile, experienced a 'calamitous die off of 1.7 million industrial pigs' in 1982 that was caused by a lack of fodder, widespread sickness among animals due to poor husbandry conditions and a devastating outbreak of foot-and-mouth disease. Lucrative meat exports were kept up, however, to satisfy Western creditors that secured the GDR's economic survival. Soon, the population started to complain about food shortages.[58] Adding to this was the dubious bookkeeping of the administrative command economy that consistently tried to emphasize plan fulfilment while hiding incompetence, failure and the resulting losses. With the state heading for default, it was eventually given respite in 1983 by a shady one billion Deutschmark-deal brokered with its neighbouring rival, the Federal Republic of Germany. The underlying economic and ecological problems remained unresolved.[59] Paired with mass civil protests, this led to the GDR's demise in 1989. In the ensuing years, wild boars have thrived and garden pigs largely disappeared across the reunited country while their industrial brothers remain bound by the chains of exploitation.

Northern paths

A region of Europe that arguably combines many of the experiences detailed above is the Nordic countries that comprise Norway, Sweden, Finland,

---

[55]Fleischman, *Communist Pigs*, p. 139.

[56]Fleischman, *Communist Pigs*, pp. 141–2.

[57]See the chapter 'A Plague of Wild Boars' in Fleischman, *Communist Pigs*, pp. 145–66.

[58]Fleischman, *Communist Pigs*, p. 169.

[59]Cf. Maximilian Graf, 'Before Strauß: The East German Struggle to Avoid Bankruptcy During the Debt Crisis Revisited' *The International History Review* 42(4) (2019), pp. 737–54.

Denmark and Iceland. As Taina Syrjämaa underlines in her concluding remarks to an edited volume on *Animal Industries* in this part of the world, these 'have not grown as a self-evident, automatic process, but have been in many ways intertwined with such huge and complex phenomena as nationalism and the overall modernisation of societies'. During the first half of the twentieth century, the high-modernist appeal of technologization and centralized control had also slowly caught on in the Nordic countries: 'Animal production was considered a pathway to higher national income and a stronger society with healthier citizens' – just as in the examples discussed above.[60] Increasing the availability of animal protein is commonly perceived 'to be part and parcel of the climb up the "development ladder"' within modernization theory, the editors highlight in their introduction. Consequently, global meat production has increased more than threefold since the 1960s.[61] This development, however, is accompanied by substantial issues with sustainability and by ethical dilemmas surrounding the exploitation of not only sentient but also intelligent creatures. Citing two philosophers – Egbert Hardeman and Henk Jochemsen – the authors name five evolutionary characteristics of industrialized agriculture:

> The first is 'mechanisation', whereby human and animal labour is replaced by machines and technological procedures. The second salient development is 'intensification', meaning an increase in production per animal. The third characteristic of industrialisation is 'specialisation', whereby farms specialise in one type of animal, instead of rearing different species of livestock. Fourth, 'science and technology' assume a leading role within agronomic research, which considers an increase of productivity as its main goal. And finally, the industrialisation of agriculture has led to the 'increased scale' of farming, and farms have increasingly come to resemble factories. On the cultural and economic level, the central aspect of this process is a drive for efficiency and profit.[32]

This is the basis for a critical assessment of the status of post-Second World War agriculture through the example of Holland. The authors argue

---

[60]Taina Syrjämaa, 'Epilogue', in Taina Syrjämaa, Marja Jalava, Taija Kaarlenkaski, Otto Latva, Eeva Nikkilä and Tuomas Räsänen (eds), *Animal Industries. Nordic Perspectives on the Exploitation of Animals since 1860* (Berlin and Boston: De Gruyter, 2024), pp. 261–3, here pp. 261–2.

[61]Marja Jalava, Taija Kaarlenkaski, Otto Latva, Eeva Nikkilä, Tuomas Räsänen and Taina Syrjämaa, 'Introduction: Towards a history of animal industries in the Nordic countries', in Taina Syrjämaa, Marja Jalava, Taija Kaarlenkaski, Otto Latva, Eeva Nikkilä and Tuomas Räsänen (eds), *Animal Industries. Nordic Perspectives on the Exploitation of Animals since 1860* (Berlin and Boston De Gruyter, 2024), pp. 1–19, here pp. 2, 4.

[62]Marja Jalava et al., 'Introduction', p. 2 – originally published as Egbert Hardeman and Henk Jochemsen, 'Are There Ideological Aspects to the Modernization of Agriculture?' *Journal of Agricultural and Environmental Ethics* 25(5) (2012), pp. 657–74, here p. 659.

that practices lack social and ecological sustainability due to a widespread 'vulnerability to ideology' that is characterized by a quasi-religious belief in technology-based solutions on the way of modernization. The government plays a leading role in this development.[63] Fields like science and technology studies (STS) have long recognized that promises of a 'technological fix' tend to create path dependencies that are almost impossible to overcome.[64] As the idea of the 'sunk-cost fallacy' underlines, commitment to large-scale investment is often upheld beyond sensible measure. The Nordic countries were no exception, with Denmark leading the way in livestock-based production since the 1870s.[65] Meanwhile, Norway had a historically strong focus on fishing and whaling (as touched upon in Chapter 6), and it has expanded its fish farms since the 1970s not least to feed animal populations around the world.[66] With regard to the larger geographic region of Fennoscandia that not only comprises the Scandinavian countries and Finland, as the name suggests, but also parts of today's Russia – especially Karelia and the Kola Peninsula, one is confronted with strong nomadic traditions in reindeer herding.[67] For the latter region, Andy Bruno has studied the environmental impact of the militarization and industrialization of the Soviet Arctic where railroad construction, apatite mining and the collectivization of animals followed the imperative of expansion in the name of progress. These practices have proven harmful to humans and non-humans alike through deforestation, pollution and the destruction of traditional animal husbandry.[68]

In the Finnish case, the connections to its Slavic neighbour run deeper, of course. Since 1809 and until its declaration of independence following the Russian Revolutions of 1917, it had been a formally autonomous part of the Russian Empire as the Grand Duchy of Finland. Its economy was dominated by agriculture. According to Taina Syrjämaa, breeding animals that arrived

---

[63]On the seductiveness of the 'technological bluff' as 'a sole and unique source of human improvement and progress', see Hardeman and Jochemsen, 'Are There Ideological Aspects', p. 665.

[64]Cf. Max Oelschlaeger, 'The Myth of the Technological Fix' *The Southwestern Journal of Philosophy* 10(1) (1979), pp. 43–53. For an all-around stimulating discussion, see the edited volume Martina Heßler and Heike Weber (eds), *Provokationen der Technikgeschichte. Zum Reflexionszwang historischer Forschung* (Paderborn: Ferdinand Schöningh, 2019).

[65]Marja Jalava et al., 'Introduction', pp. 9–10.

[66]Marja Jalava et al., 'Introduction', p. 11. On the Norwegian case, see also the chapter by Terje Finstad and Eirik Magnus Fuglestad 'Reassembling agro-human orders: Antibiotics in animal agriculture, 1940s–2000s' in the same edited volume, pp. 115–32.

[67]For an overview of how nomadic traditions intertwine humans with their animals, see Sanna Valkonen, Áile Aikio, Saara Alakorva and Sigga-Marja Magga (eds), *The Sámi World* (London: Routledge, 2022).

[68]Andy Bruno, *The Nature of Soviet Power. An Arctic Environmental History* (Cambridge: Cambridge University Press, 2016). Apart from this, a range of ethnographic studies exist that explore socio-ecological change in herding communities, like David G. Anderson, *Identity and Ecology in Arctic Siberia. The Number One Reindeer Brigade* (Oxford: Oxford University Press, 2000).

in the country from Scotland in the early 1860s signalled a new stage of transnational mobility and formed a 'vanguard of modernisation'. These animals marked 'a fundamental transition from rural self-sufficiency to commercialised monetary economics' that connected the country 'to international markets and the production logic of animal industries, which thrived in more rapidly industrialised and more urbanised countries of the future Global North'. With the goal of enrichment and nation-building, she continues, 'Finland joined a colonial mindset although it did not possess colonies itself.'[69] Initially, the focus was on dairy cattle which also came from Northern Germany, Denmark and Sweden. With time, however, the offspring of those animals was propagated as breeding stock as they had already become accustomed to Finnish conditions.[70] The promotion of milk production was in line with the trend in industrializing countries, and Finland soon rose to be the global leader in per-capita milk consumption.[71]

As Marja Jalava underlines, a decreasing world market price for grain motivated the switch to dairy production. Its waste products like skimmed milk and whey could now be used to feed pigs whose numbers had dwindled in Finland due to the masses of cheap US-American pork that Europe imported from Chicago since the 1860s. Many Finnish agricultural experts, Jalava states, considered its swine production 'poorly developed' and 'a national disgrace compared to other Nordic countries, particularly Denmark that had started to export bacon to Britain in the 1860s, with the result that it ruled the market by the 1910s'.[72] New breeds 'that matured and reproduced quickly' had once originated from China and made their way across Asia to Europe and the Americas where they then formed 'the basis for the modern industrial pig'.[73] Diverging practices in keeping these animals throughout the millennia

---

[69]Taina Syrjämaa, 'Multispecies mobilities and human belief in progress', in Taina Syrjämaa, Marja Jalava, Taija Kaarlenkaski, Otto Latva, Eeva Nikkilä and Tuomas Räsänen (eds), *Animal Industries. Nordic Perspectives on the Exploitation of Animals since 1860* (Berlin and Boston: De Gruyter, 2024), pp. 25–43, here p. 43.

[70]Taina Syrjämaa, 'Multispecies mobilities', p. 39.

[71]Taija Kaarlenkaski, 'Exploring the roots of high milk consumption in Finland', in Taina Syrjämaa, Marja Jalava, Taija Kaarlenkaski, Otto Latva, Eeva Nikkilä and Tuomas Räsänen (eds), *Animal Industries. Nordic Perspectives on the Exploitation of Animals since 1860* (Berlin and Boston: De Gruyter, 2024), pp. 45–61. On the industrial development in the United States, see Kendra Smith-Howard, *Pure and Modern Milk. An Environmental History since 1900* (New York: Oxford University Press, 2014).

[72]Marja Jalava, 'Knowledge in the service of profit: Pig fattening performance testing in the first half of the twentieth century', in Taina Syrjämaa, Marja Jalava, Taija Kaarlenkaski, Otto Latva, Eeva Nikkilä and Tuomas Räsänen (eds), *Animal Industries. Nordic Perspectives on the Exploitation of Animals since 1860* (Berlin and Boston: De Gruyter, 2024), pp. 63–79, here pp. 66–7.

[73]See Brian Lander, Mindi Schneider and Katherine Brunson, 'A History of Pigs in China: From Curious Omnivores to Industrial Pork' *The Journal of Asian Studies* 79(4) (2020), pp. 865–89, here p. 866. For context on the evolution in the United States, see J. L. Anderson, *Capitalist Pigs. Pigs, Pork and Power in America* (Morgantown: West Virginia University Press, 2019).

– generally speaking, pigs in Europe continued to forage freely in forests and interbred with wild boars while their Chinese counterparts were penned, selectively bred and fattened – created the preconditions for this success story. In pre-modern China, pigs played an important part in the domestic economy which only started to switch to large factory farms under the reform communism of the late 1980s. Eventually, breeds that were genetically adapted to industrial conditions made their way from Europe and the United States back to China.[74] By implementing these new types, organizations like the Finnish Pig Breeding Association (founded in 1908) strove not only for profitability in domestic production, but also for food security. Ultimately, Jalava writes, 'the goals of pig breeding were dictated by the markets that also seemed to dictate the survival of the nation'.[75] This asked for an all-round rethinking of living conditions.

In her research, Eva Nikkilä has aimed to explore the experiences of sows within the spatial confinement of the pigsty at the beginning of the twentieth century. By looking at the nest-building behaviour of pregnant pigs she presents a pattern that both domesticated and wild swine have in common. In her reading, the animals' respective adaptations to their immediate environment reveal their true agency.[76] Around 1900, farms were growing, and the materials of farrowing pens started to change. Although concrete became favoured by architects and planners as a signifier of modernity that promised sturdiness and hygiene, it was contested among pig farmers for its problems in practice: 'Excessive use of concrete and stone had led to cold and damp environments, which tested the health and well-being of pigs and brought about new health problems, including respiratory diseases, that were associated with modern buildings.'[77] Contemporary design was not to everyone's taste, yet it offered more control over the animal and its interactions. This was paramount for efficient breeding. In the process, the sows' natural behaviour to roam freely before giving birth was inhibited. While still uncommon in Finland during the first half of the twentieth century, farrowing pens were soon replaced with crates that reduced the available space even further, but helped avoid that the mothers squashed their young.[78]

In the interwar years, Finland aimed to secure self-sufficiency while profiting from exports. Industrialization in animal rearing happened in a

---

[74]Lander, Schneider and Brunson, 'A History of Pigs in China', pp. 869–77.

[75]Jalava, 'Knowledge in the service of profit', p. 68.

[76]Eeva Nikkilä, 'Building a Nest in Human-Built Spaces: Tracing the Experiences of Finnish Sows, c. 1900–1930s' *Animal History* 1(1) (2025), pp. 52–70, here pp. 55–6.

[77]Nikkilä, 'Building a Nest in Human-Built Spaces', p. 60.

[78]Nikkilä, 'Building a Nest in Human-Built Spaces', pp. 65–7.

somewhat peculiar context and was by no means a linear process, as Marja Jalava has shown: Until the 1960s, 'small-scale farms with open-air fenced pastures for pigs were in fact significantly increasing in number instead of giving way to factory-scale confinement and concentration'. This did, however, not mean that they were unproductive: 'even in these small farms it was entirely possible to handle pigs as raw material to be exploited in the process of producing standardised industrial objects and tools of the trade'. This offers important food for thought about alternative avenues. In line with the works discussed above, she concludes that 'Finnish pigs were a materialisation of a political project that aimed to maintain social stability within a republic of small farmers, so that they could be called "nationalist pigs"' – the animals, that is.[79]

---

[79] Jalava, 'Knowledge in the Service of Profit', p. 79.

8

Space monkeys and Pavlovian dogs: Animals in science and technology

Before she began her journey into earth's orbit that was destined to kill her, Laika received rations comparable to those of the human cosmonauts who followed her: 'a diet that included meat, bone broth, vegetables, fish oil, and milk'. Reportedly, this even meant 'a good Russian sausage' for dogs that were to be put on a rocket, Kurt Caswell writes.[1] On 3 November 1957 *Sputnik II* was launched, only one month after its famous predecessor and in time to celebrate the fortieth anniversary of the October Revolution on 7 November.[2] Carried at the tip of an intercontinental ballistic missile, Laika possibly watched the world grow smaller through a little window in her capsule – at least for the few hours she remained conscious before succumbing to a malfunction in the thermal control system.[3] For the Soviet Union, a dog's life was a small price to pay to demonstrate technological prowess. It was the height of the Cold War, and the Space Race served to ensure the potential for mutual destruction. As it was widely understood, in lieu of Laika there could have been a nuclear warhead fixed to the R-7 rocket. This explains the phenomenon of a 'Sputnik Shock' that many Western onlookers experienced when the earth's first

---

[1]Kurt Caswell, *Laika's Window. The Legacy of a Soviet Space Dog* (San Antonio: Trinity University Press, 2018), p. 20.
[2]Caswell, *Laika's Window*, p. 37. Until mid-February 1918, Russia was using the Julian calendar which at the time was thirteen days behind the widely accepted Gregorian calendar. Henceforth, the anniversary of the October Revolution was celebrated in November.
[3]In a later part of his book, the author however mentions the likelihood that Laika's window was covered by a plastic fairing, making it impossible to see through – Caswell, *Laika's Window*, p. 206. On temperature control, see pp. 213–14.

artificial satellite had successfully been launched from Kazakhstan's Baikonur Cosmodrome.[4]

All this suggests that Soviet space dogs were more than mere lab animals but protagonists in their own right.[5] Consequently, Amy Nelson has posed the central question *What the dogs did*. As mongrels that were collected from Moscow's streets, they were explicitly selected for their resilience in demanding conditions and ascribed *agency* as 'pioneers and scouts' that paved the way for human space exploration.[6] Underlying are notions of coevolution and anthropomorphization (as seen in Chapters 2 and 3) in the ways dogs interacted with humans in artificial (i.e. human-made) environments:

We know that the lives and experiences of the dogs were extensively documented – that they each had a 'passport' (complete with photograph), and that their biological processes (heartbeat, respiration and so on) and reaction to experimental situations were carefully recorded, as was what they ate, how they slept, what they did in their kennels, how they behaved on walks and how they interacted with other dogs and people.[7]

As suggested by the dietary regime above, canines stood in for people: 'they needed animals that could endure the stresses of space flight, and whose response to environmental adversity could be compared to that of humans (....) They also needed to be easy to train, monitor and care for.'[8] It thus seemed like a natural decision to choose dogs as subjects, but it was by no means self-evident. After experimenting with smaller animals like fruit flies and rodents, the US-Americans continued to train primates. In 1961, a chimpanzee named Ham (officially as an acronym for the Holloman Aerospace Medical Center) became the first great ape in space. Leading up to this were rather cruel set-ups, however, where monkeys were simply strapped into leather harnesses or restraint suits and secured with belts without spending too much time accustoming them to what lay ahead. Before the flights, they usually were anaesthetized to avoid them interfering with the instruments, but also to take off the edge and avoid suffering when something went wrong, like a parachute not opening properly. The scientists' initial reasoning for these experiments was straightforward: if a monkey could survive a flight aboard a

---

[4]For context, see Kim McQuaid, 'Sputnik Reconsidered: Image and Reality in the Early Space Age' *Canadian Review of American Studies* 37(3) (2007), pp. 371–401.

[5]Cf. Caswell, *Laika's Window*, p. 174.

[6]Amy Nelson, 'What the Dogs Did: Animal Agency in the Soviet Manned Space Flight Programme' *BJHS Themes* 2 (2017), pp. 79–99, here p. 79. On the choosing of street dogs, see Caswell, *Laika's Window*, p. 109.

[7]Nelson, 'What the Dogs Did', p. 84.

[8]Nelson, 'What the Dogs Did', p. 86.

rocket, so could a human.[9] As the missions became more complex, so did the animals' set-up and attire: monkeys received custom-fit suits that measured their physiological reactions to these extreme environments. They allowed for more freedom of movement, as these astrochimps were conditioned to perform simple tasks like pulling levers within their capsule to mimic human interaction. This was done in so-called psychomotor machines by administering 'a mild electric shock through metal plates attached to the underside of their feet' if they did not comply with their cues in time, Colin Burgess and Chris Dubbs write.[10]

Meanwhile, Soviet scientists 'considered simians unsuitable because they were highly strung, easily stressed and much less resilient than stray dogs', Amy Nelson notes.[11] Apart from this pragmatic approach, there was a strong scientific lineage that reached back to the eminent physiologist Ivan Pavlov (1849–1936) who became known for his conditioning experiments and received the Nobel Prize in 1904 for his research into the digestive system. Protégés and former colleagues of his continued to play an important role in the Soviet space programme, as did animal handlers from the circus.[12] In their eyes, dogs were 'known commodities', 'less excitable than monkeys and closer to humans in their emotional and physical reactions', Burgess and Dubbs argue.[13] It is difficult to provide an exact number of the animals involved: 'in the decade leading up to April 1961, the Soviets sponsored missions with passenger slots for more than seventy dogs', Nelson writes, 'including twenty who were put on flights between Laika's launch in 1957 and [Iurii] Gagarin's successful flight nearly four years later'.[14]

Pavlovian subjects

In an attempt to better understand animal agency – 'what the dogs did', in Nelson's framing – Matthew Adams has re-read the established literature on Pavlov's experimental set-up. Large parts of his empirical sources can easily

---

[9]Colin Burgess and Chris Dubbs, *Animals in Space. From Research Rockets to the Space Shuttle* (New York: Springer, 2007), pp. 42–5, 49. The French, in turn, decided to send cats to the brink of space – pp. 225–8.

[10]Burgess and Dubbs, *Animals in Space*, p. 171, pp. 242–4.

[11]Nelson, 'What the Dogs Did', p. 86.

[12]For some context about conditioning in the USSR, see Ann Kleimola, 'A Legacy of Kindness V. L. Durov's Revolutionary Approach to Animal Training', in Jane Costlow and Amy Nelson (eds), *Other Animals. Beyond the Human in Russian Culture and History* (Pittsburgh: University of Pittsburgh Press, 2010), pp. 164–77.

[13]Burgess and Dubbs, *Animals in Space*, p. 63.

[14]Nelson, 'What the Dogs Did', p. 88.

be accessed in translation.[15] Since 1891, Pavlov led his own department of physiology within the Imperial Institute of Experimental Medicine that was founded in St Petersburg in the spirit of Louis Pasteur's bacteriological institute in Paris (see also Chapters 2 and 3) with the support of Tsar Aleksandr III (r. 1881–94). Pavlov rose to fame and was able to expand his research to several sites with a notable budget: 'his studies were most likely the best funded in the country, his facilities the envy of many European and American visitors'.[16] Hundreds, if not thousands, of dogs suffered in the process. Pavlov managed to survive the revolutionary chaos that befell Russia in 1917 and the bloody civil war that ensued. Although he was critical of the new system, he found reliable sponsors in the Bolshevik elite that saw notable parallels between his work and their utopian plan to create the 'New Soviet Human', later satirized as the *homo sovieticus* who is indifferent, unambitious and obedient.[17]

The predominant number of Pavlov's animals was most likely stray dogs. After arriving at the laboratories, they underwent preparatory work for the experiments. To collect saliva straight from the gland in order to measure the canine's reaction to stimuli (the proverbial 'Pavlovian reflex' or 'Pavlovian response'), incisions were made in the cheek or the jaw. Others were less fortunate and had to undergo surgery where large parts of their brains were removed. Adams notes that Pavlov admitted to causing the animals to suffer and that he was willing 'to embrace the reality of emotional states in his dogs' that resulted from the scarring of the brain tissue:

> His recognition of post-traumatic depression and convulsive suffering, terms usually associated exclusively with humans, arguably reflects a profound anti-anthropocentric awareness of animal subjectivity and agency running through Pavlov's methods and analysis. Pavlov had no problem moving freely from animals to humans and humans to animals in extrapolating the psychological significance of his findings. Nor did he shy away from ascribing complex and distinct characters to dogs.[18]

Paradoxically, Adams continues, this did not hinder Pavlov to employ violence while he was exploiting his laboratory animals. The stimuli themselves were much more unpleasant and painful than generally presented: they included

---

[15]Olga T. Yokoyama (ed.), *Pavlov on the Conditional Reflex. Papers, 1903–1936* (Oxford and New York: Oxford University Press, 2023).

[16]Matthew Adams, 'Centring Animals in the History of Experimental Psychology: Pavlov and the Kingdom of Dogs' *Slavonic and East European Review* 103(1) (2025), pp. 64–92, quote p. 68. For a biographical study, see Daniel P. Todes, *Ivan Pavlov. A Russian Life in Science* (Oxford and New York: Oxford University Press, 2014).

[17]The term was popularized by Alexander Zinoviev's novella of the same title, first published in 1981.

[18]Matthew Adams, 'Centring Animals', p. 78.

flashing lights, electrocution, pricking with needles, loud noises or ingesting acid. Meanwhile, the results were not as coherent as Pavlov suggested in his publications. From this, Adams concludes that canine agency was a factor Pavlov had great trouble controlling: 'some dogs fought, growled, or attacked co-workers, others remained obdurate and unruffled by changes in stimuli or other variables; some fell asleep; others were cowed by the demands of the experiment, whimpered and refused to stand'. Pavlov sought to 'explain this away' by developing a theory of different nervous types and 'innately determined psychophysiological predispositions' during the 1920s and 1930s, yet to no avail.[19] Through their constant interaction, lab personnel and their subjects formed close human–animal bonds that were characterized by strong power hierarchies.

Much in the vein of Descartes (see Chapter 3), Pavlov understood dogs as 'complex machines governed by determined processes that are regulated by the nervous system', Nelson notes.[20] As laboratory animals, later space dogs were enhanced into biotechnological hybrids with implanted sensors that measured their vital parameters. Much like in Pavlov's experiments, lab workers assigned different temperaments which created its own array of contradictions: dogs were considered to be both unique friends and categorized servants that were potentially sacrificed for science. 'Individual characteristics and experiences', she resumes, 'shaped the agency of each dog'.[21] Training exposed them to stressful situations like vibration plates, the centrifuge or extreme temperatures. While the Pavlovian focus on conditioning through associative learning remained a 'mainstay of Soviet behaviourism, its limits became obvious:

> The methods of classical conditioning would serve to teach a dog to press a lever in response to a light in order to get a treat, but they would not convince dogs to spend a week restrained in a tiny hermetic cabin using a sanitation suit and be more or less content with their situation. Individual dogs had to identify strategies to meet the potentially devastating challenges presented by long-term sensory deprivation, restricted movement and oss of social interaction.[22]

In the end, the Soviet space dogs simply 'tried to survive by cultivating relationships with people'. Some adapted to the cruel conditions and proved resilience while others did not. In acknowledging this, Nelson points to the

---

[19]Matthew Adams, 'Centring Animals', pp. 80–4, quote p. 82.
[20]Nelson, 'What the Dogs Did', p. 88.
[21]Nelson, 'What the Dogs Did', p. 92.
[22]Nelson, 'What the Dogs Did', p. 94.

cynicism of it all as Laika and her canine comrades had learned 'that these conditions were temporary and that their human partners would care for them afterward'.[23] As we have seen, not all dogs were this lucky.

Protesting vivisection

Brian Bonhomme has shown that criticism of animal cruelty was a subversive way of addressing human suffering. Consequently, the establishment of the Russian Society for the Protection of Animals (*Rossiiskoe obshchestvo pokrovitel'stva zhivotnym*, ROPZh) in 1865 was a milestone not only for animal welfare, but also an expression of the empire's temporary liberalization in the wake of the emancipation of the serfs in 1861 that allowed for civic freedom and broader societal participation (*cf.* Chapters 2 and 3 for the British counterpart, the Royal Society for the Prevention of Cruelty to Animals, RSPCA). These societies were connected across the continent.[24] They worked to improve the treatment of urban animals like carriage horses and street dogs; they promoted humane slaughter and strove for penalties when domestic animals were mistreated. Its members condemned working-class activities 'while elite pursuits such as hunting, horse racing, and vivisection remained socially accepted and legally sanctioned', Nelson writes.[25] Apart from this classist bias, legislation focused on mistreatment witnessed *in public*.[26] Laboratories, in turn, were closed spaces – inaccessible to the uninitiated.

As outlined by Daniel P. Todes, Pavlov formulated clear rules on physiological investigation in an article on vivisection that was published in 1893: experimenters must be alert to detail, conduct several iterations of the same experiment and vary its form – in short: they have to establish a reliable empirical basis for their observations.[27] While this may sound banal, it addresses a core criticism of vivisection, namely the often haphazardly violent set-up of its interactions with live animals. In his work, Pavlov thus differentiated between *chronic* and *acute experiments*. As vivisections, the

---

[23]Nelson, 'What the Dogs Did', p. 99.

[24]Brian Bonhomme, 'Russian Compassion: The Russian Society for the Protection of Animals – Founding and Contexts, 1865–75' *Canadian Journal of History* 45(2) (2010), pp. 259–98. See also Hilda Kean, *Animal Rights. Political and Social Change in Britain since 1800* (London: Reaktion Books, 1998).

[25]Amy Nelson, 'The Body of the Beast. Animal Protection and Anticruelty Legislation in Imperial Russia', in Jane Costlow and Amy Nelson (eds), *Other Animals. Beyond the Human in Russian Culture and History* (Pittsburgh: University of Pittsburgh Press, 2010), pp. 95–112, here p. 97.

[26]Cf. Nelson, 'The Body of the Beast', p. 104.

[27]Daniel P. Todes, *Pavlov's Physiology Factory. Experiment, Interpretation, Laboratory Enterprise* (Baltimore and London: The Johns Hopkins University Press, 2002), p. 72.

latter were carried out through surgical procedures that the animals usually did not survive. Pavlov however observed that 'acute experiments conducted on a freshly operated-on and bleeding animal that was either writhing in pain or heavily narcotized so distorted normal physiological processes that they led inevitably to "crude errors"', Todes writes. This made it 'impossible to untangle the results of the operation itself from normal physiological processes'.[28] Such insights notwithstanding, Pavlov soon attracted the criticism of Baroness Vera Illarionovna Meiendorf (1847–1924), the influential head of the Russian Society for the Protection of Animals who fought to gain oversight of his experiments in 1903.[29] While her stance followed in the spirit of British activists like Frances Power Cobbe (1822–1904) who in 1875 founded the Society for the Protection of Animals Liable to Vivisection which, in 1897, would become the National Anti-Vivisection Society (NAVS), it remained peripheral to the Russian animal protection movement.[30] What is more, the society became increasingly mired in scandals like the embezzlement of funds. By the time of the October Revolution, it was already in shambles, and its activism was not helped by the Bolsheviks labelling their endeavours 'bourgeois'. Pavlov and his methods, as seen above, endured. 'Throughout the Soviet period', Amy Nelson notes, 'there would be neither organized animal protection nor legal restraints on cruelty to animals'.[31] Arguably, this lack of critical oversight from an independent institution cleared the way for scientific utopias unshackled by ethical concerns.[32]

In Great Britain, anti-vivisectionists were more successful. While their accusations were often exaggerated, as the pathologist and historian of medicine A. W. H. Bates notes, they touched on the self-perception of the medical profession. Consequently, many physicians themselves came to oppose it to avoid disrepute. It did, however, present them with a conundrum: could the suffering of animals be excused by scientific advancements? As a 'humanitarian *cause célèbre*', anti-vivisection addressed the core questions how societies 'made ethical choices', 'how science should be conducted' and

---

[28]Todes, *Pavlov's Physiology Factory*, p. 85.
[29]Unfortunately, this is relegated to only a footnote in Todes, *Pavlov's Physiology Factory*, p. 414 and, contrary to his promise, remains unmentioned in his subsequent biography *Ivan Pavlov. A Russian Life in Science*.
[30]Cf. Nelson, 'The Body of the Beast', p. 108.
[31]Nelson, 'The Body of the Beast', pp. 109–12.
[32]For a discussion of a Russian *Sonderweg* in related fields like anti-cruelty legislation and bird protection that marked a rupture with the country's orientation towards the West, see Brian Bonhomme, 'For the "Preservation of Friends" and the "Destruction of Enemies": Studying and Protecting Birds in Late Imperial Russia' *Environment and History* 13(1) (2007), pp. 71–100.

'how humans saw themselves in relation to the rest of creation'.[33] When the first such experiments were reported in Britain as performed by the French physiologist François Magendie (1783–1855) in 1824 who 'nailed a greyhound to the dissecting-table before cutting it open', it sparked not only public outcry and resentment in the face of such a vicious act, it also reminded the urban bourgeoise of the violence of the French Revolution, as some scholars have argued.[34] While the Society for the Prevention of Cruelty to Animals (SPCA) called to evaluate which experiments were permissible, other organizations like the Animals' Friend Society (AFS) aimed to have vivisections outright banned as unnecessary and wanton acts of cruelty – a definition the British courts would not follow, however. It was not before the 1876 Vivisection Act, which had been preceded by the Medical Act of 1858 to set standards for good practice, that still in the spirit of Francophobia it was 'mandated that vivisection be performed only for an original, useful purpose'.[35] Its reasoning was thus more utilitarian than based on moral concerns or humanist compassion.[36]

During the nineteenth century, the idea that animals could reason and possessed souls in the religious sense became commonly accepted. 'The Cartesian notion of animals as automata', Bates underlines, 'had little currency outside philosophy schools, and no British vivisector ever adopted this position' (cf. Chapter 3). They rather argued to what degree animals could perceive pain during experiments:

> Indeed, it would have been difficult for a physiologist to make such a claim, because the validity of experiments on animals depended on their anatomy and physiology being similar to our own: nervous systems organized and functioning like ours could scarcely be found in animals incapable of feeling the pain they so evidently reacted to. The real question was not whether animals had souls, but how closely comparable they were to the souls of humans.[37]

From this sprang various, partly romantic, strands of transcendentalist thought that inspired physicians to different degrees. Mourning deceased animal companions and the organization of funerals were not the only indicators

---

[33]A. W. H. Bates, *Anti-Vivisection and the Profession of Medicine in Britain. A Social History* (London: Palgrave Macmillan, 2017), pp. 6–7, 13–14, quotes p. 14. Pathbreaking: Coral Lansbury, *The Old Brown Dog. Women, Workers, and Vivisection in Edwardian England* (Madison: The University of Wisconsin Press, 1985).

[34]Bates, *Anti-Vivisection*, p. 16.

[35]Bates, *Anti-Vivisection*, pp. 18–19, quote p. 26.

[36]See also Judith E. Hampson, 'History of Animal Experimentation Control in the U.K.' *International Journal for the Study of Animal Problems* 2(5) (1981), pp. 237–41.

[37]Bates, *Anti-Vivisection*, p. 48.

of changing middle-class sentiments that were at odds with materialistic beliefs based in a more sober scientific worldview.[38] Soon, this new age stance brought forth more holistic lifestyles that combined anti-vivisection with vegetarianism and proclaimed to be in harmony with nature.[39] These movements failed to create a unified force, however, and with the obvious advances in the treatment of such diseases like rabies and the successful production of vaccinations by using animals, anti-vivisectionist positions were increasingly questioned:

In the twentieth century (...) when vivisection was set up as one of the pillars of experimental medicine, it could hardly remain the prerogative of a few eccentric, taboo-breaking innovators. It had to be normalized within a medical culture that based its intellectual and moral authority on the intimate relationship between professional knowledge and laboratory experimentation.[40]

As with Pavlov's laboratories, animal experiments disappeared from public view and were relegated to a highly professionalized medical elite. Organizations like the British Research Defence Society, founded in 1908, served to represent the experimenters' interests.

Pinkies and Brains

While early anti-vivisectionists were largely concerned with the societal degradation that may result from the use of companion species in laboratory experiments, they showed little mercy for less sympathetic animals like rats. Considered urban pests that carried dangerous diseases like typhus and the plague, they were known to multiply quickly and in uninviting conditions. Selling their prey to laboratories proved a lucrative business for rat catchers in big cities, and the 'Norwegian' brown rat (*Rattus norvegicus*) became a staple animal for experiments.[41] At the turn of the millennium, worldwide numbers

---

[38] Bates, *Anti-Vivisection*, pp. 57–8.

[39] See chapter 4 'A New Age for a New Century: Anti-Vivisection, Vegetarianism, and the Order of the Golden Age' in Bates, *Anti-Vivisection*, pp. 69–98. In Germany, esoteric movements were especially virulent – p. 144.

[40] Bates, *Anti-Vivisection*, p. 134.

[41] Dawn Day Biehler, *Pests in the City. Flies, Bedbugs, Cockroaches, and Rats* (Seattle and London: University of Washington Press, 2013), pp. 111–38; a useful overview of rats in research is provided by Klaudia Modlinska and Wojciech Pisula, 'The Natural History of Model Organisms: The Norway Rat, From an Obnoxious Pest to a Laboratory Pet' *eLife* (17 January 2020), https://elifesciences.org/articles/50651 [accessed on 19 April 2025].

of vertebrates used in testing were estimated at more than 100 million each year, of which around 95 per cent are thought to be rodents.[42] What started as a truly hands-on approach of providing animal stocks for study soon turned into an industry of its own, as it was shown for the United States in Karen A. Rader's book *Making Mice*. The usual response given to the question why it was ultimately these rodents that were used as 'model organisms' for research is rather straightforward:

> they are small and relatively tame animals, which makes them easy to handle, house, and feed. They breed readily and often (several times per year), and three weeks after the females have mated, good-sized litters of pups are born, which allows for a quick yield of research results, whether in terms of providing a large sample or observing generational patterns. Finally, mice are mammals with a 99 percent genetic homology to humans, and they happen to get many of the same diseases as us (cancer, heart disease, etc.), which (by extrapolation) makes it possible to track and experiment on many human health conditions in situ.[43]

The history of genetic standardization, as laid out by Rader, is more complicated, of course. A central dilemma can be subsumed in the question: 'What animals are enough like us to make laboratory results obtained from them generalizable to humans, but not so much like us that we ethically prohibit their being the subjects of experiments?'[44] To find more comprehensive answers, the author follows Clarence Cook Little (1888–1971), a Harvard graduate in zoology who received his Doctor of Science in 1914 and was focused on the still developing field of genetics, as it had been coined only in 1905. Working with inbred strains of mice at Harvard Medical School proved a viable approach in cancer research that allowed to directly trace genetic mutations. What is more, the focus on rodents helped C.C. Little and his colleagues to avoid being affected by 'politically charged animal welfare debates' with anti-vivisectionists who seemed to care little about these creatures (as pointed out above).[45]

The focus on mice was set at Harvard's Bussey Institution, a biological institute that tested the laws of Mendelian genetics in mammals. The animals originated from hobbyist breeders in 'mouse-fancier organizations' that enjoyed notable popularity in the early twentieth century. They systematically created standardized specimens. 'Fanciers thus provided scientists with both

---

[42]Katy Taylor, Nicky Gordon, Gill Langley and Wendy Higgins, 'Estimates for Worldwide Laboratory Animal Use in 2005' *Alternatives to Laboratory Animals* 36(3) (2008), pp. 327–42.
[43]Karen A. Rader, *Making Mice. Standardizing Animals for American Biomedical Research, 1900–1955* (Princeton and Oxford: Princeton University Press, 2004), p. 11.
[44]Rader, *Making Mice*, p. 22.
[45]Rader, *Making Mice*, pp. 29, 58, 151–2.

a unique mammalian material resource and a broader practical context in which mouse breeding was an accepted cultural activity', Rader writes.[46] As she continues to underline, these breeders did not have to worry about the suffering of their beloved offspring: unlike physiological experiments on cats and dogs that usually involved surgery, 'the overt suffering and/or death of these animals [i.e. rodents] was not built into the main genetic procedure of breeding'.[47] While this may have been true for the observational stage, Rader does not relay what happened to the mice afterwards, i.e. whether they were disposed of in a humane way since keeping them until the end of their natural lifespan would surely have proven financially demanding. Also, trials did not stay that innocent, as C.C. Little's forays into cancer research suggest that involved the transplantation of tumours.[48] Biologists and physicians soon joined forces and scaled up the breeding of mice.[49]

When he became the president of the University of Maine in 1922, Little managed to attract wealthy patrons for his breeding operations. In 1925, he moved on to become president of the University of Michigan which provided him with better funding opportunities. He vowed to turn it into 'a paragon of cooperative scientific research in the Midwest', as Rader relates.[50] With the rising societal attention to 'the cancer problem', Little's work gained traction. After resigning as president in 1929, he returned to Maine and founded his own research institute in Bar Harbor, the Roscoe B. Jackson Memorial Laboratory, which was named after a recently deceased donor. Little successfully catered to the local upper class and its philanthropists.[51] What he labelled 'the wise direction of a program of improvements in human biology' in assessing the work of his peer was linked to eugenic ideas and its 'racial' application. Little's controversial engagement for the American Birth Control League (ABL) and the American Eugenics Society (AES) would have deserved a more critical and distanced evaluation.[52] The prevention of hereditary diseases seemed to be a main interest here as in the recommendation of another pathologist that 'a man who has a history of multiple incidence of carcinoma in his family should not marry a woman who has the same kind of family history'.[53]

During a climate of global economic crisis, breeding standardized mice and selling them to researchers across the United States evolved as a means to keep the laboratory afloat. Since 1929, Little was perfectly connected for this

---

[46]Rader, *Making Mice*, pp. 30–3, quote p. 33.
[47]Rader, *Making Mice*, p. 36.
[48]Rader, *Making Mice*, p. 124, see also p. 182.
[49]Rader, *Making Mice*, p. 51.
[50]Rader, *Making Mice*, p. 72.
[51]Rader, *Making Mice*, p. 88.
[52]Rader, *Making Mice*, pp. 94–5.
[53]Rader, *Making Mice*, p. 192.

as managing director of the American Society for the Control of Cancer (ASCC). Mouse populations soon reached tens of thousands in his new laboratory which ultimately proved to be a goldmine – even though Little is characterized as a stark proponent of freely exchanging mice among geneticists.[54] With time, operations were further streamlined as ways were found to lower costs on animal feed by buying 'fox chow' by the tonne, setting up an increasingly reliable postal distribution system and expanding the breeding facilities. Catering more reliably to user needs put 'Jackson Lab' en route to 'monopolizing the scientific market for mice'. In 1935, this heralded 'A New Deal for Mice', as the popular *Scientific American* quipped.[55] Little did his best to advertise his laboratory along with its specially bred 'JAX mice' that had even been presented in catalogues since 1933. 'Anticancer sentiments', Rader writes, 'reached a fever pitch both in the media and on the floor of the U.S. Congress' which fostered 'a near-unanimous agreement among federal officials that cancer was a problem requiring immediate government attention'.[56] This soon turned into concrete programmes, and Little seized the opportunity to present his inbred mice as 'the biological equivalents of standardized, interchangeable parts in a well-oiled machine of biomedical research production'.[57] In 1941, 'JAX Mice' were trademarked with the U.S. Patent Office which completed their long way to becoming a commodity.[58] A devastating fire in 1947 destroyed large parts of the populations, yet it also provided further publicity for the laboratory which was rebuilt in an even more grandiose fashion to provide 'industrial-style research'.[59] Eventually, Rader summarizes Little's achievements as follows:

> The legacy of the inbred mouse as a 'model organism' today draws momentum from the choices made by Little and other early twentieth-century geneticists. In turn, these choices both shaped and were shaped by broader trends (made retrospectively even more salient) in the structure of biological research – specifically, shifts in sources of patronage and the commercialization of scientific infrastructure, including the mass production and specialized production of lab animals.[60]

The evolution and commercialization of the lab mouse reached new apogees in the decades to come with the creation of 'transgenic mice' that contain

---

[54]Rader, *Making Mice*, pp. 100–102, 117.
[55]Rader, *Making Mice*, pp. 134–5.
[56]Rader, *Making Mice*, p. 145.
[57]Rader, *Making Mice*, p. 155.
[58]Rader, *Making Mice*, p. 171.
[59]Rader, *Making Mice*, pp. 208–11, 235.
[60]Rader, *Making Mice*, p. 252.

human DNA at Harvard University in 1985 and other 'true cyborgs' through human intervention (*cf.* Chapter 3).[61] This presents its own set of ethical dilemmas as it confronts the utilitarian goals of science and medicine with the question of what is allowed to remain of natural animality.

Beyond the lab

In his concise overview on the evolution of biomedical research since the times of Antiquity, Nuno Henrique Franco shows that long-held beliefs on human and non-human organisms have only been questioned in the Age of Enlightenment thanks to 'modern scientific inquiry in the life sciences' that created 'sound knowledge on basic biological processes'.[62] As discussed above, this sparked scepticism and controversy about the faculty of animals to suffer. In 1959, the still-valid ethical principle of the '3Rs' – *Replacement, Reduction* and *Refinement* – that presses for a search for alternatives in animal research was formulated. In the late 1970s, the idea would finally gain traction and create an ongoing best practice discussion.[63] Ultimately, science has come a long way and it 'opened unlimited possibilities for the understanding of gene function and their influence in several genetic and non-genetic diseases', Franco writes. The mouse thus became 'the most commonly used animal model in our day' with 'a central role in biomedicine in the foreseeable future'.[64]

While mice advanced to a sine qua non, an essential component of modern research, ethical discussions especially surrounding the '3Rs' proved much more complicated with simians that, according to Donna Haraway, 'occupy the border zones' of nature and culture: 'The animals have been claimed as privileged subjects by disparate life and human sciences' in a number of fields like psychobiology, reproductive physiology, linguistics or behavioural ecology. 'Monkeys and apes have modeled a vast array of human problems and hopes', she notes.[65] Since the end of the nineteenth century, they had been

---

[61]Rader, *Making Mice*, pp. 258–62.
[62]Nuno Henrique Franco, 'Animal Experiments in Biomedical Research: A Historical Perspective' *Animals* (3) (2013), pp. 238–73, p. 244. See also Anita Guerrini, *Experimenting with Humans and Animals. From Aristotle to CRISPR* (Baltimore and London: The Johns Hopkins University Press, ²2022).
[63]Franco, 'Animal Experiments in Biomedical Research', p. 260.
[64]Franco, 'Animal Experiments in Biomedical Research', p. 257. For a popular account of model organisms in scientific advancement, see Jim Endersby, *A Guinea Pig's History of Biology* (London: Heinemann, 2007).
[65]Donna Haraway, *Primate Visions. Gender, Race, and Nature in the World of Modern Science* (New York and London: Routledge, 1989), pp. 1–2.

increasingly used for research on polio and syphilis, on tropical diseases like yellow fever, and for neurophysiological experiments. Physical anthropologists aimed to better understand evolution through comparative anatomy and phylogeny.[66] Often, newly founded zoological gardens offered the necessary facilities for observation (see Chapter 9). Primates, Haraway stresses, are not only interesting because of their genetic similarity to humans, but also because they possess culture that expresses itself in group dynamics. In her feminist reading, conservative human values like monogamy or heterosexuality were projected onto these animals in experimentation.[67]

After the Second World War, the National Science Foundation was established in the United States to fund civilian research projects. International Conferences that led to the creation of the International Primatological Society in 1964 brought scientists together and created strong networks to discuss interpretations of animal behaviour. According to Haraway, primate field studies had resurfaced in the 1950s accompanied by 'growing medical demand for primates as laboratory material, and the developing interest in primates as models for psychobiological questions about humans'. This phase, she notes, lasted until the mid-1970s, when funding for field research was restricted.

> In the face of deep post-war anxieties about the fate of modern civilization, the image of man the hunter dominates the first period, coupled to the equally compelling image of the mother-infant pair. Social stability was the burning question, along with a growing list of practical concerns about 'achieving' female monkeys, adequate infant care, and stress in urban environments for men adapted to low-density hunter-gatherer conditions. The stability and evolution of 'the family' informed both laboratory and field imaginations.[68]

Such a traditional understanding of gender roles was reflected in the popular literature of the time. This soon changed, however, through works like that of primatologist Jane Goodall (1934–2025) who gained important insights into the social interactions of chimpanzees and their use of tools which put them closer to humans than previously accepted. These findings were widely publicized and they questioned long-held beliefs about educability and plasticity as a supposed 'species character of *Homo sapiens*'.[69] This scientific paradigm shift happened in the climate of the Cold War with its fear

---

[66]Haraway, *Primate Visions*, p. 22.
[67]Haraway, *Primate Visions*, p. 78.
[68]Haraway, *Primate Visions*, pp. 123, 126 (quotes).
[69]Haraway, *Primate Visions*, p. 200.

of annihilation that was accompanied by student protests against the Vietnam War and environmental degradation. As Haraway stresses, their resistance 'cut deeply into ideologies of progress through science and technology and into the marriage between the human family and post-nuclear technological discourses'.[70] This drive expanded into 'manifestations of the revolution in gender' that became 'a global explosion of women's collective and personal agitation and self-expression' accompanied by demographic revolutions and scandals concerning the sexual division of labour along with access to goods and education.[71] Haraway thus points the finger at the problematic preconceptions and power hierarchies in science that repress and silence diverging or even subaltern voices.

In a scathing review of *Primate Visions*, Matt Cartmill labels Haraway's work contradictory, as distorting historical evidence, difficult to follow and a calculated provocation, however. In a postmodernist spirit, she deconstructs truth claims, convinced 'that scientists are nothing but politicians and shamans, and that objective knowledge is itself a myth cooked up by scientists to protect and enhance their power'. Cartmill notes 'a deep suspicion of ordinary language' in Haraway's work that subjects reality to an infinite number of equally valid interpretations. 'Deconstruction is not a friendly act, and Haraway's approach to science in general and to primatology in particular is an unfriendly one, which makes no effort to understand or to sympathize with the intentions of scientists.'[72] Overall, he deems her disinterested in the science behind primatology and biased, at times even hostile in her assumptions – but he also underlines the potential of such an approach: 'There are real insights and intermittent flashes of brilliance scattered through this book, and all primatologists will benefit from reading it and getting their preconceptions shaken up', thanks to 'Haraway's challenging analyses of the social, political, and empirical factors that have induced and guided the growth of feminist ideas in contemporary primatology'.[73] While sexologist Anne Fausto-Sterling acknowledges this potential of Haraway's work, she remains critical of the idea that scientific knowledge is a mere social construct: 'I do not find the so-called strong program, the claim of a completely constructivist position, convincing. But (...) I wish to use the tools of these particular social scientists to provide critical analyses of how science works.'[74]

---

[70]Haraway, *Primate Visions*, pp. 223–4.

[71]Haraway, *Primate Visions*, p. 286.

[72]Matt Cartmill, 'Primate visions: Gender, race, and nature in the world of modern science' *International Journal of Primatology* 12(1) (1991), pp. 67–75, here pp. 68–9.

[73]Cartmill, 'Primate visions', p. 71.

[74]Anne Fausto-Sterling, 'Essay Review: Primate Visions, a Model for Historians of Science?' *Journal of the History of Biology* 23(2) (1990), pp. 329–33, p. 331.

Fausto-Sterling bases this hope on the observation 'that a great intellectual gulf has opened between the historians and philosophers of science who have read the relevant feminist works (...) and those who have chosen not so much to oppose the feminist approach as to ignore it'.[75] This criticism was part of larger debates that arose between scientists and scholars in the late twentieth century. Labelled the 'science wars', it focused to a large degree on the work of French scholars like the sociologist Bruno Latour (1947–2022), who in an essayistic and provocative manner tried to fathom the limits of human insights in societal contexts. In their 1979 ethnographic study *Laboratory Life: The Social Construction of Scientific Facts*, Bruno Latour and Steve Woolgar described the inner workings of a research division of the Salk Institute for Biological Studies in La Jolla, California. Here, they consciously disassociated themselves from the practices of the lab workers, treating them like a hitherto unknown tribe whose actions are painstakingly decoded through interviews and observations. It provided food for thought by describing how scientific findings are negotiated and by observing the interactions of humans with their non-human environments and the networks they form, making it a key text of science and technology studies (STS).[76] While such a playful approach helps to question routines and preconceived notions in everyday laboratory work, it was met with bewilderment by representatives of the natural sciences due to its seemingly superficial understanding of scientific rigor and the tasks at hand. Nonetheless, it continued to inspire important concepts like that of Actor-Network-Theory (ANT) that put *agency* as a purely human – and, to a degree, beastly – phenomenon into question by highlighting interaction without being concerned about intentionality and telicity:

In this sense, it is not necessary for us to set up an opposition between things and people (...) Within *ANT*, an actor (actant) may be anything: an insect, a boat, a person, a government, the unconscious, a virus, etc. Furthermore, actors are relationally linked with one another in webs or networks. They make a difference to each other. They make each other *be*.[77]

Alan Sokal (born 1955), a physicist and mathematician, became one of the central figures of criticism of Latour and his colleagues when he managed to

---

[75]Fausto-Sterling, 'Essay Review: Primate Visions', p. 333.
[76]Bruno Latour and Steve Woolgar, *Laboratory Life. The Social Construction of Scientific Facts* (Beverly Hills: Sage Publications, 1979). Notably, the word 'social' was omitted from the title of the second edition published with Princeton University Press in 1986.
[77]Jim S. Dolwick, '"The Social" and Beyond: Introducing Actor-Network Theory' *Journal of Maritime Archaeology* 4(1) (2009), pp. 21–49, quote p. 45.

publish a nonsensical paper in the leading cultural studies journal *Social Text* in 1996 that presented quantum gravity as a social and linguistic construct.[78] From this spun a range of publications where he and his peers dug deeper into the contradictory musings of poststructuralism and deconstruction – unfortunately not without a fair share of polemics and a pedantic schoolmasterly attitude on their side. In the 1998 book *Fashionable Nonsense*, Sokal and physicist Jean Bricmont stress that while 'there is nothing shameful in being ignorant of calculus or quantum mechanics', they aim to criticize 'the pretension of some celebrated intellectuals to offer profound thoughts on complicated subjects that they understand, at best, at the level of popularizations'. Some onlookers, they continue, would consider this behaviour either 'conscious fraud' or 'self-deception'.[79] The critical objections that Sokal and Bricmont address – at times examples are marginal to the field, they are missing context, they are prone to a metaphorical or even poetic reading of concepts and at times substantiated by a problematic belief in academic authority – have been brought forth on both sides of the aisle.[80]

As a consequence of these ethical and practical disputes, the borders of humans and animals were constantly renegotiated in science and technology.[81] Concerning the achievements of the twentieth century, non-human protagonists became involuntary trailblazers in the service of progress: 'At an ever-intensifying rate, animals, insects and other forms of biological life were fired into space in the 1960s and 1970s' – disregarding the efforts of animal activists, as Colin Burgess and Chris Dubbs observed.[82] Cosmonaut dog Laika and space monkey Ham soon found their equals in the lesser-known animals that France, China and other nations sent to the stars like the Parsian stray cat Félicette in 1963 or the canine taikonaut (*yuhangyuan*) Xiao Bao ('little darling') who was successfully launched in 1966.[83] During these decades, animal experiments answered the most pressing questions about the impact of rocket flight, zero gravity or cosmic radiation. 'Life-support systems, medical monitoring and telemetry systems came of age in this period, thanks in part to the use of animals', Burgess and Dubbs write. 'They became objects

---

[78]Alan Sokal, *Beyond the Hoax. Science, Philosophy and Culture* (Oxford: Oxford University Press, 2008).

[79]See Alan Sokal and Jean Bricmont, *Fashionable Nonsense. Postmodern Intellectuals' Abuse of Science* (New York: Picador, 1998), p. 6.

[80]Sokal and Bricmont, *Fashionable Nonsense*, pp. 7–16.

[81]For a pharmacologist's critical perspective on the present and future of animal experiments, see Richard J. Miller, *The Rise and Fall of Animal Experimentation. Empathy, Science, and the Future of Research* (New York: Oxford University Press, 2023).

[82]Burgess and Dubbs, *Animals in Space*, p. 307.

[83]Burgess and Dubbs, *Animals in Space*, pp. 310–11.

of national pride and pawns in the ongoing gamesmanship of the Cold War Space Race.'[84] *Nolens volens*, they have continued this service alongside their human companions on this earth and beyond until today.

---

[84]Burgess and Dubbs, *Animals in Space*, p. 373. See also Amy Nelson, 'The Legacy of Laika. Celebrity, Sacrifice, and the Soviet Space Dogs', in Dorothee Brantz (ed.), *Beastly Natures. Animals, Humans, and the Study of History* (Charlottesville and London: University of Virginia Press, 2010), pp. 204–24.

9

Breaking free: Circuses, zoos and animal liberation

In 1999, the German punk rock band Die Toten Hosen released a song titled *Sonntag im Zoo* whose chorus translates to 'Here we are happy, me and you / Here we are free, on a Sunday at the zoo'. In the verses, giraffes smile, monkeys do gymnastics and a keeper talks to a penguin. 'The animals are full of joy and the air is full of love.' Though tongue-in-cheek, its lyrics capture the scene quite nicely: zoos were made for relaxed strolling during off-time. Here, the urban bourgeoisie and the working class met in an environment that was fashioned in aristocratic taste. The discomforting truth is presented right away by Nigel Rothfels in his history of the modern zoo, however, where gorillas die in captivity due to 'a deep sadness, even melancholy, stemming from their tragic realization of their destiny.[1] Contradictory as it may seem coming from this angle, zoos are understood as places 'for the preservation of animals' in a simulated natural environment rather than for the sheer entertainment of its human visitors. For Germany, no name is as prominent as that of Carl Hagenbeck (1844–1913), a merchant from Hamburg born to a fishmonger, when it came to recreating artificial landscapes as 'barless enclosures' where animals were allowed to roam freely. Yet this freedom was an illusion as they were still isolated not only from the observers, but also from one another by using artificial moats or rocks. Thus, 'Hagenbeck set a standard for exhibiting animals which can be seen today in the most modern exhibits in contemporary zoological gardens and aquariums,' Rothfels states – including the Hagenbeck Animal Park in his Northern German hometown.[2] What is more, in the early twentieth century, '[p]ractically every major zoological garden, circus, or

---

[1]Nigel Rothfels, *Savages and Beasts. The Birth of the Modern Zoo* (Baltimore and London: The Johns Hopkins University Press, 2002), p. 1.
[2]Rothfels, *Savages and Beasts*, p. 147.

private collector anywhere bought animals from Hagenbeck'. His activities were not limited to animals, but they also encompassed the exhibition of Indigenous people in *Völkerschauen* as 'people shows' or 'human zoos'.[3] Taken together, this was to create 'a world in miniature' with its fair share of dramatic entertainment for tens of thousands of visitors.[4]

The history of today's zoos spans from menageries at absolutist courts and botanical gardens like the Jardin des Plantes in Paris that dates back to 1635 and became the first public zoo in 1793 to more 'bourgeois' places like the Zoological Gardens of London (1828), Amsterdam (1838), Berlin (1844) and, of course, New York's Central Park (1864) to what Rothfels calls the 'new zoos' like San Diego's Wild Animal Park (1972) and Disney's Animal Kingdom near Orlando (1998).[5] This marks a trajectory from rudimentary 'animal cages' to elaborate illusions of nature and wilderness that, at least since the creation of the modern zoo in London, aimed at education, knowledge and understanding instead of presenting a sovereign's personal influence and wealth or delivering courtly entertainment.[6] This was especially owed to the activities of the newly founded zoological societies.[7] Yet as Mieke Roscher underlines, zoos continued to promote national interests and 'strengthen imperial dominion':

> In contrast to the menageries previously kept by European aristocrats, zoos offered the populace in the 'homeland' a glimpse of the Empire's power by bringing animals from the periphery to the centre for everyone to see. Zoos became visual representations of the Empire; it was the Empire they focused on. This was in contrast to the menagerie where the single monarch or aristocrat was the focal point.[8]

---

[3]Rothfels, *Savages and Beasts*, pp. 7–9, quotes pp. 8 and 9, respectively.

[4]Rothfels, *Savages and Beasts*, pp. 42–3.

[5]Rothfels, *Savages and Beasts*, pp. 18–19; dates and details were amended in accordance with publicly available information from the respective institutions. See also Harriet Ritvo, *The Animal Estate. The English and Other Creatures in the Victorian Age* (Cambridge: Harvard University Press, 1987), pp. 205–42; Helen Cowie, *Exhibiting Animals in Nineteenth-Century Britain. Empathy, Education, Entertainment* (Basingstoke and New York: Palgrave Macmillan, 2014) and Daniel E. Bender, *The Animal Game. Searching for Wildness at the American Zoo* (Cambridge and London: Harvard University Press, 2016).

[6]Rothfels, *Savages and Beasts*, p. 31.

[7]'The London Zoological Society was founded in 1826 and two years later opened the gates of its animal garden to scientifically inclined members only. The Zoological Society of Philadelphia was chartered in 1859 with similar scientific objectives, though the Civil War delayed the actual zoo opening until 1874. In Australia, the Royal Melbourne Zoological Society, which opened the first zoo, was founded in 1857. Argentina had to wait until 1907 for a zoo to open in Buenos Aires.' – Richard W. Bulliet, *Hunters, Herders, and Hamburgers. The Past and Future of Human-Animal Relationships* (New York: Columbia University Press, 2005), p. 186.

[8]Mieke Roscher, 'Comment: Animals at Court: Interspecies Relations in a Longue Durée Perspective', in Mark Hengerer and Nadir Weber (eds), *Animals and Courts: Europe, c. 1200–1800* (Berlin and Boston: De Gruyter Oldenbourg, 2020), pp. 399–414, here p. 409.

Recreating habitats was also important for research that extended to more than the breeding of endangered species for conservation, e.g. in primatology (see Chapter 8). Zoos functioned 'as a malleable laboratory that could alter its infrastructure' in line with the experimenters' needs, Dan Vandersommers argues.[9] Another, less-known aspect is the education of furriers on live creatures as it was common in Leipzig's Zoo since the turn of the century In the 1950s, it still advertised to 'visit the living fur bearing animal exhibition' in trade journals, picturing what looks like a Pallas's cat (*manul*) – rare and valuable to the eye of the professional.[10]

The functions of education, research and conservation notwithstanding, the philosopher Keekok Lee has underlined that 'the goal of entertainment is fundamental and every zoo has to bear it in mind if it is to survive'. She deems the idea that zoos could stop mass extinction through their programmes 'highly misleading and scientifically, totally, inaccurate'. This is not only owed to the sheer number of potentially endangered species (see Chapter 1), but also to the fact that zoos 'decontextualise the animal, having deliberately excluded it from that very context which embodies its evolutionary past, substituting for it an environment, so different from its original, that its evolutionary future may also be said to be more or less doomed'.[11] Destroying habitats while keeping animals on hold in zoos, waiting to return them to the wild, is truly abstruse. What is more, as Rothfels discusses at length, the catching of animals was a rather bloody affair in the long nineteenth century: usually, the mothers were killed and their young taken without much resistance. This violence extended to the inhumane treatment of Indigenous labourers, guides and helpers under colonial rule.[12] Such disregard carried over into Carl Hagenbeck's highly popular 'people shows' that, more than anything, aspired to be perceived as authentic: 'only those shows that were verified as bona fide depictions received a stamp of approval from the anthropological societies and their associates at the zoological societies whose gardens became the primary

[9]Daniel Vandersommers, 'Failed Zoo Experiments: Primatology, Aeronautics, and the Animality of "Modern" Science, 1891–1903', in Tracy McDonald and Daniel Vandersommers (eds), *Zoo Studies. A New Humanities* (Montreal et al.: McGill-Queen's University Press, 2019), pp. 65–92, p. 84.

[10]'Besucht die lebende Pelztiersammlung im Leipziger Zoo' – printed on the inside of the cover of *Festschrift. Kürschnertag des Handwerks Leipzig 1954* (=*Das Pelzgewerbe* [1] [1954]). See also Timm Schönfelder, 'Fur Trade in Turmoil: Pelt Commodification in Leipzig from Fin de Siècle to Sovietization', in Magdalena Eriksröd-Burger, Heidi Hein-Kircher and Julia Malitska (eds), *Consumption and Advertising in Eastern Europe and Russia in the Twentieth Century* (Cham: Palgrave, 2023), pp. 113–34, here p. 121.

[11]Keekok Lee, 'An Animal: What is it?' *Environmental Values* 6(4) (1997), pp. 393–410; quotes pp. 401, 404, 407, respectively.

[12]Rothfels, *Savages and Beasts*, pp. 62, 68–9.

sites for Hagenbeck's exhibitions of people'.[13] Hagenbeck, meanwhile, had little interest in the people themselves, as Rothfels stresses:

> it must be stated very clearly that the shows were never organized to benefit indigenous peoples, and what wealth they gained from them was an insignificant portion of the often extraordinary profits that the shows could reap (...) Similarly, there seems to have been little effort on behalf of Hagenbeck and his agents to follow up on their charges after they had been returned to their homes to see if the tour had had any lasting negative effects on the people – for example, the transmission of diseases. The indigenous people were only valuable insofar as they remained 'native', and after the shows, they were returned to their homes with little fanfare.[14]

This sobering evaluation of Hagenbeck's treatment of humans put his practices with animals even more into question. His way of displaying colonialism – the last exhibition of 'exotic peoples' that carried his family's name was presented in 1931 as *Kanaks of the South Seas* at the Oktoberfest in Munich – raised serious doubt about the underlying scientific rigor of his endeavours.[15] Unsurprisingly, such racism prevailed in the 'Third Reich' with its own take on eugenics and 'racial hygiene' that not only brought incommensurable suffering onto people, but also funded animal breeding efforts like the famous Heck cattle in an attempt to revive the lost species of the aurochs (as shortly mentioned in Chapter 7). 'The Nazi fixation on concepts of extinction occurred at a time when there was a noticeably significant reduction in biodiversity in the country', Joshua Schuster notes, 'with a marked dwindling in numbers of wild animals, while the numbers of domesticated animals increased at a rapid pace.'[16] To derive from this observation a holistic interest in conservation, however, would lead too far.

The Heck brothers Lutz (1892–1983), director of Berlin's zoological garden, and Heinz (1894–1982), director of Hellabrunn Animal Park in Munich, who themselves were part of a larger dynasty, aimed at recreating 'a romantic Germanic landscape' in all its supposed vitality and wildness.[17] Lutz Heck had become a patron member of Hitler's paramilitary SS (*Schutzstaffel*) already in

---

[13]Rothfels, *Savages and Beasts*, p. 92.
[14]Rothfels, *Savages and Beasts*, p. 140.
[15]Anne Dreesbach, 'Colonial Exhibitions, "Völkerschauen" and the Display of the "Other"' *European History Online* (3 May 2012), https://www.ieg-ego.eu/en/threads/backgrounds/european-encounters/anne-dreesbach-colonial-exhibitions-voelkerschauen-and-the-display-of-the-other [accessed on 6 May 2025].
[16]Joshua Schuster, *What Is Extinction? A Natural and Cultural History of Last Animals* (New York: Fordham University Press, 2023), p. 144.
[17]Schuster, *What Is Extinction?*, pp. 148–9.

1933 and was a friend of Hermann Göring, who among many other positions carried the title of 'Reich Master of the Hunt' (*Reichsjägermeister*). According to Anke Hilbrenner, they were 'tied by their mutual passion for big game hunting' while both dreamed of creating a 'German primeval forest' with 'primeval German animals' in Nazi-occupied Belarusian-Polish Białowieża.[18] Heck reportedly demonstrated his racist inclination and lack of compassion on New Year's Eve of 1939 when he 'organized a "hunting event" for members of the SS at the Warsaw Zoo':

> Heck and his fellow SS men killed indiscriminately all kinds of wild animals that were caged in the zoo. This undignified slaughter of domesticated animals clearly shows that they were perceived as part of the enemy community and considered unworthy by the SS men compared to the animals in German zoos. Their killing induced a symbolic humiliation of the Polish zoo management, the staff of the Warsaw Zoo, especially the 'Zookeeper's Wife' Antoni[n]a Żabińsk[a] and, moreover, of the people of Warsaw and the Polish national 'us'.[19]

'The Nazi regime sought biopolitical power over all life and death, seeking control over extinction in both directions, such that species could be made and unmade at will', Schuster writes with regard to the work of the Heck brothers. 'Acts of murder contributed to the same motive to Germanicize the landscape as acts of de-extinction.'[20]

Eastern imperialisms

As the preceding paragraphs have shown, entrepreneurs like Heck and Hagenbeck were not only relentless in their treatment of people and animals, but they represented imperial ambitions and delivered a kind of blueprint for conservation in service of the nation. This impetus could also be observed to the east, as in the Russian capital St Petersburg, where city representatives aimed to promote their zoo as a showcase of empire in a globalizing world

[18]Anke Hilbrenner, 'Barred Emotions: Human-Animal Relations in Soviet Zoos' *Slavonic and East European Review* 103(1) (2025), pp. 139–57, here p. 148. See also Thomas M. Bohn, Aliaksandr Dalhouski and Markus Krzoska, *Wisent-Wildnis und Welterbe. Geschichte des polnisch-weißrussischen Nationalparks von Białowieża* (Köln: Böhlau, 2017), especially pp. 157–78.
[19]Hilbrenner, 'Barred Emotions', pp. 148–9. Here, Hilbrenner refers to Diane Ackermann's 2007 book *The Zookeeper's Wife. A War Story* about the Holocaust in Warsaw.
[20]Schuster, *What Is Extinction?*, p. 151. On the continuities and ruptures of zookeeping in post-war Germany, see J. W. Mohnhaupt and Shelley Frisch, *The Zookeepers' War. An Incredible True Story from the Cold War* (New York: Simon & Schuster, 2019).

while its owners aimed to make a profit. Originally founded as a private menagerie in 1865, one year after the Moscow Zoo, by Sophia (1813–87) and Julius Gebhard (*c.*1817–71), who were of Dutch-Prussian descent and had experience in the entertainment business, it even became a destination of the Japanese delegation known as the 'Iwakura Mission' that visited the United States, Europe and, last but not least, the Russian Empire between 1871 and 1873 in search for inspiration to modernize. As Anton Kotenko notes, both St Petersburg and Moscow had by then become part of a global space of exchange, following Western European examples in the way animals were exhibited.[21] In Japan, this orientation towards Europe and the United States was a defining trait of the Meiji Restoration that had opened the country since the late 1860s (as mentioned in Chapter 2). Consequently, Ian Jared Miller has argued that the showcasing of 'Western civilization' was a key function of Tokyo's Ueno Park Imperial Zoological Garden that was created as the first of its kind in East Asia in 1882. It left an indelible mark not only on Japanese leisure culture, but also on science through the advent of Darwinism and Linnean nomenclature in the public consciousness. The author thus speaks of 'ecological modernity' to underline the 'doubled process of intellectual separation and social transformation'.[22]

These Western influences notwithstanding, it becomes clear from the beginning of Miller's *The Nature of the Beasts* that the titular animals were understood in a notably different way than by such people like Heck and Hagenbeck:

Ecological modernity began to quicken in Japan when Udagawa Yōan completed his *Botany Sutra* (*Botanika kyō*) in 1822, an act of translation that claimed revolutionary social and scientific consequences. It was in that short essay that Udagawa (1798–1846), already a noted translator of Western medical and scientific texts at the age of twentyfour, proposed the Japanese word for 'animal' that is still used today. The characters that he chose for the word – *dōbutsu* – signify a moving or animated thing, a description that he linked with breath, air, and lifeforce: ideas that share important elements with both the Latin term *anima* and the Buddhist recognition of affinity between people and animals. It was a choice that signaled the young scholar's careful engagement with botanical and zoological texts, foreign and domestic.[23]

---

[21]Anton Kotenko, 'For fame and fortune: the origins of St Petersburg's zoo, 1865–1871' *Urban History* 52(4) (2025), pp. 604–21, https://doi.org/10.1017/S0963926824000269.
[22]Ian Jared Miller, *The Nature of the Beasts. Empire and Exhibition at the Tokyo Imperial Zoo* (Berkeley: University of California Press, 2013), pp. 2–3, quote p. 3.
[23]Miller, *The Nature of the Beasts*, p. 25.

This marked a break with traditional Chinese nomenclature in favour of Western taxonomy. While humans were situated at the top of the *dōbutsu*, they were still set apart due to their 'capacity for intelligent thought (*chinō*)'.[24] Such differences extended to concepts of nature and culture that were mirrored in the design of zoos and animal parks. Another aspect that Miller highlights is the simultaneous development of zoos and penitentiaries in Japan and the West: 'Rather than shifting objects into public view, these institutions – the one like the other – enclosed them (…) always available for observation.'[25] The act of looking makes humans complicit to suffering. Not only are animals framed by their cages, John Berger argued, they have become 'isolated from each other (…) utterly dependent upon their keepers', passively 'waiting for a series of arbitrary outside interventions'.[26] What is more, Miller writes, Tokyo's increasingly popular Ueno Zoo was discovered as 'a useful social tool, a means of communicating with – and bringing order to – urban crowds such as those that had rioted against the government' after the end of the Russo-Japanese War in 1904–5 (see also Chapter 6).[27]

Manufacturing consent among zoo visitors was representative of Japan's nationalist ambition as it began 'its fitful, violent transformation into an industrial and imperial power', as Miller coins it.[28] In the spirit of domination, Ueno even featured a collection of trophy animals that were captured from theatres of war across East Asia: 'Children could feed treats to purebred warhorses (*gunba*) ridden into battle by Japanese officers or (…) mules and donkeys used by enlisted men to transport supplies.'[29] In the early twentieth century, the zoo was constantly expanding, attracting ever more visitors. Along with this, rare exotic animals were exhibited as signifiers of expansionist power and global prestige. This, Miller argues, generated a new 'natural history' which was written from the imperial perspective of the metropolis:

> This metropolitan 'natural history' was singular rather than plural. It reframed diverse cultures, ecologies, and fauna as components of a unified Japanese empire or icons of Japanese national accomplishment. The fiction of unity was especially important in a multiethnic, multinational

---

[24]Miller, *The Nature of the Beasts*, p. 27.

[25]Miller, *The Nature of the Beasts*, p. 40.

[26]John Berger, *Why Look at Animals?* (London and New York: Penguin, 2009), pp. 33–5.

[27]Miller, *The Nature of the Beasts*, p. 48.

[28]Miller, *The Nature of the Beasts*, p. 61.

[29]Miller, *The Nature of the Beasts*, p. 62. On the zoological gardens' exhibition of military animals as symbols and propagators of 'total war', see pp. 95–119; on the ensuing 'great zoo massacre' – pp. 120–62. Cf. on Great Britain: Hilda Kean, *The Great Cat and Dog Massacre. The Real Story of World War Two's Unknown Tragedy* (Chicago and London: The University of Chicago Press, 2017) and with a global outlook John M. Kinder, *World War Zoos. Humans and Other Animals in the Deadliest Conflict of the Modern Age* (Chicago: The University of Chicago Press, 2025).

empire such as Japan's, and we need to pay close attention to its appeal as well as its costs if we hope to understand how the Japanese empire generated consent in the home islands.[30]

Like in the West, zoos presented a scientifically based order of the world where every animal – including the human visitors – had its place. In stark contrast to Hagenbeck, however, there were no exhibitions of 'exotic people'. It stands to question whether this truly was because of differences in Japan's philosophy and religious culture that extended to diverging perceptions of nature–culture boundaries (as discussed in Chapter 2) or due to more practical reasons. In the following decades, commentators noted that this understanding of the world changed as a result of the country's opening and modernization: 'the new symbolic economy instituted a powerful social fiction in which animals and nature were re-imagined as alien to the lives of most Japanese', Miller notes. Intellectuals like the liberal journalist who went by the pen name of Hasegawa Nyozekan (born Yamamoto Manjirō, 1875–1969) criticized, in 1939, that 'nature has become a thing apart' and that such a separation was 'something new for the Japanese' who now ran the risk of losing their identity. This, Miller continues, was 'one of the central ironies of ecological modernity' in which zoos played a major role:

> Even as the externalization of nature accelerated, the idea of nature, itself a human fabrication, was seen as a wellspring of authentic humanness, something that had to be rediscovered in order to recover one's true self in a world that seemed increasingly denatured and artificial.[31]

By conveying such a romantic ideal of nature, zoos served as an important counterpoint in urban architecture during a period of intense industrialization. At the same time, animals were increasingly commodified, in Miller's understanding, by being presented behind glass, much like display cases in modern department stores.[32] Since the late 1920s, Ueno also followed Hagenbeck's example to create an 'illusion of liberty' by building open cages that would allow visitors 'to indulge in the fantasy of a direct, authentic encounter with nature'.[33]

---

[30]Miller, *The Nature of the Beasts*, p. 63.
[31]Miller, *The Nature of the Beasts*, p. 67. For a discussion of the concept, see Paul Warde, Libby Robin and Sverker Sörlin, *The Environment. A History of the Idea* (Baltimore: Johns Hopkins University Press, 2018).
[32]Miller, *The Nature of the Beasts*, p. 72.
[33]Miller, *The Nature of the Beasts*, p. 76.

From zoos to the circus

Usually, the exhibition and training of animals went hand in hand, as Anke Hilbrenner shows through the story of Soviet zoologist and children's book author Vera Chaplina (1908–94) who famously kept the lion cub Kinuli in her Moscow communal appartement where it was 'raised like an infant' along with her seven-year-old boy. As an analogy to human behaviour, she aimed to demonstrate that animals could be conditioned and educated in accordance with societal needs. Her books became bestsellers; they were translated into many languages and published in 'the non-socialist abroad'. 'Chaplina even received letters from school classes in the USA who wrote to her after perestroika,' Hilbrenner stresses.[34] Such boundary crossings – that simultaneously reinforced traditional gender stereotypes of motherhood – were also at the heart of the Soviet circus. Throughout times of changing cultural politics, its widespread popularity allowed its performances to maintain a uniquely ambiguous distance from official political messaging, while serving as a comical mirror that offered a valve for frustration and thus arguably strengthened social cohesion.[35]

While Carl Hagenbeck primarily understood the circus as a way to promote his business, he also experimented with behavioural training that would test present his stock: 'Hagenbeck wanted to do away with the whip, club, red-hot irons, pistols, and metal bars by carefully selecting animals that seemed to have an aptitude for learning tricks', Nigel Rothfels writes, 'training them through praise and bits of meat and only occasionally reprimanding them with a whip when the animals became sloppy or careless'. For the World's Columbian Exposition in Chicago in 1893, he developed a show that was to rival the fabled exploits of the Roman coliseum – a nod to the antique cradle of the circus.[36] Through his pavilior, which attracted more than a million visitors in Chicago, and ensuing stays in metropolises like New York, Hagenbeck became recognized as one of the major contemporary figures in animal training. This was also due to his carefully cultivated, if generally exaggerated, reputation of employing new, more compassionate methods: 'That image, which fully exploited ideas of the humane trainer walking with confidence among his pupil animals – animals that respect, admire, but more than anything love

[34]Hilbrenner, 'Barred Emotions', pp. 143–5.
[35]Cf. Miriam Neirick, *When Pigs Could Fly and Bears Could Dance. A History of the Soviet Circus* (Madison: University of Wisconsin Press, 2012).
[36]Rothfels, *Savages and Beasts*, pp. 143–50. On the evolution of the animal spectacle, see Linda Kalof, *Looking at Animals in Human History* (London: Reaktion Books, 2007).

their keeper – came to its eventual apotheosis in Hagenbeck's groundbreaking Animal Park' in Hamburg, Rothfels observes.[37]

As a form of mass entertainment, the circus reached its 'golden age' in Europe and the United States in the decades around the turn of the century. This profitability of the trade allowed Hagenbeck to sell 'entire groups of performing animals, prepared with certain standard acts, along with cages and wagons for transportation'.[38] Eventually, Rothfels identifies a 'striking disjuncture' between the commercial nature of Hagenbeck's business and public perception:

> Hagenbeck's park was simply neither a paradise for animals nor an ark for their protection. In most cases, it was a holding station for animals brought from all over the world which were waiting to be shipped to buyers (...) Hagenbeck's park was specifically designed to meet those desires [of the public for entertainment] as a type of a proto-Disneyland where horses, ostriches, and zebras pulled carts around and camel, elephant, and tortoise rides were available to all who paid for the pleasure.[39]

As Susan Nance shows in her history of the American circus, what began as 'experimental animal exhibitions' with menagerie wagons that carried an array of common along with a few exotic animals across the country, soon grew into a well-managed mass spectacle with a large human and animal workforce. The elephant became a key creature to the American circus during the nineteenth century as it was not only a major attraction, but also systematically used as an animal machine that carried material and helped raise the circus tents. Human and animal performers existed 'in symbiosis'. Nance upholds that 'animal celebrity' was more than a way of making profit; it served as boundary-making between nature and culture during a time of national self-discovery.[40]

Nance's 'cultural and management history', as she classifies it, starts with the advent of the first elephant in the United States from Calcutta in 1796, commonly referred to as 'Betsy'. The pachyderm soon became an object of curiosity and local lore about her alleged exploits: 'Although these competing narratives were often untrue in the details, they were honest in their metaphorical comparison of a juvenile elephant with the early American republic, a creature at once compelling, volatile, and fragile', Nance observes.

---

[37]Rothfels, *Savages and Beasts*, pp. 155–6, quote p. 161.
[38]Rothfels, *Savages and Beasts*, p. 180.
[39]Rothfels, *Savages and Beasts*, p. 186.
[40]Susan Nance, *Entertaining Elephants. Animal Agency and the Business of the American Circus* (Baltimore: The Johns Hopkins University Press, 2013), pp. 1–4, 7.

Betsy became 'a vehicle for patriotic nostalgia about the primitive earnestness of the early republic's citizens'.[41] She also proved to be a highly profitable asset for her exhibitors who did not tire of propagating her prowess, supposedly in the spirit of education. There is, however, some confusion with the second elephant that arrived in the young republic and was called by the same name. While the first one was lost to history probably due to illness, the second Betsy's (or Betsey, as the author herself is incoherent in her spelling) fame even continued to attract a crowd after she was shot and killed by an unknown intruder in her barn which only 'enhanced her notoriety and the public's emotional identification with her':

> Once the flesh was removed from Betsey's bones, her owner arranged for her skeleton to be assembled and exhibited, now without the expense of watering or feeding – what great economy! And indeed, spectators did pay twenty-five cents to see the bones of the 'unfortunate Elephant that was shot the 26th of July last, in District of Maine, [and] so well known by the public.' These were the foundations of the industry in elephant celebrity, which would boom in the antebellum years.[42]

The development of the circus was closely connected to hippodrome shows that appeared in Britain in the 1770s and made their way across the ocean in the 1790s. These soon featured acrobats and clowns in addition to trick riders and were considered a 'wholesome' form of entertainment by many (if not most) citizens.[43] When these former horse circuses included elephant performers that had been 'named and promoted (…) as noted entertainers', which made them 'the most famous animals in nineteenth-century America', this created a wide range of new possibilities for interaction: improved storytelling and artistry now addressed religious and patriotic values, asserting 'a citizen's right to be a consumer of animals and the exotic' – similar to the role zoos began to play in nation-building.[44] Meanwhile, 'a second set of stories functioned as children's morality tales in a kind of performed animal fable'.[45]

In competition for paying spectators, elephants also executed spectacular high-risk acts that were dangerous to humans and animals alike thanks to a strict training regime that employed 'punishment and painful consequences'.[46]

---

41 Susan Nance, *Entertaining Elephants*, p. 16.
42 Susan Nance, *Entertaining Elephants*, p. 38.
43 Susan Nance, *Entertaining Elephants*, p. 42.
44 Susan Nance, *Entertaining Elephants*, pp. 45, 61, respectively.
45 Susan Nance, *Entertaining Elephants*, p. 61.
46 On the intricacies of animal training see Susan Nance, *Entertaining Elephants*, pp. 70–103, quote p. 72.

Mid-century audiences began finding elephants advertised posing on pedestals and the backs of other elephants, walking on elevated planks or large circumference tightropes, standing on their heads, and serving as platforms for other performing animals (...) The financial viability of these more complex performances was facilitated by a corresponding decrease in the cost of producing representations of the new acts in visual patter in graphic handbills, broadsides, and souvenir pamphlets.[47]

Such a variety of programmes was not only extremely popular, but also incredibly profitable for larger companies that managed to travel across the nation and cater to big audiences. In the United States, this interaction of man and elephant marked a breakthrough in entertainment.[48] But criticism about the conditions of training and husbandry grew louder during the nineteenth century (as seen in the preceding chapters). Newspaper reports and children stories questioned 'the vicious brute cliché' of the elephant, bluntly stating that 'circus and menagerie trainers were cruel, ignorant men out for profit'.[49] Throughout the decades, the living conditions of these animals improved only marginally, however: 'They are still confined the majority of the time, now in box vans as often as rail cars. They are still broken for training and steered with elephant hooks', Nance observes for the years after the Second World War. The situation of animal handlers was equally precarious – they were subjected 'to destructive or unpredictable elephants and additionally to open criticism by fellow circus workers and the public'.[50] With the advent of animal rights, circuses have largely lost their credibility to 'speak for elephants'.

As Nigel Rothfels has argued in *Elephant Trails*, opinions among experts about the humanity of circuses and zoos differ decidedly: while many consider zoos to be within a grey area that could see a lot of improvement in animal keeping, there is a clear dividing line between those that want to see animal performances in circuses outright banned and those that regard them as a valid form of art and entertainment.[51] This, of course, is also based in the fact that zoos have come to be identified more with science and conservation than with mere amusement. In an industrialized world, as Margo DeMello noted,

[47]Susan Nance, *Entertaining Elephants*, p. 65.

[48]On the roots and evolution of this relationship, see Jane Buckingham and Piers Locke (eds), *Conflict, Negotiation, and Coexistence. Rethinking Human-elephant Relations in South Asia* (New Delhi: Oxford University Press, 2016).

[49]Susan Nance, *Entertaining Elephants*, p. 130, and pp. 175–207. See also her essay *Animal Modernity. Jumbo the Elephant and the Human Dilemma* (Basingstoke and New York: Palgrave Macmillan, 2015).

[50]Susan Nance, *Entertaining Elephants*, pp. 223–4.

[51]Nigel Rothfels, *Elephant Trails. A History of Animals and Cultures* (Baltimore: The Johns Hopkins University Press, 2021), pp. 152–6.

zoos and circuses allow to reconnect to a nature that is lost in daily life: 'Since animal agriculture now takes place behind the closed doors of huge factories and most Americans live either in cities or suburbs, interacting with non-companion animals has effectively become a thing of the past for the great majority of us.' While this longing for wilderness and an emotional connection to animals may help to explain the lasting appeal of animal exhibitions, environmental consciousness has notably turned in their disfavour since the 1970s. Voices against the exploitation in zoos and circuses that asked for their liberation grew louder.[52]

Clearing the ring

At the core of menageries, zoos and circuses has always been a longing for the exotic that was driven by a degree of escapism from the dreary everyday.[53] As Anne Dreesbach observed, the possibilities to satisfy this desire changed over time: 'Once it became affordable to go to where the adventure was, it was no longer necessary to have it brought from elsewhere to one's home country'[54] Tourism, however, cannot compensate the high emotionality of the circus with its *Wild and Dangerous Performances*, as Peta Tait labelled it. 'In searching for ways in which animals are like us – circus animal acts exploit our predilection for mimetic reproduction of familiar physical behaviour – we seek to confirm that animals' perceptual awareness and emotional relations mirror our own', she argues.[55] Understanding emotions had become paramount in training at the turn of the century, following the publication of Charles Darwin's 1872 treatise *The Expression of the Emotions in Man and Animals* (see also Chapter 2):

> If, as Darwin claimed, wild animal performers could be understood to have emotions that matched those of humans, then working with individuals became a process of familiarising animals with humans in order to achieve calmness in reactions while watching carefully for particular emotions to forestall unwanted behaviour. The underlying premise in accounts of animal training was that the trainer could thwart the intentions of animal

---

[52]Margo DeMello, *Animals and Society. An Introduction to Human-Animal Studies* (New York: Columbia University Press, 2012), pp. 99–122, quote p. 100.
[53]For a short discussion on the exotic as part of the 'evocation of imperial power', see Helen Cowie, 'Exhibiting animals. Zoos, menageries and circuses', in Hilda Kean and Philip Howell (eds), *The Routledge Companion to Animal-Human History* (London and New York: Routledge, 2019), pp. 298–321, here pp. 301–2.
[54]Anne Dreesbach, 'Colonial Exhibitions'.
[55]Peta Tait, *Wild and Dangerous Performances. Animals, Emotions, Circus* (Basingstoke and New York: Palgrave Macmillan, 2011), p. 7.

performers through patient observation and close attention to their facial and bodily expression.[56]

Consequently, animals had to be taken seriously as autonomous agents, and their 'perceptual awareness', as noted above, called for a humane treatment. In the limelight, trainers wanted to avoid showing gratuitous violence when dealing with their animals, much to the recognition of societies for the prevention of cruelty. Yet as Peta Tait highlights, they 'probably benefited from a cultural memory of cruder nineteenth-century menagerie acts' and from the fact that 'offstage training methods were not vigorously scrutinised' in their positive assessment.[57] The circus remained an ambiguous place throughout the twentieth century. Elephants and other wild animals were presented 'in everyday activities that made them appear playful, and as if surrogate family members'. Thus, they became part of anthropomorphized acts and 'comic performances' that 'reinforced an impression of integration into the human world beyond that required for entertainment'. Ultimately, this 'misrepresented human-elephant relations to spectators'.[58] The long list of accidents when elephants trampled or big cats attacked and mauled their handlers – 'usually men who were at some point in the production of their heroic role', as David A. H. Wilson observes – of course tells another story.[59]

Such 'humanlike physical movement delivered in performance' was criticized by advocacy groups like the New York-based Friends of Animals (FoA), which was founded in 1957 and opposed animal acts. Meanwhile, defenders of the circus argued somewhat cynically that, in contrast to zoos, animals would at least get some exercise and not suffer boredom. However, Tait argues, this was 'an artificial arrangement' as 'an animal may well have experienced distress or discomfort from any number of spatial and physical factors' like the cages where they were kept.[60] In no way did this correspond to the emotional needs of these animals. In the 1960s and 1970s, the voices of animal rights activists found a growing outlet in the media where they reached an increasingly large audience. Also, movies like the 1966 British drama *Born Free*, which was based on a non-fiction book about an orphaned lion cub that was raised and successfully reintroduced into its natural habitat in Kenya, disproved the popular belief 'that captured wild animals must go to zoos or be killed because they could not be returned to the wild'.[61] In a way,

---

[56]Tait, *Wild and Dangerous* Performances, p. 28.
[57]Tait, *Wild and Dangerous* Performances, p. 71.
[58]Tait, *Wild and Dangerous* Performances, p. 77.
[59]David A.H. Wilson, *The Welfare of Performing Animals. A Historical Perspective* (Berlin and Heidelberg: Springer, 2015), pp. 113–17, quote p. 114.
[60]Tait, *Wild and Dangerous* Performances, pp. 102–3.
[61]Tait, *Wild and Dangerous* Performances, p. 163.

the story was reminiscent of Vera Chaplina's lion cub Kinuli above, and the movie won an academy award. Seemingly, the use of animals in film and television created less backlash than their training for live performances. In the latter, Tait recognizes the influence of the social liberation movements of the 1970s on animal advocacy. Activists not only continued their work to minimize harm to animals, but they began to demand individual rights of personhood to be respected: 'Protestation against the loss of animal liberty for short-term human enjoyment led to emotionally charged public demonstrations against circus internationally by the 1980s.'[62] This fuelled discussions about animal-free circuses that focus on human artistry and symbolic substitutions of animals which last until today.

In *The Welfare of Performing Animals*, David A. H. Wilson traces the trajectory of criticism by organizations like the Royal Society for the Prevention of Cruelty to Animals (RSPCA, see Chapters 2 and 3) and the much more elusive Performing Animals' Defence League (PADL), which existed under this name from 1914 to 1968 and proposed direct action. Legislation like Britain's 1925 Performing Animals Act as 'the first and last act of its kind', which the PADL helped pass, reminded many of the Vivisection Act of 1876, however, since both did in effect not prohibit animal abuse, but allowed for its legitimization through licensing.[63] While the outcome was contested both by supporters and opponents of animal performances, protests showed strong intersectionality with other social questions like women's rights and workers' interests (see also Chapter 3). As Wilson notes, discussions became mired in political intrigue during the ensuing decades.[64] In her classic history of animal rights in Britain, Susan Nance has similarly traced their evolution since the early nineteenth century. She sees a strong link between the experience of violence – especially the potential total annihilation of the Second World War that extended into the Cold War era (*cf.* Chapter 8) – and such phenomena like veganism.[65] As a consequence of this shift in consciousness and perception, circuses devised new human-centred formats such as the Canadian Cirque du Soleil, founded in 1984, which combined acrobatics with elements of street

---

[62]Tait, *Wild and Dangerous* Performances, p. 168. For a critical discussion of the underlying concepts, see Erin E. Williams and Margo DeMello, *Why Animals Matter. The Case for Animal Protection* (Amherst: Prometheus Books, 2007), here pp. 283–336. On the development of criticism against the use of animals in motion pictures (and the effect of movie violence on children): Wilson, *The Welfare of Performing Animals*, pp. 241–9.
[63]Wilson, *The Welfare of Performing Animals*, p. 38.
[64]See also the agricultural economist Harold D. Guither, *Animal Rights. History and Scope of a Radical Social Movement* (Carbondale and Edwardsville: Southern Illinois University Press, 1998).
[65]Hilda Kean, *Animal Rights. Political and Social Change in Britain since 1800* (London: Reaktion Books, 1998), pp. 202–3.

theatre and vaudeville in an exhilarating hybrid way. They demonstrated that the potential for animal suffering is no precondition for good entertainment. As long as their liberation from the rings and menageries of this world is not completed, however, humanity has to stare into these beastly mirrors of its own cruelty.

10

Conclusion and outlook

As the many stories told in this book have shown, animal history is well past the navel-gazing of its infancy, which was surveyed in the first chapter, and it is reaching out in all directions. This also means that it is slowly overcoming its favouritism towards charismatic companions. The 'microbial turn' (as mentioned in Chapter 4) has proven that there is a strong interest in even the smallest creatures, while works about insects have gained prominence during the past years. John McNeill's *Mosquito Empires. Ecology and War in the Greater Caribbean, 1620–1914* is only one example of how our understanding of modern ecology can be reframed with a strong interest in the history of medicine, following vector mosquitoes of yellow fever and other creatures in their role as involuntary nation builders.[1] Such a view has been varied by a range of authors for other parts of the world that look at potentially devastating grain beetles in agriculture, transnational cooperation in the fight against tick-borne encephalitis or the 'epidemic agency' of animals in general.[2] For this, insights gained from health studies can be taken to inspire strong transdisciplinary synergies in the environmental humanities as a promising

---

[1] J. R. McNeill, *Mosquito Empires. Ecology and War in the Greater Caribbean, 1620–1914* (Cambridge and New York: Cambridge University Press, 2010). Unfortunately, feathered companions have also been neglected in this introduction – see, e.g., Boria Sax, *Avian Illuminations. A Cultural History of Birds* (London: Reaktion Books, 2021) and the as of now twenty different species of birds published in the Reaktion Book Animal series.

[2] See, e.g., Anastasia Fedotova, 'The Beetle Question: The Growing Problem of Insect Infestations in South Russia in the Late Nineteenth Century' *The Slavonic and East European Review* 93 1) (2015), pp. 66–95, who is an entomologist by training, or Anna Mazanik, 'Arbovirology and Cold War Collaborations: A Transnational History of the Tick-borne Encephalitis Vaccine, 1930–1980' *Journal of the History of Medicine and Allied Sciences* 79(3) (2024), pp. 254–73, and Axel C. Hüntelmann, Christian Jaser, Mieke Roscher and Nadir Weber (eds), *Animals and Epidemics. Interspecies Entanglements in Historical Perspective* (Köln: Böhlau, 2023).

incubator of ideas.[3] This may extend to newer concepts like *healthscapes* that – broadly defined – focus on the interplay of spatial, social, political, legal and administrative factors that dynamically shape interactions between people, animals, environments, epistemic systems and infrastructures with regard to health, illness and care.[4]

Closely connected to the formation and fall of empires is the history of violence which is present throughout this book – be it in the killing of wolves (Chapter 2), the mistreatment of dogs and horses in urban environments (Chapter 3), the extermination of native species like the bison (Chapter 4), hunting safaris (Chapter 5), industrial whaling (Chapter 6), inhumane slaughter practices (Chapter 7), animal experiments (Chapter 8) or cruel forms of training and exhibition (Chapter 9). As an array of studies has shown, history of warfare itself offers telling insights into human–animal relationships, not least in the everyday experience of violence, but also in the way animal companions were conditioned for the battlefield.[5] Even though our treatment of animals has seen a qualitative change since the nineteenth century through the creation of humane societies that sensitized people to their suffering, human actions remain steeped in cruelty against animals around the world. As Susan Nance has argued (see Chapter 9), the wish for non-violence sparked counter-movements like vegetarianism and veganism that have since attracted a broad following. Consequently, the question why certain animals are eaten (and how they are prepared) has also become part of a globalized food history.[6]

A contemporary argument in this discussion would be the negative impact the meat industry has on the environment. In recent historiography, debates about sustainable behaviour have found their expression in the idea of the *Anthropocene* as an age when humans have become a geologically defining

---

[3]See, e.g. Abigail Woods, Michael Bresalier, Angela Cassidy and Rachel Mason Dentinger, *Animals and the Shaping of Modern Medicine. One Health and Its Histories* (London: Palgrave Macmillan, 2017).

[4]Cf. the introductory chapter in Erika Dyck and Christopher Fletcher (eds), *Locating Health. Historical and Anthropological Investigations of Place and Health* (London: Pickering & Chatto, 2011).

[5]Hilda Kean, *The Great Cat and Dog Massacre. The Real Story of World War Two's Unknown Tragedy* (Chicago and London: The University of Chicago Press, 2017). Ryan Hediger (ed.), *Animals and War. Studies of Europe and North America* (Leiden: Brill, 2013). James L. Hevia, *Animal Labor and Colonial Warfare* (Chicago and London: The University of Chicago Press, 2018). For a more recent study, see Oksana Nagornaia, 'Animal Fighters, Animal Victims: the Animal Dimension on the Russian-Austrian Front of the First World War', in Kerstin S. Jobst, Oksana Nagornaia and Kerstin von Lingen (eds), *The Great War and the Anthropocene. Empire and Environment, Soldiers and Civilians on the Eastern Front* (Leiden and Boston: Brill, 2024), pp. 127–44.

[6]The field is a world of its own with a plethora of inspiring avenues, like Henry Buller and Emma Roe, *Food and Animal Welfare* (London et al.: Bloomsbury Academic, 2018) or Julia Malitska (ed.), 'Special Section: Dietary Reforms in the Baltic and East Central Europe, ca 1850–1950' *Baltic Worlds* 1–2 (2022), pp. 105–64.

force. While the term was rejected as a successor to the Holocene by the International Union of Geological Sciences (IUGS) in 2024, it nonetheless underlines the accelerated human influence on our planet at least since around 1952 when hydrogen bomb tests caused the worldwide spread of specific radioactive isotopes. This marker was in no way uncontested: alternative suggestions viewed the beginning of the Industrial Revolution in the mid-eighteenth century or even the dawn of agriculture more than 10,000 years ago as worthy contenders.[7] Climate change, in turn, proves to be the major challenge of our times. As a consequence, historians like Dipesh Chakrabarty have called for a planetary perspective.[8] Meanwhile, Ian Jared Miller has observed in his history of Ueno Zoo in Tokyo that humans 'struggle to come to terms with the realities of climate change, diminishing natural resources, and the rapid eradication of other species'. This crisis, he continues, 'emerges most forcefully along the frontiers where people seek to make sharp distinctions between [the] two realms' of nature and society.[9] In more concrete words, this would mean that wilderness (as encountered in Chapter 2) is at peril. From this arises the wish to recover and to rewild species as a way to embrace what has been or is at the brink of being lost. Plans to resurrect the dire wolf or the mammoth present food for thought for the future. Dolly Jørgensen aptly frames preservation and conservation projects as highly emotional endeavours driven by nostalgia, hope, fear and a fair share of guilt and grief:

In these and other cases, animal species become symbols of heritage. Animals like the North American bison, passenger pigeon, red squirrel, and polar bear have been woven into a complex relationship between cultural and natural heritage, in which the two are inexorably joined. Heritage claims that something, whether a landscape, a building, or a species, *belongs* in a place. *Belonging* in this sense means to be related or connected, to fit in a certain environment (...) belonging is constructed, negotiated, and contested through biocultural relationships rather than being a fixed category.[10]

---

7 Damian Carrington, 'Geologists reject declaration of Anthropocene epoch' *The Guardian* (22 March 2024), https://www.theguardian.com/science/2024/mar/22/geologists-reject-declaration-of-anthropocene-epoch [accessed on 28 May 2025].
8 Dipesh Chakrabarty, *The Climate of History in a Planetary Age* (Chicago and London: The University of Chicago Press, 2021).
9 Ian Jared Miller, *The Nature of the Beasts. Empire and Exhibition at the Tokyo Imperial Zoo* (Berkeley: University of California Press, 2013), p. 17.
10 Dolly Jørgensen, *Recovering Lost Species in the Modern Age. Histories of Longing and Belonging* (Cambridge and London: The MIT Press, 2019), p. 8.

This sense of belonging may ultimately be the central aspect of animal history which is so deeply focused on relationships and interactions between humans and non-humans ranging from charismatic megafauna to companions, predators and 'pests'. 'The whole concept of species itself is a historical construction', Jørgensen underlines.[11] The re-negotiation of their delineation as boundary-making will prove to be a constant task of writing animal history for generations of scholars to come. To grasp localized practices of autochthonous communities, approaches that go beyond human-made written sources have the potential to be especially inspiring. As such, anthropological fieldwork has been an indispensable and ever-expanding informant (as seen in Chapter 2).[12] Queer ecologies may also disrupt established binaries.[13]

Ultimately, it will become ever more difficult for historians – especially those active in the environmental humanities – to remain within the theoretical and methodological confines of their field. Any step beyond our disciplinary boundaries will help to further decolonize our studies and to mitigate human hubris. As scholars of animal history, we should therefore confidently embrace the polyphony of human and non-human voices to find new ways of approaching our research. Maybe it is in the midst of the jungle where we are right at home.

---

[11]Jørgensen, *Recovering Lost Species in the Modern Age*, p. 9. For a philosophical elaboration on the existence of an ontological divide, see Matthew Calarco, *Zoographies. The Question of the Animal from Heidegger to Derrida* (New York: Columbia University Press, 2008) and, more generally, Nik Taylor and Tania Signal (eds), *Theorizing Animals. Re-thinking Humanimal Relations* (Leiden and Boston: Brill, 2011).

[12]Thiemo Breyer and Thomas Widlok (eds), *The Situationality of Human-Animal Relations. Perspectives from Anthropology and Philosophy* (Bielefeld: transcript, 2018).

[13]Grace van Deelen, 'What Is Queer Ecology? Queer Theory Expands Our Relationship with Nature' *Sierra* (3 June 2023), https://www.sierraclub.org/sierra/what-is-queer-ecology [accessed on 2 September 2025].

Bibliography

Act Establishing Yellowstone National Park *National Archives* (1872), https://www.archives.gov/milestone-documents/act-establishing-yellowstone-national-park.

Adams, Matthew, 'Centring Animals in the History of Experimental Psychology: Pavlov and the Kingdom of Dogs' *Slavonic and East European Review* 103(1) (2025), pp. 64–92.

Adamson, Peter and G. Fay Edwards (eds), *Animals. A History* (New York: Oxford University Press, 2018).

An Introduction to the African Convention on the Conservation of Nature and Natural Resources (Gland and Cambridge: IUCN, 2004).

Anderson, David G., *Identity and Ecology in Arctic Siberia. The Number One Reindeer Brigade* (Oxford: Oxford University Press, 2000).

Anderson, J. L., *Capitalist Pigs. Pigs, Pork and Power in America* (Morgantown: West Virginia University Press, 2019).

Anderson, Virginia DeJohn, *Creatures of Empire. How Domestic Animals Transformed Early America* (New York: Oxford University Press, 2004).

Arch, Jakobina K., *Bringing Whales Ashore. Oceans and the Environment of Early Modern Japan* (Seattle: University of Washington Press, 2018).

Ardrey, Robert, *The Hunting Hypothesis. A Personal Conclusion Concerning the Evolutionary Nature of Man* (New York: Atheneum, 1976).

Bates, A. W. H., *Anti-Vivisection and the Profession of Medicine in Britain. A Social History* (London: Palgrave Macmillan, 2017).

Beck, Laura and Maurice Saß (eds), *Hunting Troubles. Gender and Its Intersections in the Cultural History of the Hunt* (Cham: Palgrave 2024).

Beckert, Sven, Ulbe Bosma, Mindi Schneider and Eric Vanhaute, 'Commodity Frontiers and the Transformation of the Global Countryside: A Research Agenda' *Journal of Global History* 16(3) (2021), pp. 435–50.

Bender, Daniel E., *The Animal Game. Searching for Wildness at the American Zoo* (Cambridge and London: Harvard University Press, 2016).

Berger, John, *Why Look at Animals?* (London and New York: Penguin, 2009).

Berger, Stefan, Heiko Feldner and Kevin Passmore (eds), *Writing History. Theory and Practice* (London: Bloombsury Academic, ³2021; first published in 2020).

Biehler, Dawn Day, *Pests in the City. Flies, Bedbugs, Cockroaches, and Rats* (Seattle and London: University of Washington Press, 2013).

Blakeslee, Nate, *American Wolf. A True Story of Survival and Obsession in the West* (New York: Broadway Books, 2018).

Blanchette, Alex, *Porkopolis. American Animality, Standardized Life, and the Factory Farm* (New York: Duke University Press, 2020).

Bogdanov, Konstantin A. (ed.), 'M nistr, zaitsy, memy, ili kak sozdaiutsia i chem derzhatsia nauchnye soobshchestva' *Novoe literaturnoe obozrenie*

140(4) (2016), https://www.nlobooks.ru/magazines/novoe_literaturnoe_ obozrenie/140_nlo_4_2016/.

Bohn, Thomas M., Aliaksandr Dalhouski and Markus Krzoska, *Wisent-Wildnis und Welterbe. Geschichte des polnisch-weißrussischen Nationalparks von Białowieża* (Köln: Böhlau, 2017).

Bonhomme, Brian, 'For the "Preservation of Friends" and the "Destruction of Enemies": Studying and Protecting Birds in Late Imperial Russia' *Environment and History* 13(1) (2007), pp. 71–100.

Bonhomme, Brian, 'Russian Compassion: The Russian Society for the Protection of Animals – Founding and Contexts, 1865–75' *Canadian Journal of History* 45(2) (2010), pp. 259–98.

Brandler, Jacob, 'Do "Animals" Have Histor(ies)? Can/Should Humans Know Them? A Heuristic Reframing of Animal-Human Relationships' *Journal of Animal Ethics* 12(2) (2022), pp. 148–57.

Brantz, Dorothee, 'Recollecting the Slaughterhouse' *Cabinet* (4) (Fall 2001), pp. 118–23.

Brantz, Dorothee, 'Stunning Bodies: Animal Slaughter, Judaism, and the Meaning of Humanity in Imperial Germany' *Central European History* 35(2) (2002), pp. 167–94.

Brantz, Dorothee, 'Animal Bodies, Human Health, and the Reform of Slaughterhouses in Nineteenth-Century Berlin' *Food and History* 3(2) (January 2005), pp. 193–215.

Brantz, Dorothee (ed.), *Beastly Natures. Animals, Humans, and the Study of History* (Charlottesville and London: University of Virginia Press, 2010).

Brantz, Dorothee, 'Animals in Urban-Environmental History', in Sebastian Haumann, Martin Knoll and Detlev Mares (eds), *Concepts of Urban-Environmental History* (Bielefeld: transcript, 2020), pp. 191–201.

Breyer, Thiemo and Thomas Widlok (eds), *The Situationality of Human-Animal Relations. Perspectives from Anthropology and Philosophy* (Bielefeld: transcript, 2018).

Brown, Frederick L., *The City Is More Than Human. An Animal History of Seattle* (Seattle and London: University of Washington Press, 2016).

Bruno, Andy, *The Nature of Soviet Power. An Arctic Environmental History* (Cambridge: Cambridge University Press, 2016).

Buckingham, Jane and Piers Locke (eds), *Conflict, Negotiation, and Coexistence. Rethinking Human-Elephant Relations in South Asia* (New Delhi: Oxford University Press, 2016).

Budiansky, Stephen, *The Nature of Horses. Their Evolution, Intelligence and Behaviour* (London: Weidenfeld & Nicolson, 1997).

Buller, Henry, and Emma Roe, *Food and Animal Welfare* (London et al.: Bloomsbury Academic, 2018).

Bulliet, Richard W., *Hunters, Herders, and Hamburgers. The Past and Future of Human-Animal Relationships* (New York: Columbia University Press, 2005).

Burgess, Colin and Chris Dubbs, *Animals in Space. From Research Rockets to the Space Shuttle* (New York: Springer, 2007).

Burke, Peter, *The French Historical Revolution. The Annales School, 1929–2014* (Cambridge: Polity Press, 2015; first published in 1999).

Calarco, Matthew, *Zoographies. The Question of the Animal from Heidegger to Derrida* (New York: Columbia University Press, 2008).

Carrington, Damian, 'Geologists Reject Declaration of Anthropocene Epoch' *The Guardian* (22 March 2024), https://www.theguardian.com/science/2024/mar/22/geologists-reject-declaration-of-anthropocene-epoch.

Carruthers, Jane, 'Review of Black Poachers, White Hunters: A History of Hunting in Colonial Kenya' *African Studies Review* 49(3) (2006), pp. 102–4.

Cartmill, Matt, 'Primate Visions: Gender, Race, and Nature in the World of Modern Science' *International Journal of Primatology* 12(1) (1991), pp. 67–75.

Cartmill, Matt, *A View to a Death in the Morning. Hunting and Nature through History* (Cambridge and London: Harvard University Press, 1993).

Caswell, Kurt, *Laika's Window. The Legacy of a Soviet Space Dog* (San Antonio: Trinity University Press, 2018).

Chakrabarty, Dipesh, *The Climate of History in a Planetary Age* (Chicago and London: The University of Chicago Press, 2021).

Challenger, Melanie, *How to Be Animal. What It Means to Be Human* (Edinburgh: Canongate, 2021).

Chimaira – Arbeitskreis für Human-Animal Studies (ed.), *Human-Animal Studies. Über die gesellschaftliche Natur von Mensch-Tier-Verhältnissen* (Bielefeld: transcript, 2011).

Costlow, Jane and Amy Nelson (eds), *Other Animals. Beyond the Human in Russian Culture and History* (Pittsburgh: University of Pittsburgh Press, 2010).

Cowie, Helen, *Conquering Nature in Spain and Its Empire, 1750–1850* (Manchester: Manchester University Press, 2011).

Cowie, Helen, *Exhibiting Animals in Nineteenth-Century Britain. Empathy, Education, Entertainment* (Basingstoke and New York: Palgrave Macmillan, 2014).

Cowie, Helen Louise, *Victims of Fashion. Animal Commodities in Victorian Britain* (Cambridge and New York: Cambridge University Press, 2022).

Cowie, Helen Louise, *Animals in World History* (New York and London: Routledge, 2025).

Cronon, William, *Nature's Metropolis. Chicago and the Great West* (New York and London: W. W. Norton, 1991).

Cronon, William, 'The Trouble with Wilderness or, Getting Back to the Wrong Nature' *Environmental History* 1(1) (1996), pp. 7–28.

Cronon, William, *Changes in the Land. Indians, Colonists, and the Ecology of New England. 20th-Anniversary Edition* (New York: Hill and Wang, 2003; first published in 1983).

Crosby, Alfred W., *The Columbian Exchange. Biological and Cultural Consequences of 1492. 30th Anniversary Edition* (Westport and London: Praeger, 2003; first published in 1972).

Crosby, Alfred W., *Ecological Imperialism. The Biological Expansion of Europe, 900–1900* (Cambridge: Cambridge University Press, ^{2}2004; first published in 1986).

Darwin, C. R., *The Expression of the Emotions in Man and Animals* (London: John Murray, 1872).

Datta, Venita, *Heroes and Legends of Fin-de-Siècle France. Gender, Politics, and National Identity* (New York: Cambridge University Press, 2011).

de Asúa, Miguel and Roger French, *A New World of Animals. Early Modern Europeans on the Creatures of Iberian America* (London and New York: Routledge, 2016; first published in 2005).

Dejung, Christof, David Motadel and Jürgen Osterhammel (eds), *The Global Bourgeoisie. The Rise of the Middle Classes in the Age of Empire* (Princeton: Princeton University Press, 2019).

DeMello, Margo, *Animals and Society. An Introduction to Human-Animal Studies* (New York: Columbia University Press, 2012).

DeMello, Margo (ed.), *Speaking for Animals. Animal Autobiographical Writing* (New York and Oxon: Routledge, 2013).

Demuth, Bathsheba, *Floating Coast. An Environmental History of the Bering Strait* (New York: W. W. Norton, 2019).

Derrida, Jacques, 'And Say the Animal Responded?', in Cary Wolf (ed.), *Zoontologies. The Question of the Animal* (Minneapolis and London: University of Minnesota Press, 2003), pp. 121–46.

Descola, Philippe, *In the Society of Nature. A Native Ecology in Amazonia* (Cambridge: Cambridge University Press, 1994).

Descola, Philippe, *The Ecology of Others* (Chicago: Prickly Paradigm Press, 2013).

Descola, Philippe, *Beyond Nature and Culture* (Chicago: The University of Chicago Press, 2014).

Di Cesare, Donatella, *Heidegger and the Jews. The Black Notebooks* (Cambridge: Polity Press, 2018; first published in Italian in 2014, translated by Murtha Baca).

Dinzelbacher, Peter, 'Animal Trials: A Multidisciplinary Approach' *The Journal of Interdisciplinary History* 32(3) (2002), pp. 405–21.

Dixon, Simon, 'Horse-Racing in Nineteenth-Century Russia' *Slavonic and East European Review* 98(3) (2020), pp. 464–503.

Dolin, Eric Jay, *Fur, Fortune, and Empire. The Epic History of the Fur Trade in America* (New York: W. W. Norton, 2010).

Dolwick, Jim S., '"The Social" and Beyond: Introducing Actor-Network Theory' *Journal of Maritime Archaeology* 4(1) (2009), pp. 21–49.

Dreesbach, Anne, 'Colonial Exhibitions, "Völkerschauen" and the Display of the "Other"' *European History Online* (3 May 2012), https://www.ieg-ego.eu/en/threads/backgrounds/european-encounters/anne-dreesbach-colonial-exhibitions-voelkerschauen-and-the-display-of-the-other.

Dyck, Erika and Christopher Fletcher (eds), *Locating Health. Historical and Anthropological Investigations of Place and Health* (London: Pickering & Chatto, 2011).

Ekman, Paul, 'Darwin's contributions to our understanding of emotional expressions' *Philosophical Transactions of the Royal Society of London. Series B, Biological Sciences* 364(1535) (2009), pp. 3449–51.

Endersby, Jim, *A Guinea Pig's History of Biology* (London: Heinemann, 2007).

Fagan, Brian, *The Intimate Bond. How Animals Shaped Human History* (New York and London: Bloomsbury, 2015).

Fausto-Sterling, Anne, 'Essay Review: Primate Visions, a Model for Historians of Science?' *Journal of the History of Biology* 23(2) (1990), pp. 329–33.

Fedotova, Anastasia, 'The Beetle Question: The Growing Problem of Insect Infestations in South Russia in the Late Nineteenth Century' *The Slavonic and East European Review* 93(1) (2015), pp. 66–95.

Fenske, Michaela and Bernhard Tschofen (eds), *Managing the Return of the Wild. Human Encounters with Wolves in Europe* (London and New York: Routledge, 2022).

Ferrari, Arianna and Klaus Petrus (eds), *Lexikon der Mensch-Tier-Beziehungen* (Bielefeld: transcript, 2015).

Few, Martha and Zeb Tortorici (eds), *Centering Animals in Latin American History* (New York: Duke University Press, 2013).

Fitzgerald, Deborah, *Every Farm a Factory. The Industrial Ideal in American Agriculture* (New Haven and London: Yale University Press, 2003).

Fitzmaurice, Malgosia, *Whaling and International Law* (Cambridge: Cambridge University Press, 2015).

Fleischman, Thomas, *Communist Pigs. An Animal History of East Germany's Rise and Fall* (Seattle: University of Washington Press, 2020).

'Forum: Liudi i drugie zhivye sushchestva' *Antropologicheskii forum* 62 (2024), pp. 11–224.

Franco, Nuno Henrique, 'Animal Experiments in Biomedical Research: A Historical Perspective' *Animals* (3) (2013), pp. 238–73.

Frawley, Jodi and Iain McCalman (eds), *Rethinking Invasion Ecologies from the Environmental Humanities* (London and New York: Routledge, 2014).

Frieze, Donna-Lee, 'New Approaches to Raphael Lemkin' *Journal of Genocide Research* 15(3) (2013), pp. 247–52.

Fudge, Erica, *Quick Cattle and Dying Wishes. People and Their Animals in Early Modern England* (Ithaca: Cornell University Press, 2018).

Gieser, Thorsten, *Living with Wolves. Affects, Feelings and Sentiments in Human-Wolf-Coexistence* (Bielefeld: transcript, 2024).

Gissibl, Bernhard, 'Das kolonisierte Tier: Zur Ökologie der Kontaktzonen des deutschen Kolonialismus' *WerktstattGeschichte* 56 (2010), pp. 7–28.

Gissibl, Bernhard, *The Nature of German Imperialism. Conservation and the Politics of Wildlife in Colonial East Africa* (New York and Oxford: Berghahn, 2016).

Govaerts, Sander, 'Wolves and Warfare in the History of the Low Countries, 1000–1800' *Low Countries Historical Review* 137(1) (2022), pp. 4–27.

Graf, Maximilian, 'Before Strauß: The East German Struggle to Avoid Bankruptcy during the Debt Crisis Revisited' *The International History Review* 42(4) (2019), pp. 737–54.

Griffin, Emma, *Blood Sport. Hunting in Britain since 1066* (New Haven and London: Yale University Press, 2007).

Griffin, Roger, 'Fascism's Modernist Revolution: A New Paradigm for the Study of Right-wing Dictatorships' *Fascism* 5(2) (2016), pp. 105–29.

Gross, Eva M., Nilanga Jayasinghe, Ashley Brooks, Gert Polet, Rohan Wadhwa and Femke Hilderink-Koopmans, *A Future for All. The Need for Human-Wildlife Coexistence* (Gland: WWF, 2021).

Guerrini, Anita, *Experimenting with Humans and Animals. From Aristotle to CRISPR* (Baltimore and London: The Johns Hopkins University Press, ²2022).

Guither, Harold D., *Animal Rights. History and Scope of a Radical Social Movement* (Carbondale and Edwardsville: Southern Illinois University Press, 1998).

Hacquebord, Louwrens, 'Three Centuries of Whaling and Walrus Hunting in Svalbard and Its Impact on the Arctic Ecosystem' *Environment and History* 7(2) (2001), pp. 169–85.

Hampson, Judith E., 'History of Animal Experimentation Control in the U.K.' *International Journal for the Study of Animal Problems* 2(5) (1981), pp. 237–41.

Haraway, Donna, *Primate Visions. Gender, Race, and Nature in the World of Modern Science* (NewYork and London: Routledge, 1989).

Haraway, Donna, *The Companion Species Manifesto. Dogs, People, and Significant Otherness* (Chicago: Prickly Paradigm Press, 2003).

Haraway, Donna J., *When Species Meet* (Minneapolis and London: University of Minnesota Press, 2008).

Hardeman, Egbert and Henk Jochemsen, 'AreThere Ideological Aspects to the Modernization of Agriculture?' *Journal of Agricultural and Environmental Ethics* 25(5) (2012), pp. 657–74.

Hediger, Ryan (ed.), *Animals and War. Studies of Europe and North America* (Leiden: Brill, 2013).

Heitzer, Enrico and Sven Schultze (eds), *Chimära mensura? Die Human-Animal Studies zwischen Schäferhund-Science-Hoax, kritischer Geschichtswissenschaft und akademischem Trendsurfing* (Berlin: Vergangenheitsverlag, 2018).

Helfant, Ian M., *That Savage Gaze. Wolves in the Nineteenth-Century Russian Imagination* (Boston: Academic Studies Press, 2018).

Herbert, Ulrich, 'Europe in High Modernity. Reflections on aTheory of the 20th Century' *Journal of Modern European History* 5(1) (2007), pp. 5–21.

Hess, Earl J., 'The Animal-Human Relationship in War. Cavalry Horses andTheir Riders in the American Civil War' *Animal History* 1(1) (2025), pp. 71–90.

Heßler, Martina and Heike Weber (eds), *Provokationen der Technikgeschichte. Zum Reflexionszwang historischer Forschung* (Paderborn: Ferdinand Schöningh, 2019).

Hettling, Manfred, 'Bürger, Bürgertum, Bürgerlichkeit (English Version)' *Docupedia-Zeitgeschichte* (8 June 2016), http://docupedia.de/zg/hettling_buerger_v1_en_2016.

Hevia, James L., *Animal Labor and Colonial Warfare* (Chicago and London: The University of Chicago Press, 2018).

Hilbrenner, Anke, 'Barred Emotions: Human-Animal Relations in Soviet Zoos' *Slavonic and East European Review* 103(1) (2025), pp. 139–57.

Holzberger, Helena andTimm Schönfelder (eds), 'Special Issue: Crossing Boundaries. Human-Animal Relationships inTsarist Russia and the Soviet Union' *Slavonic and East European Review* 103(1) (2025).

Horowitz, Roger, *Putting Meat on the American Table. Taste, Technology, Transformation* (Baltimore: The Johns Hopkins University Press, 2006).

Howell, Philip, *At Home and Astray. The Domestic Dog in Victorian Britain* (Charlottesville: University of Virginia Press, 2015).

Hüntelmann, Axel C., Christian Jaser, Mieke Roscher and Nadir Weber (eds), *Animals and Epidemics. Interspecies Entanglements in Historical Perspective* (Köln: Böhlau, 2023).

Isenberg, Andrew C., *The Destruction of the Bison. An Environmental History, 1750–1920* (Cambridge: Cambridge University Press, 2000) [now available as the twentieth-anniversary edition, ibid. ²2020].

Isenberg, Andew C., 'From the Periphery to the Center: North American Environmental History' *Global Environment* 12 (2013), pp. 80–101.

Isenberg, Andrew C. (ed.), *The Oxford Handbook of Environmental History* (New York: Oxford University Press, 2014).

Johnson, Sarah (ed.), *Animals. Themes in Environmental History 4* (Knapwell: White Horse Press, 2014).

Johnson, Sarah (ed.), *Farming. Themes in Environmental History 6* (Knapwell: White Horse Press, 2016).

Jones, Ryan Tucker, *Empire of Extinction. Russians and the North Pacific's Strange Beasts of the Sea, 1741–1867* (Oxford and New York: Oxford University Press, 2014; online edition: Oxford Academic), https://doi.org/10.1093/acprof:oso/9780199343416.003.0008).

Jones, Ryan Tucker, *Red Leviathan. The Secret History of Soviet Whaling* (Chicago and London: The University of Chicago Press, 2022).

Jones, Ryan Tucker and Angela Wanhalla (eds), *Across Species and Cultures. Whales, Humans, and Pacific Worlds* (Honolulu: University of Hawai'i Press, 2022).

Jørgensen, Dolly, *Recovering Lost Species in the Modern Age. Histories of Longing and Belonging* (Cambridge and London: The MIT Press, 2019).

Josephson, Paul R., *Totalitarian Science and Technology* (Amherst: Humanity Books, 2005).

Kaljundi, Linda, Anu Mänd, Ulrike Plath and Kadri Tüür (eds), *Baltic Human-Animal Histories. Relations, Trading, and Representations* (Berlin et al.: Peter Lang, 2024).

Kalof, Linda, *Looking at Animals in Human History* (London: Reaktion Books, 2007).

Kalof, Linda (ed.), *The Oxford Handbook of Animal Studies* (New York: Oxford University Press, 2017).

Kalof, Linda and Amy Fitzgerald (eds), *The Animals Reader. The Essential Classic and Contemporary Writings. Second Edition* (London and New York Routledge, 2022).

Kalof, Linda, Brigitte Resl, Bruce Boehrer, Matthew Senior, Kathleen Kete and Randy Malamud (eds), *A Cultural History of Animals*. 6 vols. (Oxford and New York: Berg, 2007).

Kaltmeier, Olaf, Antoine Acker, León Enrique Ávila Romero and Regina Horta Duarte (eds), *Biodiversity. Handbook of the Anthropocene in Latin America II* (Bielefeld: Bielefeld University Press, 2024).

Kaltmeier, Olaf, María Fernanda López Sandoval, José Augusto Pádua and Adrián Gustavo Zarrilli (eds), *Land Use. Handbook of the Anthropocene in Latin America I* (Bielefeld: Bielefeld University Press, 2024).

Kean, Hilda, *Animal Rights. Political and Social Change in Britain since 1800* (London: Reaktion Books, 1998).

Kean, Hilda, *The Great Cat and Dog Massacre. The Real Story of World War Two's Unknown Tragedy* (Chicago and London: The University of Chicago Press, 2017).

Kean, Hilda and Philip Howell (eds), *The Routledge Companion to Animal-Human History* (London and New York: Routledge, 2019).

Kete, Kathleen, *The Beast in the Boudoir. Petkeeping in Nineteenth-Century Paris* (Berkeley and Los Angeles: University of California Press, 1994).

Kinder, John M., *World War Zoos. Humans and Other Animals in the Deadliest Conflict of the Modern Age* (Chicago: The University of Chicago Press, 2025).

Kindler, Robert, 'Robben töten. Jagdpraktiken, Anthropomorphismus und Sozialdisziplinierung im Nordpazifik', in Iris Därmann and Stephan Zandt (eds), *Andere Ökologien. Transformationen von Mensch und Tier* (München: Wilhelm Fink, 2017), pp. 101–20.

Kindler, Robert, *Robbenreich. Russland und die Grenzen der Macht am Nordpazifik* (Hamburg: Hamburger Edition, 2022).

Kirksey, Eben (ed.), *The Multispecies Salon* (New York: Duke University Press, 2014).

Kompatscher, Gabriela, Reingard Spannring and Karin Schachinger, *Human-Animal Studies. Eine Einführung für Studierende und Lehrende* (Münster and New York: Waxmann, 2017).

Kotenko, Anton, 'For fame and fortune: the origins of St Petersburg's zoo, 1865–1871' *Urban History* 52(4) (2025), pp. 604–21, https://doi.org/10.1017/S0963926824000269.

Krüger, Gesine, Aline Steinbrecher and Clemens Wischermann (eds), *Tiere und Geschichte. Konturen einer 'Animate History'* (Stuttgart: Franz Steiner Verlag, 2014).

Lander, Brian, Mindi Schneider and Katherine Brunson, 'A History of Pigs in China: From Curious Omnivores to Industrial Pork' *The Journal of Asian Studies* 79(4) (2020), pp. 865–89.

Lansbury, Coral, *The Old Brown Dog. Women, Workers, and Vivisection in Edwardian England* (Madison: The University of Wisconsin Press, 1985).

Latimer, Joanna, 'Review: Donna Haraway, "Manifestly Haraway"' *Theory, Culture & Society* (26 June 2016), https://www.theoryculturesociety.org/blog/review-donna-haraway-manifestly-haraway.

Latour, Bruno and Steve Woolgar, *Laboratory Life. The Social Construction of Scientific Facts* (Beverly Hills: Sage Publications, 1979).

Lee, Keekok, 'An Animal: What Is It?' *Environmental Values* 6(4) (1997), pp. 393–410.

Lee, Paula Young (ed.), *Meat, Modernity, and the Rise of the Slaughterhouse* (Durham: University of New Hampshire Press, 2008).

Lekan, Thomas M., *Our Gigantic Zoo. A German Quest to Save the Serengeti* (New York: Oxford University Press, 2020).

Lipp, Benjamin and Sabine Maasen, 'Techno-bio-politics. On Interfacing Life with and Through Technology' *Nanoethics* 16 (2022), pp. 133–50.

London, Jack, 'The Other Animals', in id., *Revolution and Other Essays* (New York: The Macmillan Company, 1910), pp. 237–66.

Lorimer, Jamie and Clemens Driessen, 'From "Nazi Cows" to Cosmopolitan "Ecological Engineers": Specifying Rewilding through a History of Heck Cattle' *Annals of the American Association of Geographers* 106(3) (2016), pp. 631–52.

Losos, Jonathan B., *The Age of Cats. From the Savannah to Your Sofa* (London: William Collins, 2023).

MacDonald, David B., 'Pushing the Limits of Humanity? Reinterpreting Animal Rights and "Personhood" through the Prism of the Holocaust' *Journal of Human Rights* 5(4) (2006), pp. 417–37.

MacKenzie, John M., *The Empire of Nature. Hunting, Conservation and British Imperialism* (Manchester: Manchester University Press, 1988).

MacKenzie, John M., 'Militarism, Hunting, Imperialism: "Blooding" the Martial Male' *The Journal of Imperial and Commonwealth History* 38(1) (2010), pp. 160–2.

Majumdar, Rochona, *Writing Postcolonial History* (London and New York: Bloomsbury Academic, 2010).

Malcolmson, Robert and Stephanos Mastoris, *The English Pig. A History* (Rio Grande, Ohio and London: Hambledon, 1998).

Malitska, Julia (ed.), 'Special Section: Dietary Reforms in the Baltic and East Central Europe, ca 1850–1950' *Baltic Worlds* 1–2 (2022), pp. 105–64.

Mallet, Marie-Luise (ed.), *Jacques Derrida. The Animal That Therefore I Am* (New York: Fordham University Press, 2008; first published in French in 2006).

Mangan, J. A. and Callum McKenzie, *Militarism, Hunting, Imperialism. 'Blooding' The Martial Male* (London: Routledge, 2010).

Marris, Emma, 'New York Is Wilder Than You Think' *The New York Times* (15 March 2024), https://www.nytimes.com/2024/03/15/opinion/free-new-york-wild.html.

Marvin, Garry, 'Wolves in Sheep's (and Others') Clothing', in Dorothee Brantz (ed.), *Beastly Natures. Animals, Humans, and the Study of History* (Charlottesville and London: University of Virginia Press, 2010), pp. 59–78.

Marvin, Garry, *Wolf* (London: Reaktion Books, 2012).

Marvin, Garry and Susan McHugh (eds), *Routledge Handbook of Human-Animal Studies* (London and New York: Routledge, 2014).

Masius, Patrick and Jana Sprenger (eds), *A Fairytale in Question. Historical Interactions between Humans and Wolves* (Knapwell: White Horse Press, 2015).

Mazanik, Anna, 'Arbovirology and Cold War Collaborations: A Transnational History of the Tick-borne Encephalitis Vaccine, 1930–1980' *Journal of the History of Medicine and Allied Sciences* 79(3) (2024), pp. 254–73.

McDonald, Tracy and Daniel Vandersommers (eds), *Zoo Studies. A New Humanities* (Montreal et al.: McGill-Queen's University Press, 2019).

Mckenzie, Callum, '"Sadly Neglected" – Hunting and Gendered Identities: A Study in Gender Construction' *The International Journal of the History of Sport* 22(4) (2005), pp. 545–62.

McNeill, J. R., *Mosquito Empires. Ecology and War in the Greater Caribbean, 1620–1914* (Cambridge and New York: Cambridge University Press, 2010).

McQuaid, Kim, 'Sputnik Reconsidered: Image and Reality in the Early Space Age' *Canadian Review of American Studies* 37(3) (2007), pp. 371–401.

McShane, Clay and Joel A. Tarr, *The Horse in the City. Living Machines in the Nineteenth Century* (Baltimore: The Johns Hopkins University Press, 2007).

Medvedev, Zhores A., *Soviet Agriculture* (New York and London: W. W. Norton, 1987).

Melville, Elinor G. K., *A Plague of Sheep. Environmental Consequences of the Conquest of Mexico* (Cambridge: Cambridge University Press, ²1997; first published in 1994).

Merchant, Carolyn, *The Columbia Guide to American Environmental History* (New York: Columbia University Press, 2005).

Miller, Ian Jared, *The Nature of the Beasts. Empire and Exhibition at the Tokyo Imperial Zoo* (Berkeley: University of California Press, 2013).

Miller, Richard J., *The Rise and Fall of Animal Experimentation. Empathy, Science, and the Future of Research* (New York: Oxford University Press, 2023).

Modlinska, Klaudia and Wojciech Pisula, 'The Natural History of Model Organisms: The Norway Rat, from an Obnoxious Pest to a Laboratory Pet *eLife* (17 January 2020), https://elifesciences.org/articles/50651.

Mohnhaupt, J. W. and John R. J. Eyck, *Animals under the Swastika* (Madison: University of Wisconsin Press, 2022) [German first edition: Jan Mohnhaupt, *Tiere im Nationalsozialismus* (München: Hanser, 2020)].

Mohnhaupt, J. W. and Shelley Frisch, *The Zookeepers' War. An Incredible True Story from the Cold War* (New York: Simon & Schuster, 2019) [German first edition: Jan Mohnhaupt, *Der Zoo der Anderen: Als die Stasi ihr Herz für Brillenbären entdeckte & Helmut Schmidt mit Pandas nachrüstete* (München: Hanser, 2017)].

Moon, David, Nicholas B. Breyfogle and Alexandra Bekasova (eds), *Place and Nature. Essays in Russian Environmental History* (Cambridgeshire: White Horse Press, 2021).

N. N., 'Hare Today and Gone Tomorrow' *openDemocracy* (7 July 2014), https://www.opendemocracy.net/en/odr/hare-today-and-gone-tomorrow.

Nagel, Thomas, 'What Is It Like to Be a Bat?' *The Philosophical Review* 83(4) (1974), pp. 435–50.

Nagornaia, Oksana, 'Animal Fighters, Animal Victims: The Animal Dimension on the Russian-Austrian Front of the First World War', in Kerstin S. Jobst, Oksana Nagornaia and Kerstin von Lingen (eds), *The Great War and the Anthropocene. Empire and Environment, Soldiers and Civilians on the Eastern Front* (Leiden and Boston: Brill, 2024), pp. 127–44.

Nance, Susan, *Entertaining Elephants. Animal Agency and the Business of the American Circus* (Baltimore: The Johns Hopkins University Press, 2013).

Nance, Susan, *Animal Modernity. Jumbo the Elephant and the Human Dilemma* (Basingstoke and New York: Palgrave Macmillan, 2015).

Nance, Susan (ed.), *The Historical Animal* (Syracuse: Syracuse University Press, 2015).

Nance, Susan, *Rodeo. An Animal History* (Norman: University of Oklahoma Press, 2020).

Nash, Roderick Frazier, *Wilderness and the American Mind* (New Haven: Yale University Press, ⁵2014; first published in 1967).

Neirick, Miriam, *When Pigs Could Fly and Bears Could Dance. A History of the Soviet Circus* (Madison: University of Wisconsin Press, 2012).

Nelson, Amy, 'The Legacy of Laika. Celebrity, Sacrifice, and the Soviet Space Dogs', in Dorothee Brantz (ed.), *Beastly Natures. Animals, Humans, and the Study of History* (Charlottesville and London: University of Virginia Press, 2010), pp. 204–24.

Nelson, Amy, 'What the Dogs Did: Animal Agency in the Soviet Manned Space Flight Programme' *BJHS Themes* 2 (2017), pp. 79–99.

Nikkilä, Eeva, 'Building a Nest in Human-Built Spaces: Tracing the Experiences of Finnish Sows, c. 1900–1930s' *Animal History* 1(1) (2025), pp. 52–70.

Oelschlaeger, Max, 'The Myth of the Technological Fix' *The Southwestern Journal of Philosophy* 10(1) (1979), pp. 43–53.

Pacyga, Dominic A., *Slaughterhouse. Chicago's Union Stock Yard and the World It Made* (Chicago and London: The University of Chicago Press, 2015).

Pearson, Chris, *Dogopolis. How Dogs and Humans Made Modern New York, London, and Paris* (Chicago and London: The University of Chicago Press, 2021).

Pennycook, Alastair, *Posthumanist Applied Linguistics* (Oxon and New York: Routledge, 2018).

Peters, Florian, 'Von totalitären Schäferhunden und libertären Mauerkaninchen. Alles von Relevanz? Ein Beitrag über zweifelhafte wissenschaftliche Standards und die angezogene Handbremse in der akademischen Debattenkultur' *Zeitgeschichte-online* (1 February 2016), https://zeitgeschichte-online.de/kommentar/von-totalitaeren-schaeferhunden-und-libertaeren-mauerkaninchen.

Plamper, Jan, 'The History of Emotions: An Interview with William Reddy, Barbara Rosenwein and Peter Stearns' *History and Theory* 49(2) (May 2010), pp. 237–65.

Plamper, Jan, *The History of Emotions. An Introduction* (Oxford: Oxford University Press, 2015; first published in German as *Geschichte und Gefühl. Grundlagen der Emotionsgeschichte* in 2012).

Pravilova, Ekaterina, *A Public Empire. Property and the Quest for the Common Good in Imperial Russia* (Princeton: Princeton University Press, 2014).

Price, Lloyd, 'Environmental and Animal History', in Stefan Berger, Heiko Feldner and Kevin Passmore (eds), *Writing History. Theory and Practice* (London: Bloomsbury Academic, ³2021; first published in 2020), pp. 253–72.

Rader, Karen A., *Making Mice. Standardizing Animals for American Biomedical Research, 1900–1955* (Princeton and Oxford: Princeton University Press, 2004).

Regan, Tom, *The Case for Animal Rights* (Berkeley and Los Angeles: University of California Press, 2004; first published in 1983).

Renner, Andreas, *Nordostpassage. Geschichte eines Seewegs* (Hamburg: mareverlag, 2024).

Richards, John F., *The World Hunt: An Environmental History of the Commodification of Animals* (Berkeley: University of California Press, 2014).

Ritvo, Harriet, *The Animal Estate. The English and Other Creatures in the Victorian Age* (Cambridge: Harvard University Press, 1987).

Ritvo, Harriet, *Noble Cows and Hybrid Zebras. Essays on Animals and History* (Charlottesville and London: University of Virginia Press, 2010).

Robichaud, Andrew A., *Animal City: The Domestication of America* (Cambridge and London: Harvard University Press, 2019).

Rome, Adam, 'Conservation, Preservation, and Environmental Activism: A Survey of the Historical Literature' *National Park Service* (16 January 2003), https://www.nps.gov/parkhistory/hisnps/NPSThinking/nps-oah.htm.

Roscher, Mieke, 'Comment: Animals at Court: Interspecies Relations in a Longue Durée Perspective', in Mark Hengerer and Nadir Weber (eds), *Animals and Courts: Europe, c. 1200–1800* (Berlin and Boston: De Gruyter Oldenbourg, 2020), pp. 399–414.

Roscher, Mieke, André Krebber and Brett Mizelle (eds), *Handbook of Historical Animal Studies* (Berlin and Boston: De Gruyter, 2022).

Rothfels, Nigel (ed.), *Representing Animals. Theories of Contemporary Culture* (Bloomington: Indiana University Press, 2002).

Rothfels, Nigel, *Savages and Beasts. The Birth of the Modern Zoo* (Baltimore and London: The Johns Hopkins University Press, 2002).

Rothfels, Nigel, *Elephant Trails. A History of Animals and Cultures* (Baltimore: The Johns Hopkins University Press, 2021).

Russell, Edmund, *Greyhound Nation: A Coevolutionary History of England, 1200–1900* (Cambridge: Cambridge University Press, 2018).

Sahrhage, Dietrich and Johannes Lundbeck, *A History of Fishing* (Berlin and Heidelberg: Springer, 1992).

Saraiva, Tiago, *Fascist Pigs. Technoscientific Organisms and the History of Fascism* (Cambridge and London: The MIT Press, 2016).

Sax, Boria, *Animals in the Third Reich. Pets, Scapegoats, and the Holocaust* (New York and London: Continuum, 2000).

Sax, Boria, *Avian Illuminations. A Cultural History of Birds* (London: Reaktion Books, 2021).

Scheer, Monique, 'Are Emotions a Kind of Practice (and Is That What Makes Them Have a History)? A Bourdieuan Approach to Understanding Emotion' *History and Theory* 51 (2) (2012), pp. 193–220.

Schönfelder, Timm, 'Fur Trade in Turmoil: Pelt Commodification in Leipzig from Fin de Siècle to Sovietization', in Magdalena Eriksröd-Burger, Heidi Hein-Kircher and Julia Malitska (eds), *Consumption and Advertising in Eastern Europe and Russia in the Twentieth Century* (Cham: Palgrave, 2023), pp. 113–34.

Schönfelder, Timm, 'Constructing Masculinities: Bear Hunting in Tsarist Russia Toward the Fin de Siècle', in Laura Beck and Maurice Saß (eds), *Hunting Troubles: Gender and Its Intersections in the Cultural History of the Hunt* (Cham: Palgrave, 2024), pp. 259–74.

Schönfelder, Timm, 'Review of Ryan Tucker Jones: Red Leviathan. The Secret History of Soviet Whaling' *Jahrbücher für Geschichte Osteuropas* 72(3) (2024), pp. 511–13.

Schönfelder, Timm, *Animals in Russian and Soviet History* (Oxford Bibliographies, New York: Oxford University Press, 2026), doi: 10.1093/obo/9780197768709-0058.

Schulte, Christiane, 'Der deutsch-deutsche Schäferhund – Ein Beitrag zur Gewaltgeschichte des Jahrhunderts der Extreme' *Totalitarismus und Demokratie* 13 (2015), pp. 319–34.

Schuster, Joshua, *What Is Extinction? A Natural and Cultural History of Last Animals* (New York: Fordham University Press, 2023).

Scott, James C., *Seeing Like a State. How Certain Schemes to Improve the Human Condition Have Failed* (New Haven and London: Yale University Press, 1998).

Serpell, James, *In the Company of Animals. A Study of Human-Animal Relationships* (Cambridge: Cambridge University Press, ²1996; first published in 1986).

Silkenat, David, *Scars on the Land: An Environmental History of Slavery in the American South* (New York: Oxford University Press, 2022).

Singer, Peter, *Animal Liberation* (London: Bodley Head, 2015; first published in 1975).

Smalley, Andrea L., *Wild by Nature. North American Animals Confront Colonization* (Baltimore: John Hopkins University Press, 2017).

Smith-Howard, Kendra, *Pure and Modern Milk. An Environmental History since 1900* (New York: Oxford University Press, 2014).

Sokal, Alan D., 'Transgressing the Boundaries: Toward a Transformative Hermeneutics of Quantum Gravity' *Social Text* 14(46/47) (1996), pp. 217–52.

Sokal, Alan, *Beyond the Hoax. Science, Philosophy and Culture* (Oxford: Oxford University Press, 2008).

Sokal, Alan and Jean Bricmont, *Fashionable Nonsense. Postmodern Intellectuals' Abuse of Science* (New York: Picador, 1998).

Speitkamp, Winfried and Stephanie Zehnle (eds), *Afrikanische Tierräume. Historische Verortungen* (Köln: Rüdiger Köppe Verlag, 2014).

Sramek, Joseph, '"Face Him Like a Briton": Tiger Hunting, Imperialism, and British Masculinity in Colonial India, 1800–1875' *Victorian Studies* 48(4) (2006), pp. 659–80.

Stange, Mary Zeiss, *Woman the Hunter* (Boston: Beacon Press, 1997).

Steinhart, Edward I., *Black Poachers, White Hunters: A Social History of Hunting in Colonial Kenya* (Oxford: James Currey, 2006).

Sullivan, Sian, '"Hunting Africa": Trophy Hunting, Neocolonialism and Land' *The Land* 31 (2022), pp. 22–7, 58.

Swart, Sandra, *Riding High. Horses, Humans and History in South Africa* (Johannesburg: Wits University Press, 2010).

Swart, Sandra, *The Lion's Historian. Africa's Animal Past* (Johannesburg: Jacana Press, 2023).

Syrjämaa, Taina, Marja Jalava, Taija Kaarlenkaski, Otto Latva, Eeva Nikkilä and Tuomas Räsänen (eds), *Animal Industries. Nordic Perspectives on the Exploitation of Animals since 1860* (Berlin and Boston: De Gruyter, 2024).

Tague, Ingrid H., *Animal Companions. Pets and Social Change in Eighteenth-Century Britain* (University Park: Penn State University Press, 2015).

Tait, Peta, *Wild and Dangerous Performances. Animals, Emotions, Circus* (Basingstoke and New York: Palgrave Macmillan, 2011).

Taylor, Katy, Nicky Gordon, Gill Langley and Wendy Higgins, 'Estimates for Worldwide Laboratory Animal Use in 2005' *Alternatives to Laboratory Animals* 36(3) (2008), pp. 327–42.

Taylor, Nik and Tania Signal (eds), *Theorizing Animals. Re-thinking Humanimal Relations* (Leiden and Boston: Brill, 2011).

'The Ladies' Kennel Association – 100 Not Out!' *Our Dogs*, https://www.ourdogs. co.uk/News/2004/November2004/News261104/lka.htm.

Thomas, Keith, *Man and the Natural World. Changing Attitudes in England 1500–1800* (London: Allen Lane, 1983).

Thompsell, Angela, *Hunting Africa. British Sport, African Knowledge and the Nature of Empire* (New York: Palgrave Macmillan, 2015).

Timofeeva, Oxana, *The History of Animals. A Philosophy* (London: Bloomsbury Academic, 2018; first published in Russian in 2017).

Today in History – June 30. Yosemite, *Library of Congress*, https://www.loc.gov/ item/today-in-history/june-30.

Todd, Zoe, 'Fish pluralities: Human-animal relations and sites of engagement n Paulatuuq, Arctic Canada' *Études/Inuit/Studies* 38(1/2) (2014), pp. 217–38.

Todes, Daniel P., *Pavlov's Physiology Factory. Experiment, Interpretation, Laboratory Enterprise* (Baltimore and London: The Johns Hopkins University Press, 2002).

Todes, Daniel P., *Ivan Pavlov. A Russian Life in Science* (Oxford and New York: Oxford University Press, 2014).

Turner, Lynn, Undine Sellbach and Ron Broglio (eds), *The Edinburgh Companion to Animal Studies* (Edinburgh Edinburgh University Press, 2018).

Uekötter, Frank, 'Green Nazis? Reassessing the Environmental History of Nazi Germany' *German Studies Review* 30(2) (2007), pp. 267–87.

Uekötter, Frank, *The Greenest Nation? A New History of German Environmentalism* (Cambridge and London: The MIT Press, 2014).

Valkonen, Sanna, Áile Aikio, Saara Alakorva and Sigga-Marja Magga (eds), *The Sámi World* (London: Routledge, 2022).

van Deelen, Grace, 'What Is Queer Ecology? Queer Theory Expands Our Relationship with Nature' *Sierra* (3 June 2023), https://www.sierraclub.org/ sierra/what-is-queer-ecology [accessed on 2 September 2025].

Vandersommers, Dan, Thomas Aiello and Susan Nance, 'Animal History: A Brief Introduction to Its Past and Future' *Animal History* 1(1) (2025), pp. 5–12.

Vanderwees, Chris, 'Companion Species under Fire: A Defense of Donna Haraway's *The Companion Species Manifesto*' *Nebula* 6(2) (2009), pp. 73–81.

Vialles, Noëlie, *Animal to Edible* (Cambridge: Cambridge University Press, 1994; first published in French as *Le sang et la chair. Les abattoirs du pays de l'Adour* in 1987).

Vigil, Ralph H., Frances W. Kaye and John R. Wunder (eds), *Spain and the Plains. Myths and Realities of Spanish Exploration and Settlement on the Great Plains* (Niwot: University of Colorado Press, 1994).

Viola, Lynne, *Peasant Rebels under Stalin. Collectivization and the Culture of Peasant Resistance* (New York and Oxford: Oxford University Press, 1996).

Waldau, Paul, *Animal Studies. An Introduction* (New York: Oxford University Press, 2013).

Walker, Brett L., *The Lost Wolves of Japan* (Seattle: University of Washington Press, 2005).

Warde, Paul, Libby Robin and Sverker Sörlin, *The Environment. A History of the Idea* (Baltimore: Johns Hopkins University Press, 2018).

Warren, Louis S., *The Hunter's Game. Poachers and Conservationists in Twentieth-Century America* (New Haven and London: Yale University Press, 1997).

Warren, Wilson J., *Meat Makes People Powerful. A Global History of the Modern Era* (Iowa City: University of Iowa Press, 2018).

Weber, David J., *The Spanish Frontier in North America* (New Haven: Yale University Press, 1992).

Whitehead, Hal and Luke Rendell, *The Cultural Lives of Whales and Dolphins* (Chicago and London: The University of Chicago Press, 2015).

Wiens, John J., 'How many species are there on Earth? Progress and problems' *PLOS Biology* 21(11) (20 November 2023), doi: 10.1371/journal.pbio.3002388.

Williams, Erin E. and Margo DeMello, *Why Animals Matter. The Case for Animal Protection* (Amherst: Prometheus Books, 2007).

Wilson, David A. H., *The Welfare of Performing Animals. A Historical Perspective* (Berlin and Heidelberg: Springer, 2015).

Winkler, Martina, *Das Imperium und die Seeotter. Die Expansion Russlands in den nordpazifischen Raum, 1700–1867* (Göttingen: Vandenhoeck & Ruprecht, 2016).

Wischermann, Clemens, Aline Steinbrecher and Philip Howell (eds), *Animal History in the Modern City. Exploring Liminality* (London et al.: Bloomsbury, 2019).

Wolf, Cary (ed.), *Zoontologies. The Question of the Animal* (Minneapolis and London: University of Minnesota Press, 2003).

Woods, Abigail, Michael Bresalier, Angela Cassidy and Rachel Mason Dentinger, *Animals and the Shaping of Modern Medicine. One Health and Its Histories* (London: Palgrave Macmillan, 2017).

Worboys, Michael, Julie-Marie Strange and Neil Pemberton, *The Invention of the Modern Dog. Breed and Blood in Victorian Britain* (Baltimore: The Johns Hopkins University Press, 2018).

Yokoyama, Olga T. (ed.), *Pavlov on the Conditional Reflex. Papers, 1903–1936* (Oxford and New York: Oxford University Press, 2023).

Index

Acknowledgements

Writing the manuscript that became this book has been an intense experience. It included sleepless nights when I lay awake wondering how to do justice to such a lively field that I myself was only beginning to enter professionally. I am grateful to my dear fellow historian Flora Roberts who recommended me to the series editors in the most gracious terms as a reliable author for a thematic introduction on animal history. With her exceptional optimism she pushed my confidence beyond its narrow boundaries. I received two rounds of very helpful and reassuring expert opinions on the book treatment by hitherto unidentified peer reviewers, at least one of whom also read the final manuscript. They challenged me to widen my scope beyond a European-centred initial suggestion and improved the final product in substantial ways. The unexpected level of praise by the two reviewers of the final text was truly a feast for sore eyes after months and months of concentrated reading and writing.

My esteemed colleagues at the Leibniz Institute for the History and Culture of Eastern Europe (GWZO) in Leipzig, including my head of department Matthias Hardt, were kind enough not to interfere with my plans but to trust in my ambitions. When our institute's director Maren Röger asked to see a draft of the manuscript at the halfway point, her laconic remark that I seemed to be knowing what I was doing was enough for me to push on through the valleys of doubt and frustration one must cross on such a journey. Luisa Raquel Ellermeier lent her carefully trained editor's eye to the chapter on the Columbian Exchange, and her warm words proved to be a much-appreciated source of motivation. Heather Roller and Ian Helfant were two very attentive conversation partners about animals, resource use, and sustainability when I visited Colgate University in the autumn of 2023. My Siberian cats Maksim and Kasparov remained bravely by my side at any hour, taking shifts whispering what felt like feline words of wisdom and compassion. The series editors and the editorial staff at Bloomsbury Academic were understanding, supportive, and highly professional throughout the process. I am deeply indebted to all the people named and forgotten. This book is dedicated to my mother, who along with my grandparents instilled an affection for animals in me from a young age.